CHATEAUBRIAND

Chateaubriand

FRIEDRICH SIEBURG

CHATEAUBRIAND

TRANSLATED FROM THE GERMAN
BY VIOLET M. MACDONALD

ST MARTIN'S PRESS
NEW YORK

First Published in United States 1962
First Published in Germany
Translation Copyright © George Allen & Unwin Ltd 1961
Library of Congress Catalog Card No. 62-8271

PRINTED IN GREAT BRITAIN

59583

CONTENTS

ILLUSTRATIONS

I

ADVENT OF AN ARTIST
IN HIS EPOCH

BURIAL OF AN EGOIST

THIS is the story of a great romantic writer, whose best work was his own life, and it might be summed up by beginning at the end —with his burial, that is, and the grave that is still there for the world to see. For his last resting place he had set his heart on a lonely rock in the sea, facing the town of Saint-Malo. He had been born within the grey walls of that ancient city, and the ceaseless thudding of the waves against the cliffs had been the lullaby of his earliest childhood. When his long life came to an end he was buried according to his known desire.

The funeral was a solemn event; the entire population of the little harbour town and many people from the country round crowded on to the ancient ramparts and the cliff-tops to watch the little procession battling its way against the storm. The clergy lining the route had hard work to hold their surplices together, and the wind tore away the clouds of incense from the censers. Twelve sailors bore the coffin to the little rocky islet at the lowest ebb of the tide; the guns mingled their thunder with the howling of the gale that was scouring the July sky. The troops ordered to the ceremony presented arms, and the coffin was lowered into the rock-hewn grave to the strains of mournful music. A granite slab, a cross, nothing more—no name, no epitaph—the great man had willed it so. His pride, his love of dignified solitude could tolerate none but the voice of the sea, always true to itself in storm and calm.

His grave might serve as an image of himself and of his life: it is lonely, romantic, a little theatrical. François-René de Chateaubriand lies buried on a rock washed by the sea and separated by it from the land, but the place is close to the coast, within reach of human affairs—not far out in the immeasurable ocean like the deathbed rock of his great counterpart Napoleon. It is a bare and nameless place, but everybody knows he is buried there—the great writer, the statesman, the traveller, the lover and hater. The simple cross can be seen from the shore, within a few strokes of the oar from the world with its curiosity and its hero-worship. The solitude is on no inhuman scale, it is a pleasing solitude, within easy approach. One of his enemies, of whom in his lifetime he had as many as friends, declared that his ideal would have been 'a monk's cell upon a stage'. He would have liked, that is, to combine all the advantages of a hermit's life with those of fame and popularity, without burdening himself with the responsibilities of either. His ambition did in fact conflict to the very end with his pride; his pleasure in the good things of life waged a ceaseless struggle with his *weltschmerz*, of which he was the most exquisite, most eloquent portrayer of all time.

A devoted friend, Joubert, said of him: 'He wrote only for others and lived only for himself.' Could there be a better definition of egoism? Stendhal called him 'the king of egoists'. But the contradictions in a soul of genius are not so easily defined. Joubert's observation applies equally to the artist. Chateaubriand was an artist, and the condition of an artist is one to which all other human conditions are necessarily subordinate. The artist can only live for himself and through himself, whatever the nature of his life. Egoism is his formula—a formula of which nobody has so far succeeded in finding a definition. None of his works, neither *Atala* nor *René*, neither the *Spirit of Christianity* nor *The Martyrs*, can compare as a work of art with his own life, which explains why his recollections, the *Mémoires d'outre-tombe*, have outlived everything else that he wrote and are looked upon even today as one of the peaks of French literature.

APPETITE AND SATIETY

The life of no other French writer so greatly resembles that of

Goethe, though it never attained the same completeness. The short novel *René*, which Chateaubriand wrote at the beginning of his career, as an emigrant in England, has often been compared to *Werther*, but Goethe fought his way resolutely through the perilous stage in which his hero came to grief, whereas Chateaubriand never attained the simple, active relation to life, and to his time, which helped Goethe to overcome his crises and cataclysms. Chateaubriand's ambition and his desire for action were intense; they were forever undermining the foundations of his existence. Like a sorcerer of his Celtic homeland, he deliberately called up the tempest that would destroy what little order he contrived now and then, almost against his will, to introduce into his life.

His life presents a riddle. How could a man be so avid of life and at the same time so bored with it? His craving for experience drove him to explore the forests of America and roam about the East. He aspired to honours and influence, and was not satisfied till he had occupied the Embassies of Berlin, London and Rome. He fought cleverly, persistently and energetically to obtain the post of Minister of Foreign Affairs, and initiated the campaign against Spain with the victory of Trocadero. He loved women and aroused violent passions in them: his relations with Pauline de Beaumont, Delphine de Custine, Natalie de Noailles, Cordélia de Castellane, and above all his unbroken association with Juliette Récamier, belong to the *grandes passions* of that half-century. Their secret, personal side may well have been deep and ecstatic, but they were also a part of public life; people talked of these love affairs as they talked of artistic and military events. Byron alone has ever succeeded to the same degree in interesting the outside world in events belonging by rights to the sphere of intimacy. Chateaubriand was the originator of a colourful, suggestive mixture of love, literature and politics forming a single stream of romantic exaltation. His whole being seemed bent on absorbing the greatest possible share of the world and of life—and yet his perpetual state of boredom, of which he complained only too readily, was more than a pose.

His partiality for visiting famous graves and deserted ruins and wandering alone in the shadow of vast antiquities imbues his literary style with the most admirable purity and sincerity. He followed no fashion, he created one. The peculiar nature of his imagination is apparent in the fact that for his genius to become articulate he must be able to grasp the idea of death, of the decline and decay of time, so to speak with his hands; he must hear the rushing of the stream of history and visualize the features of a human face. Everything he invented was second-rate; whenever he made his passion speak and spring to life again he was great. But he could not be satisfied with an inner life nourished by itself alone, he cast wide the line of his desire and was often disappointed by the meagre capture it brought him.

His boredom was genuine, and the many love dramas, political storms and literary sensations he kindled could not save him from a feeling of profound disgust. This was the 'spleen', which had started on its career with Byron and was to affect a good part of the opening century. On the threshold of the epoch that was to transform the life of Christendom so completely, man had become conscious of his omnipotence and his impotence at one and the same time; his spirit overflowed with the fullness of life, yet he found he could not grasp this fullness and transmute it into a personal existence. Ennui and weariness haunted these submerged souls, till they ended by seeking refuge in force, in satisfied desire and appeased ambition. But the remedy proved vain, for desire would never rest and ambition would never be silenced.

Chateaubriand's pessimism and disgust, his melancholy and boredom, aroused disbelief from the first. They were compared with the vehemence of his ambitions, his thirst for recognition and his inextinguishable 'yearning for an earthly Eve', and the contradiction was ascribed to the writer's fashionable conceit. For at the beginning of the nineteenth century gaiety, freshness and a frank appetite for the good things of life were no recommendation for a poet. Pallor, dishevelled hair, a remote gaze, a background of broken amphorae, weeping willows and fallen columns were the poetic equipment of an age in which men had begun to realize that their existence might be called in question and that they might one day be evicted from the centre of creation.

The 'spleen' was a requisite of the age, though of course this did not rule out its genuineness. Chateaubriand gave his early hero René his melancholy as well as his own Christian name. He himself was René to most people for many years afterwards, as though he were in duty bound to assume the attitude he had once so incomparably described in his youthful romance: 'I was acquainted with suffering from my earliest childhood: I bore a germ of suffering within me, as a tree bears the germ of its fruit. A strange poison mingled itself with all my feelings. I am a tormenting dream. Life bores me, boredom has always consumed me; the things that interest other people do not affect me at all. Shepherd or King—what should I have done with my crook or my sceptre? I should have wearied of fame as of privation, of labour as of idleness, of good and bad fortune alike. I am virtuous without complacency; I could be a criminal without remorse. Everything bores me, I trail my boredom along with my days and spend my life yawning.'

Can pessimism be more violently expressed, can it be more closely linked with the sense of mortal decrepitude? An emotion is at work that is wholly opposed to satisfaction since everything is alike in this life. Yet the author had known hunger, and had the best cook in Europe in his service; he had always been lonely, and yet enjoyed the unreserved surrender of the most beautiful women of his time; he had fought, after his own fashion, an obstinate battle with Napoleon, and yet sung his praises more beautifully than any other writer of his day; he had served the Bourbons with exemplary loyalty while despising them; he had covered many thousands of pages with his entrancing prose, and yet hardly ever known what to do with his time. In the act of writing a Diplomatic Note to some foreign Power he was seized with the desire to hasten to the embraces of his mistress. Holding a woman in his arms, he thought of the speech he was about to make as a peer of the realm. He prided himself on having re-opened the churches of France with his book *The Spirit of Christianity*, but was he really a devout Christian? One thing is certain: he was an ardent Catholic 'because as a Frenchman one cannot be anything else'.

His style, whose wonderful emotional force and often extravagant beauty took his age by storm, is inseparable from this *taedium vitae*. No sentence overflowing with vitality but drags in its train another, mourning the decay of all beauty and greatness. In his vast correspondence, which reads like the rough draft of masterpieces, hardly any love-letters are to be found; convinced of his posthumous fame, he was careful to destroy all evidence of this kind. But it is easy to imagine how this man—undersized, we are told, with no beauty except for his magnificent head—must have appealed to women. His kindliness and simplicity in social intercourse were constantly extolled, a fact remarkable enough in a man so excessively jealous of his dignity and so apt to assume pompous attitudes—usually a sign of hypersensitive, irritable egoism. At his very first appearance in Parisian society he earned for himself the epithet 'l'Enchanteur', the Enchanter, which stuck to him all his life, and by which men and women alike referred to him with no tinge of irony.

The charm he exercised must really have been almost irresistible; even such critical observers as Madame de Boigne, Molé and Sainte-Beuve allowed themselves to be ensnared against their will by this atmosphere of melancholy chivalry. Reserved with men, he drove the women he courted to the verge of folly. His personality was so all-conquering that any woman he approached was soon aware of the suffering in store for her and yet could not escape him. He was anything but constant as a lover, and quite capable of kindling and feeding two fires at once. But because in his first approach there was always a melancholy hint of the rupture, the parting to come, he excited a species of exaltation in his victims. 'I'm crazy on him!' exclaimed the beautiful Natalie de Noailles, afterwards Duchess de Mouchy. He often deserted women with regrettable haste, but he never lied to them, since all his protestations of love, however ardent, seemed bathed in the waters of evanescence and secret mourning over the end to come, and it was precisely this that lent them their melancholy attraction.

In the daydreams of his youth, which was spent in the remoteness of the Breton castle of Combourg, he had created a feminine being out of his imagination, endowed with the features of all the girls and young women he had known. This dream creature, whom he called his Sylphide, originated in the erotic unrest by which every emotional boy of fifteen is troubled if he happens to be living among none but his nearest relations, denied all friendly intercourse with outsiders and having only the vaguest notions of the world beyond the woods and fields of his home. But soon this Sylphide of his became something more—a proof that only to a creature of his imagination would be given the power to make him happy. To none of the many women he encountered later, to whom he offered his passion and whose passion he accepted as a tribute, could he bring the fulfilment they yearned for. He aroused wild passions because he loved their violence, but he left the victims of the storm behind without remorse. The person he really loved, with whom he really sympathized up to the final dénouement, was himself. What satisfied his desire was the stirring of his emotions, not their object. How otherwise should a man interest the public, and even posterity, in his love affairs? The lover, regarded as a type, nearly always appears to be bending over his own soul, weighing the force of his feelings not by the loved one but by his ideas.

'He was not fit to be loved', wrote a woman of his day. But was not that precisely what attracted the women, was not the sublimity of the emotions he aroused due to the very fact that they were lavished without hope of total conquest of the beloved? However deep his feelings might be, his mind was entirely pre-occupied with his writing, and the idea of being able to influence the great affairs of this world. His life has sometimes been held to prove that extravagant passions are only aroused by men who are themselves unable to love whole-heartedly and to surrender themselves without reserve. If this be so, René de Chateaubriand can never have made any woman really happy. But one should in fairness remember that nearly all the women he met were unhappy at the time, and fell for him all the sooner for that very reason. Hardly any one of them was in complete harmony with herself; they bore secret wounds, they were in search of something their nature denied them, they were impetuous, morbid and restless.

Madame Récamier alone, to whom he proposed marriage

B

shortly before his death, after years of intimacy, was calm, patient, always the same. But shall we ever find the key to this most famous and best loved woman of her day? Who was ever really the object of her desire, to whom did she ever make the final sacrifice of her enchanting femininity? For all the great men that laid themselves at her feet, all the dramas she gave rise to without ever losing her quiet smile, all the unrestrained homage to her beauty, her kindness (not her cleverness) and her almost supernatural attraction that have been handed down to posterity, there is nothing to suggest that she ever belonged entirely to any man, or ever experienced any true, simple fulfilment of love.

THE DIFFICULTY OF LOVING

Juliette Récamier, the wonder of a century so rich in exceptional people, events and circumstances, alone survived her great friend. Pauline de Beaumont died in his presence; the enchanting Natalie de Noailles lost her reason; Delphine de Custine, who ended by turning satirical and embittered, and Claire de Duras, promoted to the rank of 'dear sister', both preceded him—to say nothing of his wife Céleste, whom he married shortly before emigrating without really knowing her, and for whom he could never feel any great affection. Not till their old age could this strange couple draw a little nearer to each other, and Chateaubriand never attempted to conceal the fact that this sharp-featured, over-pious creature got on his nerves to a terrible degree. She had more wit and self-irony than her somewhat consequential spouse, whose world-famed books she declared she had never read. Her jealousy was unbounded but mostly unspoken: she contented herself with referring ironically to his innumerable female adorers as 'My husband's Ladies'.

But for all her mockery she could not entirely conceal her chagrin at having been assigned the most unthankful role in her husband's life. She listened to his complaints when he was ill or convinced that he was being persecuted; she busied herself with his money affairs, which were always in a muddle and for which she had no more aptitude than he; but she knew there was nothing romantic about her. This did not prevent him as a writer, however, from making ruthless use of her diaries, letters and notes, and incorporating whole pages of them in his own work. She saw through him, she vexed him by smiling satirically at his self-conceit and his illusions, and above all, no doubt, she bored him by her complete lack of coquetry.

Madame de Boigne, who wrote the most revealing memoirs of her time, knew her well, and was highly amused by her malicious stories. But she could not refrain from remarking: 'She did her husband a great deal of harm by making his domestic life unbearable. He was always very considerate towards her, but never succeeded in obtaining peace at his own fireside.'

Céleste had the aridity of a clever wife married to a charming but inconstant husband, and chose to take a sceptical rather than a rosy view of the future. 'Nothing but misfortune can come from Pandora's Box', she used to say, and was never tired of inspiring her husband with distrust of his friends. 'She was filled with hatred,' Vitrolles said of her, 'and saw to it that her husband should always be offended with everybody.' This might have served to bring them together, for Chateaubriand himself was capable of lasting dislikes, but unfortunately she was shrewd enough to discover the weak points in his romantic attitude: 'As I'm not in the least melancholy, and am past the age when sighing is a pleasure, neither the wind nor the moon means anything to me. I like rain for the sake of my lawn, and the sun for the comfort it gives me.'

She brought this sound common sense only too often into play in the attempt to bring her husband to reason; but he was not really so unreasonable, he was merely different, living in an emotional world that was distasteful to her. She knew very well that even when he appeared to be completely under the spell of other women, he was profoundly preoccupied with himself and exclusively concerned with the changes being wrought in his personality.

He could only really love his dream, the Sylphide he had created for himself as a boy, by a sort of mythological process. 'I gave her the eyes of one girl in the village, the fresh complexion of another. The portraits of great ladies of the time of Francis I, Henry IV and Louis XIV, hanging in our drawing-room, lent me other features, and I even borrowed beauties from the pictures of the Madonna in the churches. This magic creature followed me invisibly everywhere, I conversed with her as if with a real person; she changed her appearance according to the degree of my madness: Aphrodite without a veil, Diana shrouded in azure and rose, Thalia in a laughing mask, Hebe with the goblet of youth—or she became a fairy, giving me dominion over nature. I was always altering my picture, taking one charm away to replace it by another. I altered her attire too, borrowing from every country, every century, every religion. When the masterpiece was complete, I rubbed out all my lines and colours again. My one wife turned into a multitude of wives, and in each of them I admired the beauties I had adored in the one.'

To this description, which almost amounts to the description of a disease, he adds: 'The delusion lasted two whole years, in the course of which my soul attained the highest peak of exaltation.' The image he had created could no longer be destroyed. It had become an idol and the measure of all amorous ecstasy. Even the violent feelings the youth entertained for his sister Lucile were of this unreal, over-excited nature. They admired each other, inciting each other to exceed the potentialities of their lonely youth. Lucile, with her restless sensibility, added fuel to the secret fire consuming the boy; she foresaw the future poet in him, and drove him deeper into his melancholy, for to her 'all was care, grief and pain . . . she was convinced that everybody was leagued against her'. Her obsession bound her brother all the closer to her when she appealed, with the persistence of a prophetess, to his genius, of which he himself was not yet aware. Their mutual attachment was so disordered and violent that it came natural to him later on to lay the curse of a guilty passion on his hero René and René's sister Amélie.

The children in the Chateau de Combourg were far from any such entanglement, but each loved himself in the other, and they were henceforth never free from this urge to self-reflection. In after years Lucile's mind became more and more clouded. When

René had become famous he brought her to Paris, where he lodged her with some kindly, religious people. She lived only for her brother, in whose affection she hoped to find relief from her increasing mental derangement. 'My friend,' she wrote to him, 'I have a thousand contradictory notions in my head, of things that appear to exist and yet not to exist. They affect me like objects seen in a mirror, so that one cannot be sure whether one is seeing them clearly. I don't want to have anything more to do with all that. From now onwards I am going to give myself up entirely . . . .' She died soon afterwards, probably by her own hand. Her spirit haunted her brother ever after.

THE LOVELY LIGHT OF OBSCURITY

What led Lucile to her death was closely related to the 'yawning' in which her brother allegedly spent his life: but he had an advantage over his frail sister in his robust instinct of self-preservation, which always drew him out of his shadows and obscurities into the daylight of real life. The urge to action continually dragged him back from the abyss; he wanted to be a great traveller, a great explorer, he hankered after a statesman's responsibility, he strained every fibre of his being in pursuit of outward power, and yet could never forgo the display of his weariness and resignation. He pressed his 'ladies' to use their influence with the King so that he might be sent to this Congress or entrusted with that mission, and almost at the same time he would tell them in a letter how greatly he longed to rest 'on foreign soil', or even 'seek forgetfulness in the shadow of death'.

He was always tormented by the secret longing to make of his life a work of art. But his *weltschmerz* stood in the way. 'I'm sick of life,' he wrote, 'I was sick of it in my youth. It is a malformation of my heart or my mind that I have never been able to correct. I have grown used to it, and am going my way, consumed with boredom, towards the goal I have always felt to be unattainable . . . I had only lived a few hours when the burden of time made its mark on my brow.' The last sentence is one of the exaggerations and misuses of language that so often laid him open to the mockery of his contemporaries. The wish to regard himself as unalterable and appear to have been thus planned and formed by the Creator led him more than once to transgress the laws of taste. He knew himself well enough: 'Although I was always on the verge of boredom, I was capable of attending to the smallest details, for I had inexhaustible patience. Even if the thing I was doing tired me, my obstinacy was stronger than my weariness. I never gave anything up, the accomplishment of which was worth while.'

That was true. He could work with thoroughness, he could display astonishing diligence, returning persistently to the attack, but he never clearly recognized the advantage of a restricted target. What Goethe called 'the challenge of the day', the regular fulfilment of a chosen task with all its difficulties, great and small, was foreign to him. Although he was active in a wider sphere than Goethe, he did not derive the same mental benefit from his activity. Goethe knew that action is of use to the artist only if he sets definite limits to his activity, and never loses sight of his final purpose. His almost mysterious sense of order, which no accident could disturb, was entirely wanting in the great Frenchman, whose daemon drove him to seek satisfaction of his 'insatiable longing for happiness' in politics, although he knew full well that his passions and yearnings could not be appeased by diplomatic activity. Goethe discharged the duties of his modest ministerial post in order to retain control of his limitless genius. Chateaubriand became Minister of Foreign Affairs of a great and powerful country in order to open fresh fields to his genius, to extend the bounds of his life and succeed in taking a hand in the fortunes of the human race.

To widen his existence, not to deepen it. It was not the development of his personality that attracted him but its dispersal over an immeasurable field. Goethe limited himself because of his abundance, Chateaubriand squandered himself from boredom, discontent and lack of ideas. He had ideals in which he believed, for which he fought chivalrously, and which he was incapable of betraying, but he lacked the guiding principle that might have traced a path for his spirit. He had no definite mental conception capable of producing harmony from the dangerous complexity of human thought, feeling and action. He was a Legitimist out of loyalty, he adhered to the Throne out of chivalry, he defended religion from a sense of tradition, but he never succeeded in extracting a moral, a doctrine, or even a theory from these three attitudes. In spite of his many essays on historical, religious and political subjects, he never produced anything—in comparison with contemporaries such as Joseph de Maistre and de Bonald—resembling a system or even a theoretical proposition.

It should always be remembered, however, that he began to write at the end of the eighteenth century, and it was as an emigrant, moreover, that he took up his pen. In his poverty-stricken years as a refugee in London his spirit knew only two supports, which he had brought with him into exile, namely the philosophy of the eighteenth century and the Breton nobleman's feeling for tradition. These two possessions waged a hard battle in his heart as well as his brain. Neither lost but neither won. Poetic fiction intervened in overwhelming fashion and created a new kingdom, which Chateaubriand conquered for French literature.

Years later another great writer, Benjamin Constant, defined a position intended to represent his own, but which expresses Chateaubriand's genius far better: 'If I am to be reproached for not having defined religious feeling more precisely, I would ask how one can precisely define those of our moral sentiments which because of their vagueness and depth defy every effort of speech. How can one define the impression of a dark night or a virgin forest, of the wind moaning among ruins or over graves, of the sea, losing itself in endless distance? How can one define the emotion that seizes one on reading the songs of Ossian, at the sight of St. Peter's, when meditating on death or realizing the harmony of sounds and forms? How can one define the condition of reverie, that inner trembling of the soul, in which all the powers of sense and thought are lost in a mysterious transfusion?'

Chateaubriand himself did not attempt to define these emotions, but his expression of them was so penetrating that French literary style was caught up in it as a shore is overrun by waves. It could be said that the language itself was astonished at its own capacity.

All that Rousseau had once felt and could only half express because his painful coming to terms with himself and society stood in the way, all the convulsions of nature that re-echo in the human breast, man's urge to plumb the infinity of his own spirit and to suffer from it as an angel suffers from his wings, all these things found expression through Chateaubriand. He loosened the tongue of the century and paved the way for the romantic triumphs that came after him and altered human consciousness for good and evil.

It is easy to see why many of his books are no longer readable today. The discovery of human personality, which he greeted with the shout of the mariner sighting land at last, is now complete; passions have abdicated; the barriers against which his characters were hurled by their inner tumults have long been broken down; guilt, which was such a powerful motif in his romances, has taken other directions: it no longer resides in the conscience of the individual, but must be attributed to circumstances and conditions. But he remains the great writer of the turn of the century, even if much of his influence was transmitted through Byron, who is inconceivable without his great French neighbour.

His individualism formed a counterpart to Napoleon's autocracy, and he always felt it to be so; but suffering, which found no place in the great ruler's character, was his particular sphere, in which he dwelt alone. The hero of romance, with his wild locks, his faraway gaze, victim and yet lord of his destiny, gloomy-minded, filled with the despair that he contrived to transmute into charm, is entirely a type of his creation. Add to this the rebel for whom even crime may be a road to freedom, and we have the captivating, picturesque outlaw who has had his assured place in literature ever since. Of the hero of his early novel he says: 'To feel innocent, and be condemned by law, seemed to René a sort of triumph over the social order.' This revolt was alive in the author himself and gave him his inward and outward independence.

His life alternated between highly paid government posts and troublesome money difficulties. In spite of high pay, royal gifts, enormous allowances, loans, sales and auctions, he never achieved wealth. Material cares pursued him even in his old age, but they had no power over him. His sense of honour, often tinged with arrogance, and his almost senseless thirst for independence, made it easy for him to send in sensational resignations, retire from highly paid posts of honour, call off advantageous agreements, auction his library and take his gold-embroidered Court uniform to the dealer in old clothes. In spite of all the high offices, titles and honours, in spite of the Orders, Eagles, Crowns, Fleeces and Ribbons with which the favour and respect of sovereigns decorated him, there was always something of the gypsy in him, secretly opposed to the recognized order of things. The artist in him often conquered the society lion.

The certainty of being an artist influenced him as much as the fact of being a Breton nobleman, a Grand Seigneur of a province that had come into the possession of France only late and reluctantly. His pride of birth took a peculiar form: he had no wish to be distinguished by his company or his tricks of speech, he practised no social exclusiveness, he wished for no honours or titles because he felt himself the equal of all the great ones of this world. His loyalty to the Throne was not rooted in his intelligence, for he could seldom approve the conduct or the politics of the restored Bourbons—in fact, when he went over to the Opposition later on he was something of a Liberal. But his monarchism was unshakable, the King himself could not divert him from it. His loyalty tended to isolate him at a time when everybody else trimmed their sails to the wind; his sense of honour cut him off from the multitude who disowned everything that might be to their prejudice. The haughty vicomte he could be when he chose was inseparable from the lonely artist he always was. Both were opposed to the new society that was beginning to spring up after all the heroically useless upheavals; both of them ignored the masses, which were just beginning to turn into an independent phenomenon and preparing to impose the pattern of uniformity on mankind.

His self-sufficiency offended most of those he had to deal with, and yet soon after his return from emigration he was able to command a respect such as never fell to Rousseau's lot. Although he did not realize his capacity as a writer until the period of his exile in London, he was one of those who brought back the heritage of French literature to their old country, like the Ark of the Covenant. The Revolution, which had driven out the young nobleman, had at the same time driven out a spirit that not only preserved its essence on alien soil but, as a result of its transplantation, acquired a wider social outlook and learnt to consider the world at large as a higher unit than the world of France alone.

Only one of his kind had remained in France—André Chénier, the great lyricist, who was executed literally on the last day of the Terror, although his mediocre brother had functioned as a sort of Party Poet. The remainder, including foreigners like Madame de Staël, Benjamin Constant and de Maistre, and emigrants like Rivarol, Bonald, Senancour, Senac de Meilhan and Chateaubriand, had settled in London, Hamburg, Anspach, Geneva, Neuchâtel, St. Petersburg and Philadelphia. They counted the days to their return, of course, but the best of them never lost courage, for they had taken the images of their gods with them, and although the Revolution appeared to be running its course in their absence, they were still the custodians of all that the eighteenth century had bequeathed in the way of ideas, forms and knowledge worth living for. As soon as the Revolution had accomplished its bloody work, France had need of the *emigrés* again, as trustees of a buried treasure the new age could not do without. For this reason the young Chateaubriand, who had first learnt to write in a foreign land, found his place immediately on his return.

No matter to what depths his life in exile had driven him, he did not feel that he had ever been uprooted. It was France that had lost her roots, but now that thanks to Bonaparte she was once again his motherland, he had little difficulty in recognizing her and finding his way under new conditions. Suffering balanced suffering: the Breton aristocrat had known starvation and want, the French people to whom he returned had known poverty and terror. But no comparison was called for; though the wounds inflicted by the Revolution had not yet healed, France was now greater than before. She had fought victorious campaigns, extended her territory and pinned glory to her new standard, the tricolour. Over the threshold of the new age hung, huge and intimidating, the shadow of a great soldier-statesman, hardly more than a youth, a slender General whose sudden fame had made of France, still in the throes of fever, the most powerful country of the world.

Chateaubriand's taste for greatness was not offended, therefore, when he returned to France to assume the leadership of literature. The days of humiliation were over, it lay with him and his kind to bring the literary sterility of the Revolutionary epoch to an end. He not only became a great author, he created the modern type of writer, whose life and looks are a part of public life. The autonomy of the literary personality, which contributes so much to the fascination of France, was first firmly established in him. He completed what Voltaire began. Literature became a public force; its greatest representatives, of whom he was the foremost, ranked in future with statesmen and high authorities. He endowed literary life with a style that became prevalent, was further developed by Lamartine and brought to its peak by Victor Hugo. A particular form of human freedom was thus injected into the foundations of European civilization for all time. The writer assumed his share of power as the guardian of human sovereignty, and was recognized as such. Chateaubriand might not have succeeded in doing this, had it not been for his unwavering instinct for the aristocratic life. Not that he wished to play the Grand Seigneur with a gift for writing; he was a man of letters first and foremost, but his social position being above attack, he could combine a life in consonance with tradition with a life of utmost freedom, without visible seam.

IN PRAISE OF SELF-ESTEEM

Chateaubriand's life, as we see it today, is a triumph of personality, in spite of the neglect into which many of his works have fallen. He is a phenomenon by reason of a unity of personality seldom met with today, the intensity of his love and hatred, and his attitude towards himself. He was no great innovator in the realm of ideas, but his character presents a whole in its frailties and idiosyncracies. He was never anything but himself; he represents, in short, the perfect type of the artist, for he referred everything to himself, measured all happiness and all suffering by his own emotions, and proved that self-esteem is not only one of the commonest of human characteristics but an inseparable part of the artist's equipment.

Goethe often analysed the nature of conceit and praised it as a social asset. 'A conceited man,' he said to Riemer, 'can never be entirely discourteous; he wants to please, and therefore accommodates himself to others.' Of self-liking he says: 'The wish to communicate this liking to others makes one complaisant, a sense of one's own agreeableness makes one agreeable. Would to God all men were conceited, but with conviction, with moderation and in the right way, for we should then be the happiest of men in the cultured world.'

Chateaubriand met this demand too, for while he loved solitude so much that he could dally with it, and though his melancholy moods were genuine enough, on social occasions he was the delight of his friends. His playful pleasure in his own intellect entranced everybody in his company; though he listened more than he talked, everybody felt himself addressed, noticed and appreciated. The simplicity of his manners, his natural politeness and his enjoyment of other people's stories made of the man who in public life could appear so cold and consequential, a good companion easily given to innocent jests and tomfoolery. He knew how to 'accommodate' himself to others, provided those others were of the right kind.

The artist's conceit lends itself to all kinds of misinterpretation. Chateaubriand was a great artist, and yet remained the Vicomte with lofty conceptions of loyalty and honour, so lofty that they amounted to convictions. His excessive, often offensive, pride had, however, nothing to do with his feudal origin but, on the contrary, with his ability to be an artist without abandoning his station in life. The Revolution could destroy institutions, it could abolish rank, but it could not kill the consciousness of social standing.

Even Napoleon, creating a new élite of his own, was obliged to assimilate it to the social distinctions of the old order. Chateaubriand could preserve his ties with his provenance while giving free rein to the anarchy of art with which he was imbued. His nature was unyielding, but he could bow to the powers and symbols to which his forefathers had bowed. He took an almost arrogant pride in entertaining sinister ideas and evoking the violence of passion without abandoning a hair's breadth of his hereditary traditions. He felt capable of every excess, even of crime, and it is by no mere accident that the subject of incest plays a like part in his novel, *René*, as in Byron's life, but the certitude that he would never really overstep the bounds intensified his self-assurance to the point of defiance. He would have walked upon the water if such a proof of his uniqueness had been demanded of him.

He was persuaded that he was a unique phenomenon; but this had nothing to do with the thousand and one little vanities of which he was capable. Of course he could never leave himself out of the picture. Even when formulating a declaration of war he would be alive to his celebrated style, even while negotiating with a foreign potentate he looked forward to the description he would be giving that evening to his mistress—or if need be, to his wife—of this historic occasion. He could never see a ruined temple without reminding people that he himself was subject to the law of decay. He connnected every sunset with the astonishing fact that his own light must one day be extinguished, albeit in splendour. The idea of death held the balance in his breast with this dazzling sense of his uniqueness, and these meditations in the spirit of Gray's Elegy, which he so much admired, were perfectly sincere, for he was as sure of the divine spark in himself as of the vanity of all flesh.

Despondency and self-assurance both go to the make-up of the artist. Penetrated with the supremacy of his task, he is at one moment forced to realize the insufficiency of his skill, at the next he draws strength again from forces whose nature is a mystery even to himself. The lonely soul pitting itself against society and its laws fights for its life in alternating defeat and triumph. The artist's secret lies in the form that is forever being broken and remade. Diligence is not sufficient, for it is associated with the sense of exhaustion; but the certainty that the form will be fitted together again by some remote, mysterious power bearing his own features, this is the triumphant conviction, which, however short-lived the victory, gives the artist the self-assurance so offensive to his contemporaries.

Chateaubriand was a solitary by nature, but fully aware of his artistic powers. His singular childhood had accustomed him to rely on himself alone, and to consider his own feelings as the highest court of appeal. Nobody had ever disturbed his high opinion of himself; his sister Lucile had even encouraged it. Timid and yet unrestrained, like the fauna of ancient forests, he felt capable of containing the whole of creation within himself. He never wholly surrendered himself, and no matter how much he found to feed his heart and senses upon in later life, it was always with love itself that he was in love. His emotional agitation filled him with pride, he looked upon even his sufferings as a work of art, or at any rate as something that raised him above the common herd. He could love the object of his emotions to the point of licentiousness for the sake of the image of himself that she reflected; the radiant reflection increased his stature and fed his pride.

His devotion to public affairs tended in the same way to further his persistent preoccupation with himself. He served them for honour's sake, and honour was to him entirely his own personal affair. The victory of the good cause mattered less to him than the satisfaction of his sense of honour and his chivalrous loyalty. In the hour of danger he was always on the spot; in the hour of reward he was not at hand. This too was an effect of his pride. His high-souled attitude to the principle of Legitimacy was undoubtedly concerned with that principle, but it also enhanced his sense of being personally great and independent. His finest hour was always one in which the Crown had nothing left to hope for and nothing more to bestow. The Mighty Ones with whom he had to deal soon became aware of the arrogance this attitude concealed, and this may well have been the reason why he had so few friends.

He was very chary of the trust he reposed in other people. Though as a writer he had restored the power of speech to his generation, he was reticent as regards personal communication. He was always so preoccupied with himself that he had acquired little knowledge of human nature in general. His habit of sub-merging himself in the fount of his ego, whenever an impression or a stimulus reached him from the outer world, had weaned him so radically from consideration of his fellow men that there was now only one man left to interest him, and that was himself. He regarded the passions that convulsed him as exclusively characteristic of himself; he alone, so he believed, was capable of these inner tumults, these yearnings and exaltations. He was convinced that he wept tears such as no other mortal had wept before him, he took the melancholy of all creation to be the work of his own heart, he made the uncertainty that rules our life an element of his personal tragedy.

He saw his literary work in the same light: 'Among the French authors of my day I am so to speak the only one whose life corresponds to his work. I have been a traveller, a soldier, a statesman, a publicist. It was in forests that I sang of the forest, on board ship that I pictured the sea; I was at the front when I wrote of the profession of arms; it was in exile that I learnt what exile means, in Courts, offices of state and Assemblies that I made a study of Princes, politics and laws. But ever since the reign of Louis XIV our writers have too often been isolated people whose talents were fitted to express the spirit of their epoch but not to deal with its events. If I was destined to live, I was intended to represent the principles, the ideas, the events, the catastrophes, the epic of my time in my own person, all the more in that I have witnessed an end and a beginning of a whole world, and because the opposite characters of this end and beginning were mingled in my own ideas. I found myself between two centuries, at the confluence, as it were, of two great rivers. I plunged into their troubled waters, reluctantly deserting the familiar shores on which I was born, and swam across, full of hope, to the unknown coast on which the new generations are to land.'

He was fully alive, therefore, to the representative importance of his personality. He saw clearly that his life was inseparable from his work; he may even have had an inkling that his life would prove more enduring as a work of art than almost anything he wrote, since everything he did and recorded was illustrative of his time. No wonder if even in his most intimate impulses one can detect a sidelong glance at his own generation, or at any rate at posterity. Was he not bound to feel he was living on a stage, in front of which his own generation formed the audience? The poison of historical consciousness first excited him to an extravagant degree and then plunged him, when the intoxication subsided, in an almost crippling sense of emptiness. Even at the peak of his fame he said of himself: 'I live alone in a great house, bored, and uncertainly awaiting something I do not wish for and that will never come.'

At the age of sixty-four he wrote to the beautiful, light-minded Hortense Allart: 'My life is a mere accident, I know I ought not to have been born. Take from this accident its movement, its passion and its misfortune, and I shall have given you in one day more than others in long years. . . .' Thus in the same sentence he denies the significance of his life, of which he is usually so persuaded, and, full of self-esteem, assumes superiority over everything around him. He knows that women can be seduced by a display of suffering, that wooing is never more effective than in the guise of a melancholy pessimism, but he adds the rash boast of being a more magnificent lover than any other. His triumphs and defeats, his devotion and his egoism form a turbulent flood in which he seeks to drag with him the object of his desire.

Chateaubriand enjoyed his fame with the same dignity with which he had borne his miserable life in exile, but the sense of his unique position inspired him with some arrogant expressions that have passed into legend. His 'I and Napoleon', so often repeated, with its suggestion of two forces of equal importance, actually anticipated the coupling by posterity of these contrasting poles of a dynamic epoch; but he stung many of his contemporaries to the quick by utterances of this kind, and the coolness with which he was treated by the Royal House may be explained by examples of grandiose arrogance such as these.

'I seated the Bourbons on the Throne again.' No sovereign cares to hear utterances of this kind, even if there is a modicum of truth in them. 'I re-opened the Church to the French people', he said, alluding to his undeniably revolutionary book *The Spirit of Christianity.* Referring to his polemic *De Buonaparte et des Bourbons,* which appeared in 1814, with its disparaging 'u' in the name of the fallen hero, he declared it had been 'more useful to the King than an army of a hundred thousand men'. Then there was 'My Spanish War was a gigantic undertaking', and 'When Napoleon had done with the kings he hadn't yet done with me'. And finally 'Suppose I had died at that moment and there had been no Chateaubriand? How different would have been the fate of the world!'

The deprecation that such remarks provoke even today cannot alter the fact that this obsession with the self was a new phenomenon in intellectual life at that time. No writer of the eighteenth century would have dared to attribute to the individual, whose sovereignty was even then undisputed, the importance that Chateaubriand did. A new sense of freedom appears in these seeming extravagances of self-consciousness. Of course he could not foresee how quickly men would tire of this freedom, nor all that they would invent in order to rid themselves of this individuality again, but he foresaw that the nineteenth century, in the middle of which he died, would be, in a sense, the shortest of all centuries.

This man, so closely bound in appearance in the fetters of tradition, who knelt to a monarchy whose final disappearance he foresaw, for whom honour and loyalty were not moral but aristocratic principles, this man of letters who sought in political power the satisfaction that neither love nor literary fame could afford him, this René who never seemed to talk of anybody but himself, declared in his old age: 'Nobody has ever really known the bottom of my heart; most of my feelings have remained buried there, or only come to light in my works, applied to imaginary beings.' A surprising assertion in the mouth of a writer who ventured to make himself the highest court of appeal and the sole source of his own creations. But he did in fact conceal a great deal; his *Memoirs from beyond the Grave,* which have come down to us as his greatest work and belong to the peaks of world literature, are full of his personality, the effect he produced, his views, his time and his boredom. But they are unrevealing when it comes to

c

the people he loved, and sucked into the wake of his life. How discreet he is when his story leads along the edge of a great passion! However, he lived in an epoch much given to writing, and countless memorials have come down to us of his commerce with other people and his influence on them.

His lot, as he says, was cast at the meeting-point of two centuries; worlds were collapsing and rising again in fresh guise. Everybody was aware of this, everybody heard the reverberation and saw the signs, but he alone realized that all the tumult of history, all the splendour of coronations and victories, all the misery and greed of the rising masses had only one significance: to serve man and afford him a background for his grandeur and frailty. More things happen in a single brain, a single heart, than on all the battlefields, in all the Cabinet Meetings, all the Revolutions. The artist is there to make this truth visible and inescapable. Chateaubriand was an artist whose aerial flights and whose vanities all had their source in the same certainty. The mirror is the most fruitful symbol for human creative powers. Chateaubriand saw himself in the mirror; we look over his shoulder and discover a world.

II

A BRETON ARISTOCRAT

THE CASTLE ON THE HEATH

A HEAVY gale had been blowing for days, driving the waves against the ancient ramparts of Saint-Malo. Although it was only the beginning of autumn the weather had been bad for weeks. During the evening of the 3-4 September, 1768, the storm attained such force that the harbour-master ordered the alarm to be sounded for the removal to safety of the small craft rocking in the harbour. The relics of Saint-Malo had been exhibited in the Cathedral Choir for some days past, by order of the Bishop and Chapter, according to pious usage in time of peril. Despite the lateness of the hour many of the faithful had fought their way through the hurricane to the church, but their singing was drowned by the thunder of the furious sea dashing with restless force against cliffs and city walls. It was during that night, in an old house built into the ramparts, with windows overlooking the sea, that François-René de Chateaubriand was born. The storm had no difficulty in drowning his first cries, for he was a puny infant and showed little inclination to live. He was the last of ten children, four of whom had died in infancy.

Saint-Malo was at that time a wealthy, well-established city; the commerce from which it derived its importance went mostly hand in hand with war, England being nearly always the enemy. The ships' captains carried on a lucrative trade as privateers, furnished with royal letters of marque. The shipowners were also engaged in the slave trade; they sent their ships to the coasts of Guinea and sold the 'black cargo' they purchased there from the Arab man-hunters to the French planters in the colonies of the New World. Chateaubriand's father had himself made his fortune as a shipowner and merchant-captain. Although he was descended from one of the most distinguished families of the local nobility, he was too poor as a young man to buy a commission as a naval officer, and had made a career in merchant shipping. He amassed a considerable fortune, chiefly in the slave trade which, far from being tabooed, was specially assisted by the authorities. A taciturn, almost morose man, who never indulged in a pleasure and never gave way to a smile, he constantly brooded on the fact that he had been obliged in his youth to toil for rich merchants as a second steersman among rough companions—he 'whose forebears had commanded their vassals at Bouvines and held supreme command of Breton naval squadrons'. 'My father had only one passion,' his son wrote of him later, 'a passion for his name. His usual mood was one of profound sadness, which increased with age, and a habit of silence, broken only by outbursts of temper. The hope of restoring its ancient splendour to his family had made him avaricious, at the States Assembly of Brittany he treated the nobles with arrogance, he was harsh to his peasants, taciturn, despotic and threatening at home: his aspect inspired fear.' The urge to restore the lustre of his name drove him to work hard, to shrink from no transaction, and to pile gold piece on gold piece. Suddenly he presented himself, with a huge sum of money, as the purchaser of a feudal castle. His forefathers' stronghold was no more to be had, it had long since passed into the possession of the Condés, so he bought Combourg, more a fortress than a château, a tall, gloomy building with four huge corner towers, the oldest of which dated from the year 1100. He had thereby acquired the right to call himself Count of Combourg, Lord of Gaugres 'and other titles'. To his eldest son, Jean-Baptiste, he would now be able to bequeath a magnificent estate and a resplendent name; his one request to fate had been fulfilled.

René was nine years old when he moved with his mother and sisters to Combourg, where his father had hitherto been living alone. On a May morning the family took their departure from Saint-Malo, travelling in an old-fashioned coach with gilt carvings, and purple tassels on the roof. Eight horses with little bells on their necks, silver-plated harness and bright-coloured saddle-cloths drew the enormous vehicle with its load of five noisy, happy children and their mother—absorbed in her missal—through the Breton heath country. Gorse, juniper bushes and heather as far as the eye could see. Every now and then they met a long-haired, weather-beaten peasant in a broad-brimmed hat, wearing a coat of mangy goatskin and driving his lean oxen before him with shrill cries. Or they overtook a charcoal-burner with two little horses, hauling his burden to the villages. Otherwise the country was deserted, but it had a fresh tang in the spring sunshine, and above it stretched a limitless sky, in whose soft haze a few rounded clouds were drifting.

Suddenly a valley opened, the spire of a little village church came into sight, and behind it, out of a heavy mass of old trees, the dark, almost forbidding castle raised its four great towers to the sky. The towers had pointed roofs surmounting black battlements; loopholes and machicolations gave the towers a suspicious, menacing look. The bare walls of the main building were broken by a few very small windows. Everything was protected by gratings, studded with nails, crenelated, savouring of war. The owner received his family at the massive gateway; for once he was smiling, proud of introducing them to this magnificent family seat. The interior of the castle, on nearer acquaintance, turned out to be a good deal less magnificent, and its prison-like severity soon lay heavy on the children's spirits; but for the moment the fun of exploring had the upper hand. All day long they reconnoitred the spiral staircases, the secret passages, the dungeons and the granaries. In the ancient armouries they found rusty lumber covered with black cobwebs, the flooring of the galleries was rotten, everything smelt mouldy, and through the chinks in the door-frames streaks of sunlight fell like luminous bars of dancing dust. The air was full of mystery and forgotten histories. There was said to be a ghost: an old gentleman with a wooden leg might be seen coming down the turret staircase at night; sometimes the wooden leg walked alone, accompanied by a cat. But outside the castle there was space and fresh air, and an old pond bordered by gigantic oaks mirroring their tops in its calm surface. The thick underwood concealed birds in such numbers as the children had never seen. It was May, everything was in bloom, and it was a joy to rush out into the open from the silent chill of the old fortress.

René spent the most decisive years of his youth at Combourg. His father sent him for a year or two to the grammar school in the neighbouring town of Dol, but the holidays were long and frequent, and the old castle was the real background of his early development. In later life he came to know the forests of America, the deserts of Syria, the multi-coloured East, the quiet of English villages, but it was the colours, the play of light, the ever-changing aspects of nature at Combourg that he was to absorb into himself and make his own for ever. No bird would ever sing again like the birds in the beech hedges at home, no night would ever be so full of mystery as the boy's nights in the Moorish turret, no distance so alluring as the Breton heath, and no encouragement would mean so much to him, no intimacy enrich him so greatly as that of his sister Lucile, the unforgettable companion of those early years.

THE MYSTERY OF PLEASURE AND REPENTANCE

Lucile was left alone at Combourg; her three older sisters married noblemen of equal birth in the neighbouring town of Fougères, while René was sent to the Jesuits in Rennes, the capital of the province, to improve his knowledge of mathematics, his father having decided that he was to be an officer in the Royal Navy. But he pursued his studies irregularly and unmethodically; learning came easy to him, and while his slower comrades were brooding over their tasks he gave himself up to secret reading, with a fevered brain and disordered emotions. An unabridged edition of Horace was a sudden revelation of the joyous world of the ancients; the beauty of goddesses assumed a special significance, he felt the pagan breath of an unimagined freedom. He read Virgil, and then Tibullus, and a channel was suddenly dug for his indistinct emotions and mental excitement. The alders by the river mingled their rustling with the laughter of the nymphs whose white forms could be glimpsed slipping through the bushes. The gods were gods because they lived more fully, more energetically and freely than mortal men, forever threatened by the anger of superior powers.

But what was the gloom of Hades beside the pains of eternal damnation, which he found so horrifically described in the sermons of the illustrious Massillon? His teachers, who looked with suspicion on his browsings on antiquity, were only too glad to give him the run of this famous preacher's works. They did not know what the boy was looking for in these warnings, threats and promises. The ambiguous lustre of sin attracted him no less than the voluptuous contrition of the prodigal son or the beautiful sinner. The heartrending dissonances of pleasure and repentance haunted him even in his sleep. The joys of which the ancient poets sang were fleeting, and steeped in a premonition of decay; the sufferings imposed on the penitent were assuaged by the mild breath of assured forgiveness.

But what contradictions his youthful conscience had to contend with, now that the sunset glow of the classical world and the tremors of Christian emotion had made themselves felt almost at the same moment! 'A strange world rose up around me. On the one hand I guessed at secrets inaccessible to me at that age, an existence entirely different from my own, enjoyments far removed from my amusements, the obscure fascination of a sex the only members of which I had known so far were my mother and sisters; on the other hand stood terrible phantoms dragging chains, spitting fire and threatening me with eternal torments for a single unconfessed sin.'

There was no easy way out of these conflicts. What the commandments of the Church demanded of him if he was to be worthy to receive the consecrated wafer seemed to him impossible to fulfil. But to whom should he confess his unworthiness? To receive the body of the Lord in a state of mortal sin was to fling oneself irretrievably into the jaws of Hell to eternal damnation. He lay sleepless at night, his mind wandering obsessed and appalled in a realm that could wear such perplexing colours. The white goddesses smiled at him, the powerful gods, stark naked, offered him their bows and arrows, but the glow of Hell flooded ever and again over this ambiguous world, while into the dread of eternal punishment crept the secret satisfaction of suffering from a body that must one day either burn or triumph.

It fell to an understanding confessor to help the boy over this threshold, at what cost we are not told. René was one day to be an ardent eulogist of Christianity and a respectful Catholic; he was to extol the beauties of the true faith and enhance, in magnificent prose, the haloes of the martyrs that suffered a cruel death for their faith; he was to make a pilgrimage to the Holy Sepulchre, and sit at the right hand of the Pope. In his old age his confessor commissioned him to write the life of Armand de Rancé, the founder of the Trappist Order, which proved one of his finest books; but he was never to find the way to a simple, tranquil piety. He was to be many things—a wanderer, an exile, a lover, an illustrious writer, one of the great men of this world, but he was never to be a saint.

His mother was a very devout woman; in later life she was never seen without her missal, and spent many hours of the day in the castle chapel. But to how few pious mothers it is given to save their sons the painful discord between soul and body! His timid, high-strung sister Lucile became the confidante of his perplexities. Lucile was a handsome girl with raven hair and expressive eyes, the mingled ardour and melancholy of which foreshadowed mental derangement to come. She delighted in her own romantic pallor, her floating veils and loose-flying locks. Her sensibility and impetuosity made her a fit companion for the adolescent boy, with whom she often roamed hand in hand through the woods, or waited, leaning against the old wayside cross, for him to join her in an evening walk.

She always appeared to be plunged in some deep reverie or impenetrable melancholy. He knew she slept badly at night, had all-too significant dreams, sensed the approach of imaginary dangers, believed she was pursued by evil forces, and cherished a grief in her heart, of which she did not know the cause. This bound him all the closer to her; there were times when he could not bring himself to leave go of her hand; the mutual enjoyment of their melancholy made of the tenderness binding them to each

other a secret that nobody ever penetrated. Together they spun
the endless thread of their youthful *weltschmerz*, assimilating the
grand, austere landscape of the Breton heath to this unreasoning
melancholy, listening to the voice of the wind in the ancient tree-
tops, and detecting in it the tidings of a nameless grief.

They read together; his sense of form was kindled by the old
poets, to whom Homer was now added, and by the rich command
of language of the Old Testament Lamentations. They copied
out fine passages; Lucile tried her hand at verse, and when
language failed her before the beauties of nature she would say
to her brother. '*You* ought to describe that!' The words echoed in
his ear like a magic watchword, the voice of some mysterious
fairy pointing to the entrance of an unknown kingdom. Despite
his preoccupation with his Sylphide, the woman of his dreams,
endued with all the attractions and perfections he could think of,
it was Lucile's lips that framed the first hint of his vocation. The
Sprite with whom he held imaginary conversations, and whose
silhouette he altered daily according to his mood, created the
basis of his future behaviour towards women. He was to desire
and conquer many, but would never make any of them happy
because none of them would have the perfection of his dream.
But his sister pronounced the magic word that awoke the germ
of his artistic power. She confirmed his melancholy, encouraged
his youthful weariness of life and led him to cherish grief as
something to be desired rather than resisted, but she handed him,
so to speak prophetically, the means by which he could conjure
these dangers and turn them to his own use. Poetry entered
René's destiny through a door that Lucile had set ajar.

Their father had no idea of the intense inner life his two
children were leading together. Even René's desultoriness, in-
clining now to this profession, now to that, did not seem to worry
him overmuch. Was he even aware of his family around him? He
seldom exchanged a word with them, but he seems to have been
pursued by the fear of not making adequate provision for their
future. Nothing broke the monotony of his days except shooting,
of which he was passionately fond, and which allowed him to
roam alone about the moors and forests with his gun. Visitors

hardly ever came, except for a few of the neighbouring nobility on their way to Rennes, to attend the session of the Breton Parliament which was held every winter. They arrived at dusk, on horseback, pistols in holster, *couteau de chasse* at their side, followed by a servant whose horse also carried the master's valise. They begged hospitality, for the road to Rennes was a long one, and the inns few and far between. The old man received them at the gates with old-fashioned courtesy and housed them in the north tower, in the room known as Queen Christina's bedchamber, containing a huge bed with four gilt bed posts. Before they retired there was much talk of the campaigns in Hanover, family history—everybody being related to everybody else—and their eternal lawsuits. The host was friendly, almost garrulous with these compeers of his, whose exclamations at the vastness of the castle filled him with secret delight. Early next morning the children saw them riding away over the snow-covered fields, scaring up the crows, till they were lost in the haze of the limitless heath.

At other times life flowed monotonously on. The old Count began to feel the burden of his years, his left arm became almost paralysed. Shooting fatigued him more and more, and his days were long. Every morning at four, summer and winter, he got up and woke his servant, who lived in another, distant part of the castle; at five a cup of coffee was brought to him in his study. In his record chest with its unwieldy locks he kept his sugarloaf and candles— a fragment of the precious sugar and a single candle his daily allowance. Tardily, scantily the daylight made its way through the loophole in the massive wall. While his wife prayed the morning away in the chapel, the Count turned over the pages of his ancient documents to make sure he was not being cheated of any of the feudal rights due to him as Lord of Combourg. The village was small and decrepit, the peasants poor and extremely dirty, they could hardly contrive to support their miserable lives, but their landlord insisted on his rights. More and more long-forgotten privileges came to light. The living of Mont-Dole owed him one pair of white gloves per annum; the parishioners of Québriac a cake of puff paste and five pieces of silver. He was lord of various weekly markets, at the entrance to which he posted his armed serfs, to collect a toll for every animal driven in.

His rights, in his eyes, had something sacred about them; he was not ill-natured, but old corsair and slave-trader that he was, he was gradually consumed with pride of a rank that he held to be the basis of social order. He sat for hours in his dark study with its heavy table laden with old records and accounts, staring at the tapestry over the fireplace on which the family tree of the house of Chateaubriand was pictured. He seldom went to Mass; he left the chapel entirely to his wife. He still adhered to the Old Order, which in France was beginning to show cracks, but he was pious more from tradition than conviction. God, to him, was 'the first of all nobles' or 'the great Landlord up above'.

His attitude to the Crown was hardly more cordial, it was determined mainly by honour and loyalty; in politics he sided with the *Frondeurs,* who detested the Court and its manners and were infuriated by the government's attempts to lay something of the growing burden of taxation on the nobility. He was quite aware that people shrugged their shoulders in contempt when he chose to appear at Versailles. He knew that they considered him a rustic oddity, a petrified country squire; but this did not worry him, for much as he despised the capital, he was in one sense a modern man: he was a 'philosopher', a rationalist that is, who had read the works of Montesquieu and the dissenting Jesuit Raynal, and to the Countess's distress, made light of the benediction of the Church.

OWL SHOOTING

The family and the domestic staff were scattered all over the rambling castle. Young René had his room in the remotest of the four old towers; he had an endless spiral staircase to climb and then a gallery to cross, through the battlements of which could be seen the edge of the distant forest. When the gales of autumn whistled, rattling the decaying shutters, when the torn clouds scudded over the moon and the screech-owls complained, this journey to his remote bare bedroom was quite a romantic undertaking, but he was not afraid, he loved the mysterious stirrings of the dark countryside and his lonely lodging. In summer, after supper, the family sat on the castle terrace enjoying the twilight, but their peace was often disturbed by the Count—who aways kept his gun beside him—shooting at the owls as they left their hiding-places under the corbels and battlements. The shot echoed far over the quiet fields, as René and Lucile sat watching the slow paling of the sky and the appearance of the first stars.

But summer does not last long in Brittany. When the days grew short they spent the evening in the great hall, a long room hung with family portraits, one end of which was used for meals, while at the other stood a huge fireplace round which they gathered after supper. Sighing, as was her wont, the Countess lay down on her sofa, beside which stood a little round table with a single lighted candle upon it, and the children crouched in front of the fire to watch the play of the flames. The servant cleared the table and left the room. The Count then started on his usual perambulations. Wrapped in a monkish garment of white woollen material, his bony scalp hidden under a tall white cap, he deserted the fireplace to walk restlessly up and down, out of reach of the light thrown by fire and candle, his footsteps echoing in the darkness. Then he drew slowly nearer to the fire again, emerging all at once in his white garments like a ghost out of the shadow.

The children whispered to each other when he was out of sight and fell silent again as he approached. 'What have you just been talking about?' he would ask as he went by, but the children could not get a word out for fright. He went on with his rambling, and again nothing was heard but his regular footsteps, with now and then a sigh from the Countess, and the soughing of the wind. Only once, according to René, did things happen differently. One evening his father suddenly interrupted his walk, seated himself beside the children at the fireside and told them the story of his youthful hardships and his adventures as a sailor. Paris, though he had lived there, he referred to only as an abominable place, and as though it was in some foreign country. To a Breton, Greenland was not out of reach, but Paris was at the end of the world. The boy listened, deeply affected; the old man had never opened his heart so wide before. A father could suffer too, then, could discover as a child the bitterness of life and other people's lack of comprehension; he could feel the want of tenderness . . .

The Count stopped suddenly, as if he had gone too far, pulled his white cloak about him and took up his walk again. When the clock in the big tower struck ten he halted suddenly, regulated his watch, seized a big silver candlestick, lighted the candle in it and prepared to go to bed. Without a word he presented his thin cheek for the children to kiss, bowed to the Countess and left the room. He had hardly closed the door behind him when the others broke into a stream of talk as though released from a spell. They talked all together, feverishly, as if to dispel the silence the old man had left behind him.

For some reason people were inclined to lay the blame for René's early lack of decision on his imperious, unapproachable father. René did not know what he wanted, or what occupation he should prepare for. Random reading, reveries with Lucile by moonlight or in the gales of autumn, solitary rambles with a sporting gun, now and then a half-hearted attempt to write verses in the fashion of the day—all this merely irritated his sensibility and left unfed the craving for life that went hand in hand with his boredom. 'I often felt a mere cipher, incapable of ever rising above the average; then again I felt capacities in myself that had never been properly appreciated. Everything contributed to the bitterness of my disposition. Lucile was unhappy, my mother did not know how to comfort me, my father watched me incessantly in order to abuse me.'

These were unhappy years for a youth just conscious of the first stirrings of manhood and experiencing dimly the emotional disturbances that were later to make of him a great romantic writer. He toyed with the idea of suicide, but the sensible old musket misfired at the critical moment. At the naval harbour of Brest he did his best to prepare for an officer's career, but the commission which his father had been so firmly led to expect never arrived. His pious mother would have preferred her youngest child to choose the priesthood, but he felt not the least vocation for it. On the contrary, he believed himself to be entangled in so many sins of the mind that he often despaired of salvation. He pestered his parents to let him go to India or Canada, though he could not have said in what capacity, whether as explorer or merchant.

He continued to alternate between despondency and mental ferment, till one day his father sent for him: 'Sir Knight, no more nonsense! Your brother has obtained a commission for you in the regiment of Navarre. You will go to Rennes, and from there to Cambrai. Here are a hundred *louis d'or*, use them sparingly. Acquit yourself as a brave man, and never bring shame on your name.' With the trembling hand of age he picked up the sword lying on the table in front of him and held it out to his son. It was a last farewell.

FREEDOM FROM PREJUDICE LEADS TO DEATH

The road to Cambrai lies through Paris, where René's eldest brother Jean-Baptiste was living. His stay in the capital was only a brief one, but he was not long in the garrison at Cambrai either, for September 1786 saw him hurrying back to Combourg. His father was dead. The home in the old castle was broken up, his mother returned to Saint-Malo, his sisters lived henceforth in Fougères and Paris. Jean-Baptiste inherited by far the largest portion of the family fortune, all that was left for René was the modest sum of 63,000 livres. His regiment had given him un-limited leave on account of his father's death; they were not particular in those days with regard to the military duties of young noblemen—the training of the troops was preponderantly in the hands of corporals, the officers had social duties to fulfil. The young Chateaubriand was seen in Fougères, where he did not disdain the amusements of small-town society, though he spent a good deal of time reading Goethe's *Werther*, going for solitary walks, indulging in reveries among the rocks and making a great impression by his melancholy attitude on the young ladies of the pretty little township.

Paris, however, put an end to his reveries. With his sisters Julie and Lucile he had turned his back on Brittany, and hoped, now, with the help of his eldest brother, to widen his horizon in the capital, meeting fresh people and perhaps even becoming a 'philosopher', a rationalist with modern ideas, criticizing the policy of the King's ministers, talking the jargon of natural science and countering the influence of the Church with a sceptical smile. Paris was undoubtedly the capital of the world, and the new spirit, so visibly at work in England and still more in America, found its most intelligible and pleasing expression there. The sky above this greatest city of the world was no brighter or darker than usual at that moment; some people looked up at it when their eyes were sore from their daily toil, others merely to judge of the weather to come. They looked upwards because the earth had no further answer to give them, or because it had become too narrow for them. The sky was there for everybody, and its light waxed and waned according to laws that had now been thoroughly investigated and were known to every educated man.

Life in Paris was only fine and easy for the few, but the others were not mentioned. The century was enlightened, and filled with curiosity about the structure of creation, but the number of those sharing these pleasures was very restricted. Looked at closely they were a mere handful of persons following the advice of the learned Monsieur de la Mettrie—also a native of Saint-Malo—to look upon man as a machine, and were now examining, with nimble fingers, the wheels and screws that set the thing in motion. It was amusing, of course, but scientific too, in fact what is known as a game. It did not allow for any surprises, such as the eruption of a passion or a signal of distress, but in good society, with its witty conversation, the man who knew nothing of hunger or pain or unhappiness was always the most acceptable, the nearest to their ideal of elegant manners. The apprehension that the machine might suddenly sweat blood or cry out for bread was throwing a disagreeable shadow over the century and mingling a drop of bitterness in its pleasure. People felt comfortable only in a circle possessed of tact, and consorted only with persons and books that did not overstep the limits of good taste, however much explosive material they might be harbouring.

In a word, people were living in the best of all possible worlds.

It was the duty of the philosopher, however, to call this life in question, of course with as much wit and elegance as possible. It was precisely these cultured circles that prepared, with a playful gesture, the great upheaval with which the century came to an end. Nobody mentioned 'the People', and the lower classes, though their poverty cried to heaven, made no attempt as yet to shake off the yoke that weighed so grievously on their shoulders. For this they needed help from above, the leadership of superior brains, of associations so 'modern' that they quivered with impatience to reconstruct the society of their day. Ségur wrote later on, describing the situation: 'We, the young French nobility, neither mourned the past nor feared the future. We walked happily over a carpet of flowers that hid the abyss from our eyes. We laughed defiance at the old customs, the feudal pride of our fathers and their ceremonious etiquette, everything old struck us as tiresome and ridiculous. Although it was our privileges and the remainder of our former power that were being dug out under our feet, we rather enjoyed this guerrilla warfare. Because the outer walls of the building remained intact, we did not notice that the interior was being undermined. We were amused by the serious warnings of the Court and the clergy, thundering against the spirit of innovation. We applauded the republican scenes in our theatres, the philosophical lectures in our Academies and the daring works of our literary men. . . .' The first performance of 'Figaro's Wedding' was still a thing to remember. The entire Court had crowded into the boxes to watch the challenge to itself with amusement. The Duchess of Bourbon had sent her domestics to the box-office at eleven in the morning, although it did not open till four in the afternoon. The whole of distinguished society made its appearance and applauded every audacity that Beaumarchais had put into the mouths of his characters.

The young Chateaubriand had no idea that society could be so free from prejudice and inclined to progress. He was astonished by what he took for intellectual freedom but was in reality the lack of principle of a society that had given itself up for lost. He would never have thought such an amusing form of cynicism possible. Everything was disavowed, nothing was feared except to be thought old fashioned. The fiery glow of eternal punishment that had so often tormented him began to pale. If the representatives of the highest authority were themselves so unprejudiced, it could not possibly be a sin to question the compatibility of intelligence and religion. If a Chamfort, supported by the Prince of Condé and the Comte d' Artois, could call courtiers idiots and duchesses whores, and be rewarded by the laughing approval of his patrons, the respect he had cherished hitherto for the great ones of this world could not be so well-founded as he believed. Paris transformed him more and more every day; the timid Breton, who had only lately received his father's sword with respect, became a doubter who found pleasure in doubt.

Among the *esprits forts* that he admired, and soon began to imitate, the old Malesherbes carried the most weight. His granddaughter, Mademoiselle de Rosambo, had married René's brother Jean-Baptiste, so the illustrious old gentleman was so to speak one of the family, and as he now had nothing to do, and was accessible at all hours of the day, his garrulous conversation came to have a great influence on the young man's mental development. He had first held the post of Minister of Finance, and later succeeded the Comte d'Argenson as Supervisor of Literature, an appointment that amounted in practice to the Censorship. It was his duty to examine all books, journals, pamphlets and periodicals in manuscript and sanction their publication. He could forbid, confiscate and destroy anything he considered prejudicial to public order; he had command of the frontier police, and could arrest authors, publishers and hawkers of books; he had, in fact, almost unlimited means with which to combat the great intellectual offensive against the Monarchy that had been in progress since the middle of the century.

In actual fact he made little use of this power; he was a 'philosopher', and would have died rather than not march in the van of progress. He always had an uneasy feeling that the innovators, especially the younger generation, did not take him seriously, and he took enormous pains to keep up with them. It is

D

obvious that he did not quite appreciate the importance of the publications he secretly encouraged, or he would not have allowed bookstalls to be set up in the palaces of the Knights of Malta, the Duke of Orleans, Prince Conti and other dignitaries, where anti-royalist and anti-clerical works were sold with little attempt at concealment. During his term of office the most important works of Diderot, Duclos, d'Alembert and Voltaire appeared with his casual approval; he allowed the intellectual artillery to be mounted under his very eyes. He gave Rousseau access to the leaflets he should have confiscated, and banned the works of those that dared to attack the Encyclopedists. Malesherbes thus became one of the great accomplices of the upheaval of which he had as yet no suspicion, for what signs he did notice he took for a welcome regeneration of French intellectual life.

He can hardly be blamed for this receptive attitude to the new spirit, for if educated people always realized the inevitable result of the theories in which they take such a lively interest, intellectual life would come to an end. But the widespread confusion of ideas at that time is apparent in the fact that this respectable minister, out of sheer delight in 'philosophy', persistently violated his duty to the Crown, which was to defend it in the intellectual sphere. Now he was enjoying a well-earned retirement, and could read everything that was printed without racking his brains as to whether he ought to forbid this or that. He was no longer a Censor, but only an *esprit fort* devoting himself to the pleasures of reading and to family life. But the day was to come when the wind he had helped to sow would whirl him away to an appalling fate, as one of the King's three advocates, unable to avert the death sentence on the monarch demanded by the Convention. On that day he would sit in his black suit beside Louis XVI, unable for sobbing to utter a word of sense.

However, there were a few years left to him before that ordeal, and before ending up himself under the guillotine. Meanwhile he was a welcome guest in Jean-Baptiste's house. To René's great joy he was generous with his wisdom, and liked airing his views bluntly, sometimes coarsely. 'Seeing him for the first time,' wrote one of his contemporaries, 'in his brown coat with capacious pockets, his gold buttons, lace cuffs and snuff-stained shirt-frill, his badly-combed wig all awry, one could hardly believe one was looking at the great man he was.' The old gentleman found an attentive listener in René, he was no revolutionary in reality, but a liberal thinker, convinced of the necessity for thorough-going reforms—in which he was only too right—and looking to science for salvation.

Conversing with him, René became aware not only of the backwardness of his own ideas, but of the gaps in his education. He discovered the importance of Linnaeus's work, heard of the great voyages of English and French navigators, and pored over the beautiful maps the old gentleman brought with him from time to time. How immeasurable was the earth's surface, and how many blank patches there were upon it! Would it be possible to sail right round the globe; was there a north-west passage above America through which one could reach Japanese or Chinese waters by ship? The notion took firm hold of his imagination; he brooded on the satisfaction it would afford to a turbulent heart and a restless fancy, to sail unknown seas and open new routes to mankind. He devoured the reports of missionaries returning from distant lands, Raynal's *History of the Two Indies* and the tropical descriptions of Parny, who had devoted himself to correcting the false exoticism of Bernadin de Saint-Pierre; he became absorbed in the works of Tournefort and Gussieu, he frequented the King's Botanical Garden and, not content with the beauties of nature alone, sought to familiarize himself with its laws.

Malesherbes was undoubtedly the most considerable intellect within the young man's purview, but he was no poet, and René had to content himself with writers of second rank, who, however —to do them justice—could talk wittily about God and the world and were never boring. One acquaintance he made in this circle was to be of great importance to his future career; this was Fontanes, who had produced a famous translation of Pope, and in everything that he wrote afterwards remained a classical author of the eighteenth century. Despite the heights to which he rose under Napoleon, he was never so much a creator as a connoisseur, his suggestions and discoveries were always more important than his own productions, and like Socrates, who prided himself on serving as midwife at the birth of other people's ideas, Fontanes had a gift for recognizing talents, perceiving tendencies and foreseeing developments and even fashions. He had a passion for talking at richly-laden tables without neglecting his food, and his ponderous figure was far from suggesting the resilient vivacity of his mind.

Chateaubriand, who had fundamentally little capacity for masculine friendships, developed a real attachment to the 'Wild Boar', as Fontanes was nicknamed, which was to be of the greatest benefit to him in later life. Fontanes possessed the art of survival far better than his contemporaries, though he could not be accused of want of character. In good and evil fortune he was to be found at René's side, with untiring sympathy for 'the greatest egoist of his age'. Fontanes was one of those liberal spirits enamoured of reforms, provided these did not degenerate into revolutions. He would have liked to improve the world without turning it upside down and, like so many of his friends, suffered under the delusion that the stream of new ideas in which he took such a lively interest would not turn into a torrential flood. But the stream was roaring quite considerably even then, and its roar was robbing some people of their sleep.

THE BASTILLE IS STORMED

At the end of the year 1788 the Breton Parliament assembled. The air was full of rumours and scandals; everybody was talking of the Monarchy's collapsing finances, but nobody was prepared to make the slightest sacrifice. They were talking of the Necklace Affair, in which a courtesan, disguised as the Queen, had gone to a certain garden at night to receive a diamond necklace from the hands of Cardinal de Rohan. They talked of the arch-humbug Cagliostro, of Mesmer, who had discovered magnetism, and of the 'Marriage of Figaro'. The refractory Breton nobility indulged in demonstrations against the Court and the Royal Administration. The young noblemen came to blows with the students, and both sides attacked the watch. There were bloody heads as a result, but not a little laughter.

The return to Paris took place in June 1789. The country was restless; sinister gangs wandered about the highways, and nobody knew what had brought them out. In many of the villages the peasants had become audacious, holding up carriages as they drove through and demanding to see passports. The gates of Paris were closely guarded; those wishing to enter the city were minutely and suspiciously questioned as to whence and whither. Many of the tradesmen had closed their shops and were peeping inquisitively through the bars at the street. People clustered at every corner, listening to strange orators and having bills and tracts thrust into their hands. The deliberations of the States General, which the King had convened, appeared to be taking a turn for the worse. The Third Estate now had a leader who roared like a wild beast, an honest-to-God Marquis named Mirabeau, who had audaciously summoned the Third Estate to the National Assembly as the true representatives of the people. Troops were assembled all over Versailles, the garrison in Paris was likewise strengthened, there was a coming and going, a rolling of wheels, a trampling of hoofs, and over all, like the first rumbling of a storm, a murmur of human voices. But was not Paris always in a fever? Had the French known it, for centuries, in anything but a state of *fronde*, of opposition, of resistance to any authority that threatened to forbid its popular gatherings, its spreading of rumours and its noisy proclamations?

Chateaubriand believed this capricious city capable of any mad prank, but the storming of the Bastille gave him something of a fright none the less. Ever since the 12th July he had scarcely left the street, so fascinated was he by the spectacle of an excited populace, hardly certain itself whether it was acting in an outburst of high spirits or starting a revolution. Were these people, who instead of going to work were roaming up and down the street, pushing into coffee-houses and drinking without paying, breaking up furniture, smashing shop windows and seizing the goods displayed in them, insulting women, holding up elegant coaches and overturning them, cheering impromptu orators or tearing the clothes off their backs—were these brawling hordes, in which harlots, homeless creatures and drunkards were mingled, no more than a populace broken loose and having a good time because the police were nowhere to be seen, or were they Men of the Revolution, under leadership and obeying fixed orders?

While the tocsins sounded and bugle calls rang out from the beleaguered barracks, an irregular procession bearing the busts of the Duke of Orleans and of Necker—the recently dismissed Minister of Finance—both of whom were accounted 'Friends of the People'—was making its way to Versailles, before the wide front of which a division of dragoons had been drawn up under command of Prince Lambesc. The cavalrymen wore glittering breastplates and highly polished Bavarian helmets that made them look like warriors of antiquity, but this did not prevent them from being bombarded with stones and bottles by the crowd. They made their horses rear; the busts were broken to pieces in the ensuing confusion, and the demonstrators driven back. Next day all shops and business premises were closed, the citizens barred their doors and did not venture out. At the Town Hall hurried attempts were being made to form some sort of City Militia to control the rising disorder. The police stations had been stormed during the night, and the released detainees were reinforcing the mob, which was now attacking the larger prisons, some of which they had actually taken and broken open. Police Headquarters and the Invalides had been invaded and the vast quantity of arms stored there distributed among the crowd. The noisy crowd had suddenly become 'The People in Arms', and was now marching towards the Bastille, the citadel in the east quarter of the town.

Who was leading these people? Who had dictated their route and their objective? Were there plans, prepared long ago by silent conspirators, or were all these events, slowly mounting up to a catastrophe, merely a series of unfortunate concatenations and spontaneous outbreaks? Chateaubriand was filled with contempt for the creatures that captured the Bastille, an old, barely defended stronghold; in his eyes they were nothing but drunkards, prostitutes and ragamuffins. Most of his contemporaries thought otherwise, the day of the storming was to be remembered, even though the victory itself was not imposing as a feat of arms. The enormous structure with its eight round towers would have been impregnable in spite of its scanty garrison and insufficient provisioning, had Gouverneur de Launay shown the slightest fighting spirit. He preferred to parley, withdrew his guns, gave orders to close the loopholes and permitted an emissary from the Town Hall to enter, in order to convince him of the harmlessness of his intentions. He even invited two men bearing flags of truce to his dinner-table, while the crowd outside swelled ominously and attempted to set fire to one of the towers.

At last two men succeeded in destroying the chains of the drawbridge with their axes (one of them, Hulin, later commanded a division under Napoleon and obtained the title of Count), the drawbridge thundered down, the besiegers crowded into the outer courtyard and laid four guns in position before the inner door. The garrison, which up to now had made hardly any resistance, lost their heads completely and forced the aged de Launay to capitulate. The leader of the procession assured him that nobody would suffer any harm. Empty words. The Governor was struck down by the invading crowd. A butcher's lad, 'who knew how to wield an axe', hacked his head off and spitted the trophy on a pike. Three of his officers were likewise slaughtered, some of the disabled soldiers of the garrison were hanged. The victors formed a procession, bearing the Governor's head in triumph, and marched to the Town Hall, on the steps of which they were met by the President of the Merchants' Guild. He collapsed under the blows of the furious mob, which tore him in pieces and spitted his heart on a lance.

Chateaubriand witnessed all this, and began to suspect that the revolution the Philosophers had desired was not going to stop half-way. The proud words 'People' and 'Freedom', which had so noble a sound in intellectual circles, were suddenly casting threatening shadows. It dawned on him that men can invent watchwords and slogans, and lose control of them ever after. The people, whom he had so far only looked down on from the paternal citadel, assumed quite a different reality in the streets of

Paris. These were no docile peasants, bowed by their hard labour, directed by their parish priest and ignorant of the ways of the world; they were shrewd townspeople, full of scepticism, with no respect for authority, and prepared to give free rein to their instincts under the protection of numbers. What chiefly roused his indignation was the cowardice of those who thus perpetrated their cruelties, assassins emerging from the horde and disappearing into it again. Who delivered the blow? Who fired the shot? Nobody knew. The victim was nearly always struck down by an unknown hand, and once he was down everybody was eager to deliver another blow.

From the window of his hotel, the day after the storming of the Bastille, he saw two horribly mutilated heads borne past on pikes. The aged Privy Councillor Foulon, at one time Administrator of Paris, and his son-in-law Bertier, said to have neglected the provisioning of the capital, had been hunted down and torn in pieces. It was a ghastly sight to see these heads, once the ornament of the Monarchical Administration, now turned quite black from mutilation and incipient putrefaction. One had the pike thrust through its mouth, one eye was still recognizable, hanging out of its socket. The mouth of the sixty-four-year-old Foulon had been stuffed with grass, somebody having asserted that he had told those that were crying out for bread to eat grass. René flung open the window and shouted: 'Murderers! So that's what you mean by freedom!' Fortunately the uproar was so tremendous that nobody heard him; his sisters dragged him back into the room and tried to soothe him. 'If I had had a gun,' he wrote later, 'I would have shot the wretches down like wolves.' Luckily he had no gun, and the cannibal procession down below pressed on. But René was shattered as if by a stroke, he was stirred to the depths of his being. He realized all at once that he must leave the country.

This revelation came to him earlier than to most of his compeers. Old Malesherbes was confident, he thought the people must be allowed to exhaust their fury. Hadn't Rousseau declared the people to be good at heart? The differences of opinion, however, never amounted to quarrels. They were still in good society and knew what became well-bred people. Jean-Baptiste, René's brother, shared his gloomy view of the future and anticipated the worst disasters. Malesherbes, his wife's grandfather, opposed him with great eloquence. But they were destined to be conveyed to the scaffold in the same tumbril; death under the guillotine was to write FINIS under their disputes as to the usefulness or harmfulness of the Revolution. René maintained a composure during these disputes that helped him to survive. The revolutionary fanaticism of Chamfort merely made him shake his head: 'I have always wondered how a man with so much knowledge of human nature could take anything up so ardently. Didn't he know that all governments are alike?' The young man was more far-seeing than his older friends. He said to the Chevalier de Panat: 'I'm going to seek something fresh; there's nothing more to be done here. The King is lost, and you will have no counter-revolution. I shall do like the Puritans, who emigrated to Virginia. I shall go to the primeval forests; that will be better than going to Coblenz.'

He was obsessed by the idea of America. It was from there that the concept of freedom had come in its abstract form, there was no city mob there—or so he imagined—there were virgin lands and seas to be travelled; grand scenery and unspoilt humanity, new colours and sounds awaited the artist to be. Old Malesherbes did not contradict him; he studied the maps with him of an evening, read the accounts of the great navigators and travellers in detail, measured the distances, took note of the variations of temperature and put all the treasures of his knowledge and of his library at the service of the intending traveller. While the streets of Paris were filled with the noise of growing disorder or with a threatening silence, René could scent the tang of the sea breeze, which he had drawn in with his first breath in Saint-Malo. Jacques Cartier, who discovered Canada, Louis XIV's great ship's captain Duguay-Trouin, and the bold corsair Surcouf, were all born in Saint-Malo and heard the sea breaking against its familiar walls. A stale smell of blood was spreading slowly but irresistibly throughout Paris. Only the ocean could dispel it, and the ever-youthful fury of its tempests.

III

FROM PARIS TO NIAGARA

MIXING WITH INDIANS

On a spring day in the year 1791 Chateaubriand, now aged twenty-three, stepped aboard a brigantine of only a hundred and sixty tons in his home harbour of Saint-Malo. The vessel was bound for Baltimore with a party of priests. The voyage lasted three weeks and revived all the young traveller's love of the sea. He was at once on a familiar footing with the crew, and vied with them in climbing to the topmost yards. During a storm that drove all the other passengers below, he had himself lashed to the mast like Odysseus, and drenched by the seas, shouted rapturously into the uproar 'O storm! Thou art still not so magnificent as Homer pictured thee!' When the nights grew warmer he slept on deck: 'The ship rolled on a slow, dead swell, with phosphorescent sparkles streaming past her sides in the white foam. Thousands of stars glittered in the deep blue of the celestial dome—a shoreless ocean, immensity in the heavens and on the waves. Never had God affected me more by his greatness than during those nights, when I had infinity above and below me.' He gorged himself with contemplation; he began to view the splendour of creation with a freer eye, murmuring to himself his sister Lucile's words of long ago: '*You* ought to describe that!'

It was high summer when the little vessel dropped anchor off Chesapeake Bay. A longboat brought René ashore: at last he trod the soil of the New World: 'I gazed around me, and stood for a while transfixed. This continent, which had perhaps remained unknown through the days of antiquity and for many later centuries . . . its first savage vicissitudes and its later destiny since the landing of Christopher Columbus . . . its domination by the monarchies of a tottering Europe . . . the old form of society giving place here to a republic of an unfamiliar kind, auguring a change in the human spirit, and the part my country had played in these events, since these seas and coasts owed their independence in part to the French flag and to French blood. . . . A great man arising from the midst of discord and devastation—Washington, now living in a flourishing town on the very spot where William Penn had once bought a patch of virgin forest . . . these United States, giving back the Revolution to France, who had supported theirs with her arms. . . . Finally, my virgin Muse, which I had come to dedicate to Nature in her unknown, primeval garb, and the discoveries I meant to attempt in the wilderness that still spread its immeasurable kingdom behind the narrow sphere of influence of a foreign civilization—these were the thoughts that went rolling through my mind.' America, the independence of man, the inexhaustibility of Nature—elements of an experience that was to leave its imprint on his poetic genius.

His expectation of finding in the New World a sort of replica of the Roman Republic, an exemplary land of virtuous men, noble women and obedient children, was, however, soon disappointed. The United States, as the first to have declared the rights of man and to have shaken off its connections with the Throne, enjoyed unbounded moral and political esteem on the part of the French. They believed that this people had succeeded in founding a realm of virtue and reviving the ancient community of the older republics. Besides which, René had looked forward to some entirely new type of landscape, exotic scenery full of tropical luxuriance, smelling of vanilla and fluttered over by brilliant, gigantic butterflies. But on his journey from Baltimore to Philadelphia he saw the same oaks and meadows he had known in Europe; the swallows darted over the surface of the water just as they had done over the pond at Combourg. The men he came across were noisy, boastful and addicted to intoxicating liquors; the rich were very rich, the poor very poor; the hotels were badly run, one had to keep one's purse under one's pillow and have one's pistol at hand. The banks did their best to cheat newcomers, the gaming-houses, of which there were far too many, swarmed with cutpurses, ballrooms were filled with such a din that a fight might have been in progress. He looked in vain for the Indians, the 'mild savages', of whose unspoilt habits he had read such edifying accounts. At most he might see, seated in front of an inn, a silent figure wrapped in an old horse-cloth and perhaps hoping to scrounge a drop of brandy.

René spent five months in the New World. Although at a later date he was lavish with accounts and recollections, we know very little of his route or his encounters. That he once met Washington is a matter of dispute nowadays, although he has left a most convincing description of his visit to the Great Man, the idol of all freethinkers in France. That he went to New York and visited the battlefield of Lexington has been confirmed. It is certain, too, that he sailed up the Hudson and stayed for a time in Albany. A fur trader named Smith gave him a friendly reception there, and soon dissuaded him from his idea of discovering the North-West Passage. René had thought it possible to cross the continent by land and then sail along the coast towards the north, whence he might discover a sea route as far as Hudson Bay and towards Labrador. Mr Smith could not help smiling: nobody had ever succeeded in crossing the North American continent, hardly anybody had penetrated beyond the Upper Mississippi, the interior of the country was unknown, the prairie had only been seen by a few trappers who had spent all their lives in the wilderness.

Our traveller did not persist in his plans, he contented himself with an expedition to Niagara, quite strenuous and adventurous enough. He chose a Dutchman for his guide, and dressed up as a forester, letting his hair and beard grow. Thus equipped he made his way into the forests along untrodden paths towards the north. He soon came upon his first real 'savages', a few Iroquois, with whom he went hunting. But he was not long in discovering that these natives did not at all resemble the literary picture the Philosophers had drawn of them. Of course it was only too easy for the whites to corrupt these children of nature, but even without the whites they had their vices and passions, and were very far from the innocence that Rousseau attributed to any people untouched by civilization.

On a camping-ground in the midst of the forest he came upon a party of Indians of both sexes in full war-paint, surrounding a little man in an apple-green coat, with powdered hair; they were dancing to the strains of his pocket violin. This odd little fellow was a Frenchman of the name of Violet, who bought skins from the natives and paid for them with dancing-lessons. Monsieur Violet had come to America with General Rochambeau as a kitchen boy, and stayed on there after the end of the War of Independence. He felt happy among the tribes of the Six Nations, and like a true Frenchman was convinced that he was a bearer of culture.

René was now roaming through pathless forests. The primeval might of this uninhabited region taught him at every step that Nature, untrodden as yet by man, might well be innocent, but at the same time cruel and violent. The idyll gave place to grandiose brutality. His mind filled with new images of a Nature that would not allow itself to be trifled with. So even here the eighteenth century was coming to a close and surrendering to a reality that forced mankind to acknowledge its power. All that René saw in these woods sought a fresh outlet in words. Real scenery, which, however beautiful, always contains a hostile element, was introduced by him into literature. He overcame his initial discomfiture by resorting to minute observation, analysis, notes and descriptions. To the blossoming chaos of creation he opposed the first tentative outlines of figures whose idiom had not yet quite lost the accent of Rousseau's, but who had begun to stand out against a new background.

The characters in his great story *The Natchez* had begun to come alive, without yet knowing where they belonged, or what was to be their fate. The Natchez were an Indian tribe of the upper reaches of the Mississippi, with whom the French colonists had fought hard battles, and who had been mercilessly decimated by their superior weapons. The grief and hatred of a people of nature, whose destruction was inescapable, lent dark, tragical colours to the traveller's reveries as he busied himself with his pen in the woods, leaning against the trunk of some age-old maple tree. He invented the young Frenchman who was to bear his name, the René who was a younger brother to *Werther*, and nursed his melancholy in the wigwams of the Natchez, among whom he found friendship and even love. The pathetic shade of Atala, who was to be the heroine of a romantic love story and move all European readers to tears, wandered through his imagination, which was still too much affected by a superabundance of impressions to attach itself to particular objects: 'I fell into the kind of reverie that all travellers know . . . a reverie that is a fullness of the heart and an emptiness of the head, allowing one to enjoy one's mere existence in peace.'

His knapsack grew full of notes, among which the adjective 'romantic' cropped up for the first time. He used it in the attempt to seize the excitement of adventure and suggest the intensified emotion that a man is aware of in the presence of some overwhelming natural phenomenon. Storm, night—in which 'silence follows silence'—the gloom of the forests, the flight of the clouds over the sky, the shadows of the trees and the roar of the river, all these make the solitary traveller a stranger to himself; he broods over a grief that is causeless and nameless, and cannot recognize himself. He roamed aimlessly through the land: 'There is no road here, no town, no monarchy, no president, not a soul.' From Niagara he went to Fort Pitt, the future Pittsburg; he saw Ohio and Kentucky. Did he push on further? Did he venture as far as the Mississippi? He was fond of describing this river, which he called by its old name of Meschacebe, endowing it with exotic marvels and tropical beauties which it exhibits only a thousand miles farther south.

It would seem that memory, and the reading of innumerable descriptions of travel, ended by giving Chateaubriand's journey an extent that greatly exceeded the reality. But this is of little importance compared with the unique revelation of nature on which whole generations were to feast in the sequel. 'Who shall describe what one feels when one penetrates into these forests, that are as old as the world! They alone give an idea of Creation as it issued from the hand of God. The light, coming from above,

slanting through a veil of foliage, spreads through the interior of
the forest a changing and shifting twilight that lends things a
fantastic size. Everywhere there are fallen trees to be climbed over,
out of which fresh generations of trees are springing up. I seek a
way out of this solitude in vain. Deceived by a brighter light I
push through plants, mosses, lianas and the deep humus of
decaying growths. But I merely come to a clearing, due to a fallen
group of pines. Soon the forest grows dark again, the eye can
discern only the trunks of oaks and walnut trees in close array;
the farther off they are, the closer they appear to draw together:
I am confronted with the notion of endlessness.'

The journey was but a short one, it was no voyage of discovery,
no opening up of unknown deserts; but it was a road for René
into himself. It was these roamings that eventually made of him a
romantic writer. Everything was ready within him, it needed the
American experience to break out and assume a shape. A thunderstorm at night in the primeval forest, a streak of moonlight over
the river, the scent of unseen flowers, the tang of a camp fire
whose flickering light played over the bronzed face of an Indian;
the brown shoulder of a girl showing under a white deerskin; all
this would be transmuted one day and re-created in the prose that
was to carry the name of Chateaubriand round the world. The
impulse might have been fleeting, but what it released was an
unequalled poetical accomplishment, introduced to the France of
that day in the opening pages of *Atala*.

The confusion of visions and characters had not yet subsided
in his breast, but to everything that clamoured to be given a
shape he had already lent his own soul, his longings and sufferings,
his desires and hopes, his fondness for his sister Lucile, his dreams
of the Sylphide that he was to seek everywhere and never find,
and above all his half proud, half painful consciousness of loneliness and transience. The more these poetic foreshadowings
pressed upon him, the more he longed for home. Whatever might
have happened in France, from whatever past his country might
free itself, it was still the country of his speech and of the spirit he
revered. Literature spelt France for him; what he had to say could
only be said to Frenchmen. The conviction grew upon him that

the notes he had prepared under the trees of the forest could bring him fame only in the most cultured society in the world. This society did not fail him: it was driven out of the country by the Revolution, but he went with it, and returned with it when the waves had subsided.

It was delightful to roam through the wilds of the New World, but it would be more delightful still to be one day that romantic figure among the peoples of old Europe, which had discovered its genius in the wilderness. What drew René home was the major craving of his life: not only to be, but to be esteemed; to remain alone and yet have listeners; to keep his heart for himself and yet be loved; to dwell in a cell, provided the cell was on a stage. In the pathless wilderness nature is seen as the Creator planned it. But man is not nature, he is society.

IV

THE CANNONADE OF VALMY

WHEN René returned to France the country was still a Monarchy, but only in name. What had finally induced him to return? He tells us himself, circumstantially. He was the guest of a miller; the room 'was lighted only by maize cobs and bean shucks flaming on the hearth. My host's guns lying on the arms-rack gleamed in the reflection of the fire. I seated myself on a stool in the chimney corner. The miller's wife stood a big cauldron on the red-hot fire and its sooty bottom flared up in the flames.... While the potatoes for my supper were boiling beside me I whiled away the time by reading an English newspaper that had fallen to the ground between my feet. I caught sight of the words, in large print: *Flight of the King*. It was a report on the flight of Louis XVI and the unfortunate monarch's arrest at Varennes. The newspaper also spoke of the increasing number of emigrants and the rallying of army officers to the flag of the French Princes. I was conscious of a sudden revulsion in my mind: Renaud was confronted by his weakness in the Mirror of Honour at Armida; I was not Tasso's hero, but that same mirror showed me my own image in an American cabin. The clash of arms, the tumult of the world, echoed in my ears beneath the roof of a mill in an American orchard. I broke off my travels there and then, saying to myself "Return to France". Thus what I saw as a duty upset my original plans and brought about the first of those sudden reversals of which there were to be so many in my life. The Bourbons could have done without the Breton aristocrat, returning from oversea to offer them his insignificant devotion, just as they had no use for his services after he had emerged from his insignificance. If I

E

had lighted my pipe with the newspaper that changed my whole life, and continued my travels, nobody would have noticed my absence. My life was as obscure and unimportant at that time as the smoke from my calumet. It was simply a debate between myself and my conscience that flung me into the arena of the world.'

He returned home. It was not that he still believed in the old monarchy, or could have given the King, already a semi-prisoner, much hope of retaining his throne. It was the old sense of loyalty speaking. Faithful to his father's admonitions, he considered himself the champion of a king to whom no nobleman dare refuse his service in the hour of need. Loyalty was an archaic feeling, the world was busy replacing sentiments of that kind by moral principles acceptable to all. But René had been born under that sign; he was loyal to the Throne, not for its own sake but for loyalty's sake, and at every turn in his life his loyalty was to prove more or less unwelcome to the monarchs he served.

After a rough passage—whenever René entered on a fresh stage in his life the elements were bound to be raging—he arrived in France on January 2, 1792. His luggage was stuffed with manuscripts and scribbled notes on loose sheets of paper, but his pockets were empty. The captain had given him credit for his fare, and he had to wait for his mother to remit the needed sum. On the short journey to his mother's house along the high road from Le Havre, where he had landed, it was borne in on him with frightful clarity that he would not be able to remain long in France. Disorder and destruction were only too evident; many fields had been left untilled, fruit trees had been felled, cottages were falling to pieces. Worst of all, the châteaux had all been demolished, and the fine avenues leading up to them felled and chopped up for firewood. The owners, whose titles had long been abolished by law, had sought refuge in the towns, where they hoped to be less conspicuous.

But life in the towns had changed even more; clubs, so-called, had sprung up everywhere, political unions, composed of staunch adherents of the Revolution who kept a sharp eye on their fellow-townsmen. Whereas in the old days one bowed to the

Count and took one's hat off to the priest, now one cringed to the clamorous Republicans that shouted 'Down with the King!' and demanded not only his deposition but even his death. The conflict of opinion among Frenchman had reached a degree of violence unknown even in the wars of religion. Was not the King's brother recruiting forces on foreign territory, to invade France and punish the adherents of the Revolution? What was it that had just been settled in Pillnitz between the Emperor Leopold and King Frederick William? Had not France to fear the worst on account of these secret agreements and conspiracies? And wasn't one only too well aware that the threads of these intrigues reached as far as the Tuileries, even if they didn't originate there? Hadn't there even been rumours of a letter from the emigrant Duc de Broglie in which he said: 'I know the way to Paris, I shall lead the foreign armies there, and there will not be one stone of that proud capital left on another.'

War was in the air, in Anjou and the Vendée trouble had broken out because the peasants would not tolerate priests that had taken the oath of allegiance to the Constitution. This horrible Paris with its godless, radical-minded Commune seemed to be trying to usurp all power for itself. People like Pétion and Danton had taken over authority in the Town Hall and sworn to the populace that they would forbid the King and Queen to exercise their functions. The demand grew daily louder that the Crown be deprived of the right to veto the Legislative Assemblies in defiance of the Revolutionary laws.

Saint-Malo was a long way from Paris, but rumours and bad news quickly found their way there. The little town was no longer a comfortable place for the former lords of Combourg. René could not have returned to his native town at a more unfavourable moment. He would have liked to leave it at once and make his way to Germany, to the Princes' army, but it was no easy matter to leave one's country and go abroad. Many people were to be heard preaching against leaving one's homeland in the lurch, but it was easy for a champion of these ideas to talk, for 'nobody was persecuting him, he could circulate as he liked without fear of being insulted or even struck dead, nobody set fire to his house, he was not hunted down like a wild beast simply because his name was Jacob, not Peter, and because his grandfather, who had been dead these forty years, had the right to sit in a certain pew in church, with two or three lackeys in livery behind him.'

It was not really quite so simple. René was well aware that there was more in it than the difference between Jacob and Peter. He could have his title and privileges taken from him, but nobody could tear his coat of arms out of his heart and rob him of the knowledge that his forefathers had led their vassals in the Battle of Bouvines.

He would always remain an aristocrat, unable to act against his feudal instincts, he would always claim a special kind of loyalty and honour as his own, and take it for granted that one serves a lost cause as whole-heartedly as one desires public honours for oneself. René's chivalry would never lose a touch of absurdity, he would always be something of a Don Quixote, throwing himself into the breach and letting others pocket the reward. How often was he to go empty-handed while Talleyrand, reproached for this ungrateful treatment, would reply 'I supposed he had not been given anything because he did not want anything'.

His mother, his sisters, his uncle Bedée—usually so cheerful— were all hanging their heads in despondency; they lived under the shadow of a disaster that was spreading like a black cloud over the whole of France. René's decision to join the Princes' army was the right one, his place was there. But travelling costs money, and an officer going to the front must be properly equipped. His American adventure had cost him the last sou of his inheritance; an expedient must be found to enable him to take the path of honour in seemly fashion. It was then that Lucile, who had always enjoyed planning and working for her beloved brother, came forward with her marriage plan. Her friend Céleste was young and very rich, she came of a distinguished family, she was not exactly beautiful but lively and clever. She had been brought up by the Benedictine nuns in Saint-Malo, could actually talk Latin, and better still, write delightful letters, full of wit and discernment.

Lucile's part in this affair was a fateful one; she had not the slightest knowledge of human nature, or she would have suspected that her brother would never make a good husband, that he would live for passion and adventure, that he was capable of the greatest loyalty to symbols, but wholly unable to be faithful to a woman. Moreover she had gained only a very superficial notion of her future sister-in-law's fortune. Céleste was not at all rich, and was shortly to become quite poor. The girl was certainly no fool, she had an original mind, and intelligence well above the average, but she lacked the gift of affection. Severity, irony, even bitterness went to her make-up, and were soon to become apparent. But preparations were too far forward by then; René had declared his readiness for the marriage, although he knew he would never love this young woman.

Why had he not refused? Why did he not run away? It was not merely that a sense of duty towards his family compelled him to take this step; a sense of imminent catastrophe rendered him defenceless. Tomorrow or the day after he would be going to the front, he might be killed, in the end the whole of this unhappy France was bound to be ruined. At the edge of the abyss even a tie for life no longer meant very much. So the marriage was contracted; for fifty-five years Céleste was to be Chateaubriand's wife, to shoot the arrows of her wit at her unfaithful husband's 'Ladies', write clever letters to all and sundry, and assert to the last that she had never read a single one of her famous husband's books.

The young couple went first to Paris, although the capital had become a most dangerous place for any scion of the nobility wishing to emigrate and intending to join the army of the Counter-Revolution. Mireabeau was dead, but another 'voice of thunder' was to be heard, carrying the People along with it: the voice of Danton, who now that the Legislative Assembly had declared war against the Austrian Emperor, was to be seen everywhere at once trying to weld the bewildered, half-shattered land of France into a nation. Nation—a new, a mighty word, which had just made its victorious but bloody entry into the century. Now that the splendour of the Throne had grown pale and the Monarchy had reached the verge of its downfall, this new word had gained a connective force that gave the French a feeling of solidarity they had never known. War had begun, ostensibly in defence of the country against foreign intervention. 'What do they want of us, these foreigners?' was the question, now that the armed forces were no longer the property of the King. Danton and his followers called for 'audacity'—not merely bravery at the front, that is, but readiness to shed the blood that must flow in the service of the Republic. For the moment it was merely a trickle—though the guillotine had been set up, it was working sparingly and altogether legitimately—but the trickle threatened to become a river that would separate the free peoples from the unfree.

The tone in Paris had changed; René noticed it wherever he went. Uncouth manners, 'citizen' as a mode of address, a fancy for 'thee' and 'thou', inelegant clothes, a growing harshness of feature, less cheerfulness, less gossiping in the streets—all these changes showed the prevalence of 'republican virtues'. A young plebeian tyranny was springing up, full of hope, but animated by a more ferocious despotism than that of the *ancien régime,* 'for as the Sovereign People are everywhere, tyranny itself has become ubiquitous'. While Danton was attempting, with the grip of a giant, to compact the people into a nation in arms, against the dark background of the Revolution, which was still granting the King a little time to live, grotesque shadows had suddenly emerged and were slowly assuming menacing features: Marat, Chaumette, Hébert, Jacques Roux. Robespierre's hour had not yet struck.

Chateaubriand, now the poorer by many illusions but the richer by an unloved spouse, paid a visit to his fatherly friend Malesherbes to give him an account of his voyage to America, on which the old man had squandered so much good advice. But since in those days every conversation, between no matter whom, immediately turned to political events and boiled over into mutual abuse, or a furious dispute for and against, they did not linger long over America, its forests and wildernesses, its immensity and its coarse manners. The worthy man was taking more snuff than ever, his hands trembled at the mention of the proceedings at the *Hôtel de Ville* and the shocking situation of the Royal Family. Gone was the enthusiasm for that 'philosophy', whose conclusions, closely considered, were now being practised in France. No, this was

THE CANNONADE OF VALMY 71

really *not* how he had foreseen the liberation of the mind and the triumph of unprejudiced reason. He had dreamed of an order of things that would allow the social structure to retain its main outlines, and whose value would consist in eliminating errors while putting full trust in the goodness of man. But this was rank subversion, mob rule! It was certainly not for this that he had allowed himself to be insulted by the Court, in the golden age of the monarchy, as a freethinker and an unreliable government official, he whose sin had been tolerance and his vice respect for free opinion. The old man realized now what a difficult business it was to be a really liberal thinker, how much harm one must allow for and how much destruction one may bring about against one's will.

René, still not really sure that his intention of joining the Princes' army to fight against his own country was a right and just one, was astonished at such a display of wrath. Malesherbes was convinced that only armed intervention from without could tackle the evil. What did they mean by *Frenchmen,* by *Fatherland,* that new-fangled word? These cannibals were defiling the name of France. There were higher things than patriotism—human values, morality, membership of the great family of those that stand for reason and humanity, no matter what the colour of their flag. Had the subjects of the British Crown in America, although English themselves, ever hesitated to appeal to French arms for help against England? 'Any government, which instead of guaranteeing the fundamental laws, itself transgresses the rule of justice, ceases to exist, and restores man to his natural state. In such case it is right to defend oneself as one can, and seize any means capable of overthrowing tyranny and restoring the rights of each and everyone.'

So they argued. The young man maintained that one was responsible for everything that happened in one's own country, even if one had had no hand in it; one must take upon oneself the errors and even the crimes of one's country, just as one participated in its fame and basked in its glory. To the wrath of the older man he even went so far as to declare that emigration was 'stupidity and folly'. But he did eventually set out on the 'path of glory', leaving his wife in Paris in the care of his family and travelling in the disguise of a wine merchant, with the uniform of the National Guard under his overcoat. He took the mail coach to Lille and crossed the northern frontier of his country under cover of night, with the tricolour sash about his waist. This time his travels were to last seven years.

GOETHE RODE ON HORSEBACK OVER THERE

René stumbled through the bushes, and was wandering aimlessly round a cornfield when he fell in with the first patrol of the Coalition. Austrian lancers discovered him, and threatened to attack him because he was wearing the tricolour sash. He hastened to disown the Revolution, on which he had just turned his back for ever, and to declare himself an officer of the King. He detested the tricolour, which he untied forthwith and threw away, from the bottom of his heart, and yet when he thought of this episode in later years, it gave him a certain malicious satisfaction to think that the whole of Europe had soon been obliged to bow to it. Strangely complex, but thoroughly French reactions: feasting on the common glory, even if it has been achieved against one's own wishes and resistance! In Brussels, during the first stage of his new journey, he found a circle of emigrants that could well compare with Hamburg and Coblenz for great names, elegant young men and pretty women. Never in his life had he seen such a collection of new and dazzling uniforms. Everybody was a General, or at the least a General's Adjutant.

Their life was made up of ostentatious social gatherings, gossip, disputes for precedence and flippant boasting of imminent victory. The ragged gangs of the Republic, without experienced generals or even proper uniforms, would be sure to scatter at the first shot. 'Don't buy too many horses,' said a French officer to a Prussian captain of cavalry, 'the comedy can't last long; the liberty fever is evaporating in Paris as it is; the army of the Advocates is getting a good beating in the Netherlands, and we shall be home by the autumn.'

René was repelled by this arrogance; his dispute with Malesherbes was running in his head. Were these 'fashionable apes', as he called them, going to release the King from prison by main force? This society, to which he belonged by birth, suddenly seemed to him worthless, even hateful. Had these emigrants, who had after all left house and home behind them, nothing better to do than perpetuate the life of the Court, with all its undignified trifling? In any case he, personally, could not afford any luxuries; his wardrobe would scarcely allow him to accept an invitation from the Choiseuls, Polignacs or Autichamps. Once again his pockets were empty, his baggage was light. Still, he did possess the handsome white uniform of his old regiment of Navarre, in which he had served, alas, only too short a time, and white would keep cleaner in the chalky mud of Champagne than the sky-blue splendour of other regiments.

On the way from Coblenz to Trier he fell in with the columns of the deployed Prussian Army. A division of the Potsdam Guards had been drawn up facing King Frederick William, beside whom stood the old Duke of Brunswick, in supreme command of the campaign. Both of them greeted the young officer in the uniform of the old French army politely and asked whence he had come and whither he was bound. He told them he had heard of his King's misfortune in America, and had returned at once to Europe to place his sword and his blood at the service of the good, but alas much threatened cause. 'Bravo! Bravo!' exclaimed His Prussian Majesty, 'There you have the spirit of the French nobility'. Brunswick nodded approval, and everybody bowed to the young man who, in his white uniform, represented a Power already half-decayed. René was not a little moved by this reception; he would always remember it as a proof that at that time 'Honour meant as much as Country. In the year 1792 loyalty to one's oath was still considered a duty; now it has become so rare that it is regarded as a virtue'.

In Trier he was somewhat coolly received by his countrymen already enrolled in the units of the *emigrés*; they said he had arrived at the last moment in order to join in when the victory was as good as won. It was a cheap way of showing one's loyalty, to appear on the field of battle when the worst was over and the overthrow of the Parisian Mob Republic could be only a matter of days. It was not till his cousin Armand de Chateaubriand appeared on the scene and told them René had hurried there straight from the forests of America that he was accepted as a comrade.

The Army of the Princes, which was to operate in concert with the Austrian and Prussian forces, consisted of three corps; the first, which had been formed in Coblenz under the leadership of Marshals de Broglie and de Castries, amounted to 10,000 men, the second to 5,000 under the command of the Prince of Condé, while the third, rather smaller corps was under the command of the Duke of Bourbon in the Austrian Lowlands. Most of the units were formed from individual provinces and consisted almost exclusively of officers serving as common soldiers. The Breton nobility had formed seven companies wearing royal blue uniforms, an eighth consisted of young men not of the nobility and therefore only allowed to wear a dark grey one. This, notes Chateaubriand, was how 'people adhering to the same cause and exposed to the same danger perpetuated their political inequalities by revolting outward signs'. And in his Memoirs he adds 'The real heroes were the plebeian soldiers, for there was no alloy of personal interest in their sacrifice'.

They were all equally badly equipped; they were in want of essentials, even of arms. Old German arms had been given out, and there had been no time to put them in order. René fought the campaign with a musket, the trigger of which was hopelessly jammed; it was so heavy that it rubbed his shoulder raw. His knapsack contained only two shirts, but his cartridge pouch was crammed with manuscripts. For a while, as long as his physical strength would permit, he seized every opportunity to set in order the notes he had made in America, and to carry on with them. He had detached an episode from his epic *The Natchez* and made it into an independent work, a love story among Indians that later became famous under the title of *Atala*. In Trier he went in search of Roman ruins, seated himself on the ancient stones and wrote, with his heavy gun on the ground beside him. But he was soon forced to gather his things together again, stuff his papers under the brass cover of his cartridge pouch, stow his little *Homer* in his coat pocket, and seek shelter. For the celebrated autumn rain of the year 1792 had set in, which was to last a long while and play its part in the failure of the 'Campaign in France'.

Another great writer in the same army was to feel the rain and have the same need to keep his notes dry. He was by now of a certain age, and could travel in more or less comfortable conditions, as became a civilian and a Councillor of the Duke of Weimar. But the frightful weather, which made the roads impassable, foundered the horses, and bogged down guns and carriages in the mud, recognized no differences. Dysentery broke out in the army, the sick overflowed into the few remaining uninfected quarters, what little bread was left for distribution was mouldy, the water was polluted by the carcases of dead horses, friend and foe suffered hunger and want. Like Chateaubriand, Goethe spent his time looking for food in the farms and villages, but the Frankfort patrician's son had at least a horse and carriage, while the Breton nobleman had only his sore feet at his service. But they were both incorrigible artists, and found a good deal of picturesque charm in their sufferings, much to the wrath of later critics, who considered it wrong to enjoy these effective accompaniments of human slaughter. Chateaubriand notes: 'An officer's horse was hit by a bullet in the forehead; it reared up in pain and flung bloody foam from its mouth and nostrils. This rider with his sword in his hand on his wounded charger was a wonderful sight.' Goethe was more interested in the scenery: 'It's true that a few villages ahead of us went up in flames, but smoke is not amiss in a war picture.'

Both these great men had the satisfaction of not having underestimated the enemy; neither of them was surprised at the bravery of the Republicans or the superiority of their leadership. The campaign was going very badly. True, the Prussians had taken Longwy and Verdun, and the Austrians had succeeded in occupying 'France's Thermopylae' at Grand-Pré, but Dumouriez had given up the idea of marching on Chalons, and was proceeding up the Aisne to assemble his forces westward of Sainte-Ménéhould. Here he came up against reinforcements under Kellermann, and the position of the fronts was now reversed;

the Republican troops looked towards Paris, while the Prussians had their back to the capital. The engagement at Valmy was hardly a battle, it did not even come to a close engagement: the artillery played the principal part on this famous day. But the Coalition, which had been blinded by its contemptuous levity, was suddenly robbed of its illusions; the supposedly degenerate soldiers of the young Republic were showing such contempt of death, such startling enthusiasm, that the Prussian attack was held up. The wild shouts of 'Long live the Nation!' with which these young men, under their tricolour flag, were climbing the sodden slopes, while the deluge of rain poured down, was a new sound rising from a new world, Kellermann could be plainly seen, in his tricolour sash, marching ahead of his front line, stamping undismayed through the mud in his heavy riding-boots, his blue coat quite black, so thoroughly soaked was it by the rain; the plumes on his hat hung bedraggled and dripping, but he was carrying the hat in triumph on the point of his sword.

The Prussians were not defeated, but they felt so, and they desisted from any further advance. Their generals did not conceal the fact that 'an armistice was to be desired'. The general depression resembled an awakening after a drinking bout. Goethe, however, had not been idle; he 'had heard so much about the fear of powder and shot that he wanted to find out for himself what it was like'. He therefore rode into the midst of the gunfire and observed his reactions with considerable composure. On his return to his own men he found them in need of comfort. 'Thus the day had gone by, the French stood immovable, Kellermann had found a convenient position, our men were withdrawn out of firing range, and it was just as though nothing had happened. The greatest consternation spread throughout the army. Only that morning they had thought of nothing but impaling and devouring the French; I myself had been tempted to take part in this expedition by my unlimited confidence in such an army and in the Duke of Brunswick; but now everyone went his way without looking at anyone else—or if he did, it was only for the sake of cursing and swearing. Just as night was falling we chanced to form a circle, in the middle of which it proved impossible even to light a fire as we usually did; most of us were silent—one or two spoke, but nobody really knew what to think.' It was to this dismal company, awaiting an encouraging word from him, that Goethe delivered his famous verdict: 'Here and now an epoch of world history is beginning, and you will be able to say you were present.'

The new Republic, therefore, was not to be beaten; it had shown a grim, heroic face, and had become a power in the world. A moment ago, in the eyes of its assailants, it had been little more than a rabble of criminals that had dethroned the King and shut him up in prison with his family. A few weeks ago they had murdered the prisoners in the dungeons of Paris with pike and axe, massacring more than a thousand old men, women, priests, monks, nuns and others in custody, in cold blood and without judicial proceedings. The young Princesse de Lamballe, a friend of the Queen, had been hacked to pieces on a butcher's block. Was it not to be feared that the Most Christian King, and eventually the Queen, must also lose their heads? Roaring tigers, vampires, if you like. But here was something new appearing in the world, an Idea that was not to be checked by arms alone.

In a word, the Prussians, the Austrians and the Emigrants had lost courage at a single blow. They were ashamed of their rash talk of being in Paris in a few weeks, and giving the rascals a good hiding. The night following the cannonade of Valmy was filled with dark premonitions. An age of war had begun: it was to last more than twenty years, and it would be a national war from now on. These were gloomy forebodings when even the camp fire refused to burn, so wild were the wind and the rain. This made 'conditions in the open, on the hard ground, most unpleasant'. Everybody felt they were 'in a shameful, hopeless situation'.

Now began the 'ominous retreat', as Goethe called it. The distress of the *emigrés* amounted to despair, for they had seen their fellow countrymen in a new guise. All hope was lost as far as they were concerned. Chateaubriand with his useless musket had been unable to perform any heroic exploits; he was not present at Valmy, but there had been gunfire elsewhere, and a shell splinter had given him a serious flesh wound in the upper part of his thigh. It might have been even worse if his cartridge pouch had not been stuffed so full of manuscripts that it had stopped a bullet. It was raining harder than ever, they had all been foolish enough to devour upripe grapes and drink bad water. René himself fell ill, and had to drag his multifarious misery along the churned-up roads to Lorraine. His wound festered, he became feverish, and as a crowning misfortune he developed confluent smallpox.

Things could hardly have been worse; he had long ago lost all contact with the rest of his section; more than once he fell unconscious in a ditch, the tattered remains of his uniform were covered with mud, he was wrapped in an old horse-cloth that a wagoner had given him, his face was encrusted with dirt and overgrown by a straggling beard. At every moment he thought he was going to die; he lay in a fever under a hedge in the rain, murmuring words, old words, pious words, glad in a dim, half-conscious way, to feel that what he was murmuring to himself was a prayer. A consolation had visited him, of whose reality he felt assured from that hour. Human pity helped him to keep alive, charitable women rescued and tended him, kindly drivers gave him a lift here and there, and one day he arrived in Brussels.

Thus the father of French Romanticism dragged himself, with the last remnants of his strength, out of the theatre of war, carefully preserving his manuscript, while Goethe was enabled to take the whole adventure with the greatest composure imaginable. As we have seen, the historical significance of events had not escaped him, 'but fortunate is he whose breast is filled with a higher passion'. Goethe's preoccupation at that time was with the theory of colour; during the shelling of Verdun he was fortunate enough to be drawn into conversation by Prince Reuss XIV, and in the shelter of the vineyard wall—for the besieged 'were not slow to retaliate'—he was able to instruct Royalty in his theory. Besides which, owing to the fact that 'atmospheric air, vapours, rain, water and soil are always changing colour', and that during those weeks there had certainly been no lack of moisture, the poet was able to make many admirable observations, including the

study of a cannon-ball that was covered all over with a crystalline
deposit—consisting, as he quickly discovered, of pyrites, the
presence of which filled him with the greatest delight.

There was plenty of chalk too, for the entire area of war was so
to speak built on chalk, much to the liking of the Prussian
officers, since now the troops, whose appearance had lately
suffered very much, could set to work to whiten their leather
accoutrements, for which purpose chalk was always used in
barracks. The Supreme Command was greatly cheered by this
almost visible superabundance of beautiful chalk, and gave
orders that every man was to provide himself amply with this
cleaning material—no difficult task, for their haversacks were
empty. But the order was not carried out: the retreat afforded little
opportunity for gathering chalk. The troops were far too busy
scrounging food on the march, and although Goethe had long
since found his chaise again, he had great difficulty in getting
away. 'We now moved on at a funeral pace, but still we moved.
Day broke, we found ourselves in front of the town in the greatest
possible confusion: every sort of vehicle, a few cavalrymen,
countless foot-soldiers getting in one another's way on the great
square before the gates. We went to the right with our column
towards Etain, along the narrow fairway with a ditch on either
side. Self-preservation in such an enormous throng left no room
for pity or consideration. . . . Cavalrymen and infantrymen tried
to escape from the narrow, impracticable road on to the meadows,
but these too had been ruined by the rain and flooded by overflowing ditches.'

While Goethe was on this wearisome march towards Luxem-
burg, hugging the certainty that his troubles would soon be at an
end, and that domestic comfort was awaiting him, poor Chateaubriand had succeeded in finding a berth on a ship at Ostend, which
landed him on the Isle of Jersey. There he found friendly relations
who gave him hospitality, literally at the last gasp, for he was a
desperately sick man. He was coughing, spitting blood, in a high
fever again, and in need of months of nursing before he was in a
condition to continue his journey to England. When he left again
he was thin, pale and weak after his long, difficult convalescence,

and had only a few thalers in his pocket, given him by his relations. His baggage was light, therefore, as usual, but he had saved his manuscript. Even though the flame of life still burned only feebly in his emaciated body, his spirit was in the grip of a peculiar determination. He would live; he would become great. He was sure of this as he fingered the bundle of scribbled sheets; his characters took on their outlines, Chactas, Atala and Céluta began to come alive. What he would attempt to write had had its birth in the forests of the wilderness; it had defied the storms of the ocean, ripened under gunfire and found its voice in the paroxysms of fever. He had been looking for himself throughout, listening to his inmost soul, searching the starlight sky and the silence of the night, hearing the voice of the sea, and making of all these a world of poetry. What features his genius would wear he did not yet know, but he felt certain that the spirit would never desert him again. He was filled with an immense longing to be loved; but standing on the deck of the barque that was heading for Southampton, he was aware at the same time of the secret bliss of solitude. Never again, so he swore to himself, would he leave the fortress of his heart. All storms and stresses were welcome, but the citadel must remain impregnable. Thus he entered on the testing time of his London exile.

2 Chateaubriand's tomb at Grand Bé

2 Contemporary picture of the Château de Combourg

V

A STARVING MAN
EATS HIS FILL

THERE WAS MUCH TO BE LEARNT IN ENGLAND

THOUSANDS of French *emigrés* had taken refuge in London, hoping for better times; although things were not looking too good at home, and a speedy return was out of the question, most of them were in good spirits. Not many had been able to bring any pecuniary assets with them, but they were making ends meet with the self-confidence of their race; the ladies went in for trimming hats or dressmaking, the men carried on a trade of some kind, or gave language lessons, while their former domestic staffs set up as French pastrycooks or opened small hotels, at which, if the undertaking prospered, their old employers often dined free.

Far too many of them, it must be said, had quarrelled among themselves and were irreconcilably estranged; their common misfortune had not sufficed to bridge over their social prejudices; Dukes and princes looked down on the lesser nobility as before, and the political differences of the pre-revolutionary era had lost nothing of their sharpness: those that had pleaded for a Constitution and a constitutional monarchy could not hope for any pity from anarchists of the old school, while all those that accounted themselves 'philosophers' persisted in holding the people of the old school in general, and the clergy in particular, responsible for every misfortune. Pride of place, intellectual arrogance, intolerance and fanaticism pervaded this crowd of homeless creatures, who still refused to believe that anyone could dare to execute the King, institute Revolutionary Tribunals or make use of terrorism as a normal political weapon.

René, who could have taken advantage of his family con-

F

nections to mix with the highest circles of the emigration, avoided contact with his high-born countrymen. His complete independence of all class considerations, which was later to afford him so much freedom, showed itself here for the first time. He lodged in a miserable garret with another Breton, named Hingant, whom he had met on board ship. He went hungry; on an icy winter evening he once stood for hours before a shop-window full of fruit and smoked meats, painfully unable to tear himself away. There were days when he tricked his stomach by chewing straw and paper, or sucking a piece of linen soaked in water. His cough tormented him; the doctor that examined him told him he had not long to live.

Hingant was a good companion, but a trifle odd; he dabbled in magnetism, professed himself a pupil of Swedenborg, believed he was being persecuted and often burst into tears. René came home one evening to find him in bed, covered with blood; he had attempted suicide, and was removed to hospital by his friends. René had now to look for fresh accommodation, the garret being too expensive for himself alone, and he found a little bedroom whose only window overlooked an ancient graveyard. No view could have pleased him better, for he had always loved ancient tombs, ruined graveyards and funeral vaults. He gazed at the mossy stones with their weathered epitaphs, and feasted on his gloomy thoughts. But they did not appease his hunger, and a starving man cannot do good work.

So his new manuscript, a comparative history of revolutions, made slow progress. He was trying to discover a law common to all revolutions. In order to understand the catastrophe that had driven him into exile, he studied history—Greek, Roman, English—and explored epochs and continents. All this searching and browsing in books and documents afforded him genuine pleasure; he piled up an enormous heap of material, delved into difficult and preferably unknown authors, Latin, Greek, English and even Hebrew, mixed what he found in them with his own ideas and experience, with entirely personal lyrics, and even letters he had written and received. He visited libraries and record offices, and at night, by the light of a miserable candle, wrote page after page—and would have written more, had not hunger tormented him so sorely.

At last a friend, the gay, resourceful Peltier, found him a post in Suffolk, where he could teach French and go on rummaging among old records at the same time. In the villages of Beccles and Bungay he imparted the elements of his mother tongue to the schoolchildren—did any of his pupils realize later on that he had been taught by the greatest stylist of his age? He gave young ladies lessons in French literature, and studied, in his free time, in the well-stocked library of Mr Sparrow, a Beccles landowner. So there were lovers of books and scholarly reading among these people: they were not all as René had described them: 'They sell their corn, make agricultural experiments, hunt foxes or partidges; at Christmas they devour a fat goose, and sing of the roast beef of old England; they complain of the present and praise the past, which was no better, and curse Pitt and the war for sending up the price of port; they go to bed drunk and get up next day to begin the same life all over again.'

His inferior position, meagre livelihood, bad food and the perpetual necessity of being polite to the most stupid people because he was teaching their stupid, badly brought-up children, all this wounded his pride and drove him ever deeper into a mood of reserve and bitter melancholy. He had dropped his family name because the English found it unpronounceable; he now called himself Monsieur de Combourg, and rode a white pony, of no particular breed, to the various places where he gave lessons. People were very kind to him, but even their goodwill offended him. 'The sight of poverty,' he wrote in his notes, 'arouses different feelings in different people. The great, that is the rich, see it with only the greatest aversion. From these one can only expect insolent pity, or charitable gifts and courtesies, which are a thousand times worse than insults.' He believed he had discovered that in England one was condemned to isolation if one had no money. The young fugitive was well on the way to becoming a hypochondriac.

But despite his bad opinion of the English he was beginning, in the light of the tragic events in France, to compare English institutions with the conditions towards which his own country appeared to be vainly struggling. He discovered the secret of the cohesion of the English people in spite of the painful social differences prevailing among them, which was their acceptance of the authority of the law, the voluntary subjection of the individual to that law, in the formation of which each one felt he had a share: 'The miracle of a free government consists in this, that the voice of the law is all-powerful in this country, and when it speaks nobody opposes it.' It was here, as a foreigner, that he experienced the great political revelation of his life: he discovered that there was 'a bond between honour and freedom', and this realization never forsook him. It resulted later, during the Restoration, in the peculiar, not to say contradictory, attitude, which procured him few but enemies and aroused the instinctive aversion of the Bourbons: honour obliged him to serve kings that knew nothing of liberty and were incapable of realizing the majesty of the law. What he learnt in England, almost against his will, made of him in later years an outsider, and at the same time the great champion of the Restoration, the internal contradictions of which were quite clear to him, but which he served because of the sanctity of the Crown.

His recognition of the wisdom of the English political system cost him some pain, for it did not blind him to the poverty of the lowest classes, and the habit of measuring the value of human beings by their fortunes seemed to him crude and unintelligent. But the state of his own country was soon to involve him in suffering of a more immediate and personal kind. Sitting one evening in a village tavern at the same table with a stout, red-cheeked Englishman, he heard him reading a newspaper to himself, half aloud, as though reading did not come easy to him. He had just reached a report from Paris. Further atrocities, further executions! Then came the names, among them that of old Malesherbes, his daughter Madame Rosambo and her grand-children, of the Countess Chateaubriand and her husband Jean-Baptiste! They had all died on the same day under the guillotine. René stood up, staggering. People ran to his assistance. 'My brother . . .' he stammered.

And these were not the only evil tidings of those days. Soon afterwards he heard that a widespread conspiracy had been discovered, headed by the Marquis de la Rouerie. Mass arrests had followed. René's old mother had been seized and sent to Paris; his sister Julie and his young wife Céleste had also been taken and were now in prison in Rennes. His beloved sister Lucile had refused to remain behind, and insisted on being incarcerated in the same prison.

Only now that his whole family was affected, his old friend Malesherbes and his only brother executed, did the Revolution assume its full reality. So they could dare, they had the power, to drag innocent, harmless families to the scaffold! The executioners were merely doing their duty when they let the guillotine crash down; they were obeying the law! Could a State be built up on such injustice? Could men that had seized power for themselves and seriously believed they were acting for the benefit of mankind, burden themselves with such guilt?

RENÉ AND WERTHER

René resumed the name of Chateaubriand, for his emotion had betrayed him. He found a little consolation for his grief in the kindness of a clergyman of Bungay, a highly educated man who took a lively interest in the young Frenchman's studies, and having once been in North America himself, liked exchanging travellers' impressions with him.The atmosphere of the parsonage did the emigrant good; Mrs Ives, the parson's wife, often asked him to tea, and as the house was a spacious one she ended by setting apart a little room in which he could work in comfort. He gave the daughter, a young beauty of sixteen, daily lessons in French and Italian, and of an evening they all sat together, chatting. It was years since René had experienced such a sense of security and comfort; he opened his heart and let something of the world of his fancies, dreams and hopes be seen. He talked of the old castle in Brittany, the home of his childhood, raved about Lucile, his romantic sister, and her mysterious apprehensions; he described the grandiose scenery he had seen on his travels and the misery he had suffered during the campaign; in a word, he expanded as he had never succeeded in doing before.

The daughter, Charlotte, was his most attentive listener. René suddenly had the feeling that the Sylphide of his youthful fancy had been driven out by a living being. Regret at losing his dream creature was mingled with delight at having exchanged her for a being of flesh and blood. He began to realize the shattering force of love when it invades the human heart; he was aware of bliss and fear at the same time. The desire to surrender fought with the thirst for independence, but the confusion in his mind always ended by assuming the image of the lovely Charlotte. He was too bashful to declare himself, she was too innocent to dare even a glance at him, but her faltering speech, her blushes, her charming timidity were not lost on her parents. They were not displeased: the stranger was a stranger no longer, he was a gifted, distinguished young man, with a right to high hopes, who had proved, moreover, an agreeable house-mate. One evening Mrs Ives found an opportunity for a confidential talk with their French guest, in the course of which she hinted, in the most affectionate terms, that he would be welcome as a son-in-law, if . . . René burst into tears. 'Say no more!' he cried, 'I am married!'

He left the house without saying farewell, without even returning to his room, and hurried like a guilty man fleeing from justice to Beccles, where he took post to London. He could not drive the image of the girl from his mind, he felt the deepest remorse at having inflicted such humiliation on a family that had treated him with so much kindness, and he cursed his over-hastily contracted marriage, which, as he now believed, had thrown him out of his course and robbed him of potential happiness. But amid this tempest of emotions the self-conscious Chateaubriand of the future makes his appearance, his robust egoism rears its head: 'After all, if I had married Charlotte, my role in this world would have been a different one. I should have buried myself in an English county and become a sporting gentleman. Not a line would ever have flowed from my pen, I should even have forgotten my own language. . . .'

This was small comfort, however, for London depressed him

more than ever. He did, it is true, find a printer of the name of
Baylis who gave him shelter and was prepared to print his work
on the Revolution as it went on, but his loneliness was a torment
to him now, and he looked back on the days at the parsonage
as a lost paradise. He wrote endless letters to Charlotte only to
tear them up again. On solitary walks he tortured himself with
dreams of all he had lost. Soon there was no road, no wood, no
heath in the neighbourhood of London that he did not know.
Wandering sadly about, he became the man that romanticism was
later to picture as the poet smitten with *weltschmerz*. 'The most
deserted places, a field of nettles, a ditch overgrown with thistles,
things that men deem unworthy of attention, became my favourite
resorts: they were stirred even then by the breath of Byron. Leaning
my head on my hand I contemplated these despised scenes. . . .'

René was quite in his element. Sadness was a food without
which his poetic genius would have starved. He sank so deep into
this melancholy mood that his acquaintance began to doubt his
sanity. He spoke to nobody—but he had never been a talkative
man, and never would be. Of all the great romanticists of France,
he was the only silent one. The love of chatter, the urge to revel
in speech and be carried away by it as by a wave, this element
of French sociability forsook him during these depressing
months in London, if he had ever possessed it.

He heaped reproaches upon himself for his lack of candour.
Sitting by the fireside, as the guest of a man to whom he had confided so much of his origin, his past and his family, should he not
also have mentioned his marriage to Céleste? What fate was it
that always prevented him from behaving openly, hiding nothing
of his existence? He felt that he was born to misfortune and condemned to bring misfortune to others. A curse had been laid on
him 'to burn up hearts and lay them waste, so that wherever he
passed, love could not spring up again'.

In these gloomy broodings the London days dragged
monotonously along. Working at his *Essay on Revolutions*, the
outline of a youth took shape in his brain, who was to bear his
own name and embody the nature of his sufferings. The hero of
his novel *René* is undoubtedly a descendant of *Werther*, but also

a forerunner of Benjamin Constant's *Adolphe*. Goethe freed himself from his love of Charlotte by transferring it to Werther. Werther is a living person, he exists, and that is why we are affected by his ruin; that is how Goethe triumphs over his own suffering; it is an act of self-liberation through art. The French novelist did not succeed in liberating himself, for he could transfer his feelings to his hero, but not his conflicts. The René of the novel is loved by his sister in a sinful way, but he does not share this forbidden passion, he has never known of it, and has only discovered it by an unfortunate accident.

Chateaubriand brought in this guilty passion simply because he liked building up border-line situations. In *René* there is only Chateaubriand, he is the sole reality, all else is decoration. Goethe surmounts Werther's drama with a great, a grandiose stride, he prevails over the type he has created. In the Frenchman's case it is the other way round: he has at last found the formula for his own nature, and its name is René. This is to be the legend of his personality, he is to live henceforth according to the basic lines of the figure he has created, the world and posterity are to see him as René.

It was part of Chateaubriand's peculiar method of work to be constantly taking episodes out of his books and using them as independent pieces, or even, where possible, introducing them into other contexts. This tendency makes any consideration of the individual stages of his creative work very difficult. Both *René* and *Atala* are parts of the original novel begun in America and called after the Indian tribe of the Natchez. Both were then published separately, and later on actually incorporated as episodes in the *Spirit of Christianity*. Nothing Chateaubriand wrote was ever endowed with that peculiar autonomous life over which the author soon has no more control; everything expresses only himself, his entire literary work is one gigantic self-portrait, and when he considers that a further stroke of the brush is needed, he takes a fragment out of an earlier book, or from some of his letters, diplomatic notes drawn up when he was an ambassador, or Minister for Foreign Affairs, speeches delivered in the Assembly of the Peers of France, even extracts from the diaries of his witty wife, herself a skilled writer, of whom he otherwise took little notice.

The perpetual presence of his personality is the essential magic of his art. Whether he is writing a novel, the description of a journey, an essay, a treatise or an historical work, he always seems to be saying: 'Look, I have experienced, seen, dreamed, thought and fashioned all this, and my pilgrimage on this earth is still an enigma to me. Why am I alive, when I have no wish to live? Why have I been endowed with this skill, when I am unable to give my own existence the bliss of completeness?'

The René of the novel roams through the woods of America as his author had done. He makes friends with a red warrior and marries his delicate, innocent sister Céluta, who had fallen passionately in love with him at first sight. But 'the emptiness that had formed in my inmost soul could no longer be filled. René had been cursed by a decree of heaven, which constituted at once his torment and his genius. He awoke passions, but could not return them; he was a burden on the earth he trod, it bore him unwillingly. . . .' And he complains: 'If only I had been able to share the feelings that animated me with some other being! O God, if only Thou hadst given me a wife after my desire! If only Thou hadst drawn an Eve for me out of myself, and brought her to me . . . I was alone, alone on the earth!'

But what if he had not been alone? For loneliness and misanthropic soliloquy were his element, it pleased him to feel that he had created the 'mal du siècle', he had his hands full of what he called his unhappiness. 'I no longer wanted to die, now that I was really unhappy. My suffering was an occupation that took up all my time, to such an extent was my heart composed of weariness and misery.' And a little later—still in London—he says 'My suffering, by reason of its unusual nature, brought with it its own cure: one enjoys that which is not common to all, even when it represents a misfortune'.

A REAL FRIEND AT LAST

His life at that time was certainly not calculated to inspire him

with energy and confidence. He was writing assiduously at his
Essay on Revolutions, without ever meeting a soul except the
eccentric printer who was printing it bit by bit. He was reading,
living among mountains of books: the study of foreign conditions
and personalities had to take the place of contact with reality. But
the lessons he drew from history were not encouraging either:
'One is bereft of one's illusions without having had any gratifica-
tion; desires still exist, but no more illusions. . . . One lives with a
full heart in an empty world, and without having tasted any
delight one is satiated with everything.' It was with feelings such
as these that he found history repeating itself eternally in revolution after revolution. A breath of nihilism was exhaled by this
perpetual confirmation that all revolutions are alike and repeat the
same errors and crimes. What he wrote at that time represents a
complete *démenti* of the eighteenth century with its belief in
progress and the perfectibility of human nature. He ridiculed the
'system of perfection' on the subject of which Chamfort had once
raved to him.

Decades later, he was to judge this work harshly: 'A chaos, a
jumble of everything, Jacobins and Spartans, the Marseillaise and
the songs of Tyrtaeus, a voyage to the Azores and the Circum-
navigation of Hanno, praise of Jesus Christ and criticism of the
monks, the golden verse of Pythagoras and the fables of Monsieur
de Nivernais, Louis XIV, Charles I, lonely wanderings, views,
misfortunes, melancholy, suicide, politics, a fragment from the
beginning of *Atala*, Robespierre, the Convention, polemics on
the subject of Zenon, Epicurus and Aristotle: all this in a turbulent,
bombastic style, full of grammatical errors and foreign, barbaric
interspersions.' It was easy for the old Chateaubriand to judge the
young one with severity: perhaps he no longer remembered how
difficult it had been at that time to stand so decidedly aloof from all
Parties as the young *emigré* had succeeded in doing.

His unconcern with recent events was actually astonishing.
History was unchangeable, he said, and 'a man who is convinced
that there is nothing new in history loses his desire for innova-
tions, a desire that I hold to be one of the greatest plagues by
which Europe is visited at the present day. Enthusiasm is born of

ignorance; when the latter is cured the former dies down of itself; knowledge of things is an opium that cures enthusiasm only too speedily.' It was power itself that he distrusted; the idea of total liberty seized him ever and again like a fit of dizziness: 'One may carp as much as one likes, coin phrases, utter witticisms, but humanity's greatest misfortune is still to have laws and a government. All government is of the devil, all government is a yoke.' But he thinks again, and adds: 'All the same it is better to obey a compatriot who is rich and enlightened than an ignorant mob burdening us with every sort of evil.'

Here, as usual, he speaks of a thousand things, and yet in reality only of himself. 'The word "I",' he confesses, 'crops up everywhere in the Essay. This is because the book was written for my own sake, and for me alone. The word "I" is always conspicuous with authors that have been persecuted by other men, and have spent their lives far removed from them.' The hesitant speech of an isolated intellect, given to too much reading and too little living, lends the work a strange charm, most vividly apparent in the bare patches of piled-up erudition. The religious accents are as contradictory as they are striking, the childish philosophizings, frivolous anecdotes, long series of anti-Christian arguments taken from the writings of Volney, Diderot, Voltaire and Bayle, the immature jibes of intruding cynicism, scarcely conceal the fact that the author is approaching Christianity, if not intellectually at least in spirit. He does not believe, but he thirsts for belief.

He had dedicated his work provocatively 'to all parties', with the result that he pleased none. 'What a charlatan!' exclaimed the Abbé Siéyès, 'Were you able to read it to the end?' His good old uncle, who had tended him so devotedly in Jersey after the campaign, spoke anxiously to the Prince of Bouillon about this nephew of his, who appeared to have fallen a victim to 'modern philosophy'. 'There are only too many of that sort,' the great man assured him. This was also the opinion of the high and mighty *emigrés* in London, with whom Chateaubriand had no contact anyhow. The distress the book caused the Chateaubriand family was more serious. His old mother, his two sisters and his young wife had been at liberty again since the 9th Thermidor, but they had suffered too much under the Revolution while they were in prison to take any pleasure in an 'objective analysis' of it. The absent son, husband and brother, who should have been refined by suffering, had turned out to be an evil-minded, confused thinker, quoting whole pages from the atheists who had brought all these misfortunes about, and was attempting if not exactly to justify the Revolution, at least to assign it a meaning in history. The ladies' distress was great, his mother shed many tears, while his sister Lucile did her best to defend him. None of them had actually read the book.

Chateaubriand, none the less, had caught the attention of the French in London. Not, it is true, of the Princes and their unbending adherents, but at least of those that were prepared to learn something, for good or evil, from the drama that had driven them from home. He was given the *entreé* of the beautiful Mrs. Lindsay's drawing-room, and became acquainted with men of high standing such as Malouet, Montlosier, Mallet du Pan. He made friends with the Chevalier de Panat, who had belonged to the emigrant circle in Hamburg and had much to say on the subject of Rivarol. Panat 'was justly famed for his wit, his grubbiness and his greed. He belonged to that *élite* of good taste that used to sit observing French society with their arms crossed, like a pit audience at the theatre. Idlers, whose mission in life consisted in observing everything and passing judgement on everything; they exercised the same function as newspapers today, but without their great influence on the masses.'

It was in this circle that Chateaubriand first met a young and very pretty woman, who was later to write a number of spiteful things about him in her memoirs. The daughter of the Marquis d'Osmond, last Ambassador of the French Monarchy to the Court of St. James's, who had stayed on in London as an *emigré*, she had been married very early to a Monsieur de Boigne, who had amassed a huge fortune in India and might now, thanks to his marriage, have played a part in high society. The family contented themselves, however, with relieving him of a good deal of his fortune: father-in-law, mother-in-law and brother-in-law were provided with large pensions, and his young wife made life hell

for him till he had settled a yearly income on her of 100,000 francs
and retired for good to one of his estates in Savoy. Madame de
Boigne could now devote herself entirely to politics, society life
and great men. Since she was virtuous, her friendships were almost
as durable as her enmities. Even now, when she was barely grown-
up, she was admired for her discerning judgement; she prided
herself on her intuition in the matter of power, and in this emigrant
circle she was the first to draw attention to the youthful General
Bonaparte, who had quelled a royalist rising in Paris three years
earlier, and been appointed Governor of Paris by Barras as a
reward. Since then he had won several brilliant victories in Italy,
and even the most embittered of the *emigrés* could no longer deny
that he had enormously increased the prestige of France throughout the world.

However, it did not look as though this young hero intended
to lend a hand to the re-introduction of monarchy in France.
The reaction that set in on the overthrow of Robespierre on the
9th Thermidor had raised the hopes of the Monarchists; the
elections in May, 1797, had brought a surprisingly great number of
Moderates and Royalists to the top. A supporter of constitutional
monarchy, Barthélemy, had a seat in the Directory that was now
ruling France, and the Council of the Five Hundred had elected
as their president General Pichegru, the conqueror of Holland,
who had long been engaged in a conspiracy against the Republic.
But the Directory were not blind: although the Constitution had
forbidden the presence of mobile troops in the capital, they
recalled Augereau's Division of the army in Italy and established
a Dictatorship on the 4th September (Fructidor), to which the
royalist elements were sacrificed. Very harsh measures were
resorted to, the prisons were soon filled, 8,000 of the clergy alone
were deported, and if the guillotine had still been working,
Robespierre might just as well have remained alive. Many people
had breathed again too soon, the good old times did not seem to be
returning after all, and what the Directory had called the achievements of the Revolution were obviously there to stay.

A fresh wave of *emigrés* arrived in London, among them that
witty, distinguished man Fontanes, with whom Chateaubriand

had become acquainted during his first stay in Paris just before the outbreak of the Revolution, and who had guided his first steps among the 'Philosophers'. Fontanes was no less corpulent than before, and looked more than ever like a wild boar, so that the nickname still clung to him. He had achieved the miracle of surviving the Reign of Terror; he had hidden from sight among the crowd, and then stuck out his head a little too soon. The turn of affairs on the 18th Fructidor had taught him that France had not yet seen the end of her troubles. He was exiled, and had now to wait in London till the people at home had come to their senses. As a man of tradition, a writer in a severely classical style, an adherent of stable institutions even in the intellectual sphere, any extravagance, any disturbance of balance, was distasteful to him. He was disgusted with a freedom that refused to remain within the limits of institutions based on good manners.

Chateaubriand was delighted to see him again, and to find he had lost none of his old cordiality. From him he obtained the first positive account of the state of things in France and of what hope there might be in future for a country still in the throes of crisis after crisis. France was utterly sick of the Revolution, the country was poor and languishing, but it had gained a new kind of self-consciousness, aware that it had changed the world and that its example would never cease to preoccupy mankind. Religion, said Fontanes, was not extinguished; on the contrary, among the mass of the people there was a thirst for righteousness and reverence that only need a little encouragement to become an outspoken desire. René listened half incredulously, half eagerly, as he roamed the outskirts of London with his friend, supping with him in village inns and wayside taverns, and walking endlessly up and down the streets of the great city at night.

Fontanes studied the *Essay on Revolutions* and dipped into the manuscript of *The Natchez* and the pages of *Atala* and *René*; then, suddenly attracted, buried himself in this chaos of reveries, elegies, and grandiose descriptions of nature, and although he did not conceal from his protégé that his academic taste was often offended by this new style, he soon acquired the certainty that a new literary epoch was dawning. Fontanes was too clear-sighted a connoisseur of literature to let the over-luxuriance of the prose distract him from the originality of its core. René, for his part, realized at once the value of this friendly but incorruptible criticism; he knew he had something decisive to learn from it. He was no longer alone, he had found, if not a master, at least a teacher; his life as a writer had begun. To the scoffers that smiled at the unbridled style of his *protégé*, Fontanes retorted, with the authority of the man that wrote the most immaculate French of his time, 'Never mind, he'll outstrip us all!' René was not to enjoy this support for long, however, for Fontane's expulsion was soon revoked. He decided to start on his homeward journey, going first to Hamburg, whence he wrote to the friend he had left behind 'The things you have read to me, especially lately, are wonderful. Work, my dear friend, work, and you will become famous. You can. The future is yours.'

VI

NAPOLEON'S SUNRISE

THE WRITER IS CONVERTED

THE century was drawing to its close. Man is accustomed to think in periods, round numbers appeal to his sense of harmony; time, whose endless course has often enough disquieted him, assumes organic shape. The fancy that such an immense unity as a century is making its last rotation like a wheel, affords a mere mortal, whether spectator or victim, a touch of pride, as though he himself had given it the final push. He is only too willing to believe that he will gain by stepping from one epoch to the next; he still hopes for some sort of break that will mark the end of certain developments and modes of life and the beginning of a new sequence. Depression and expectation hold the balance between them: what must one fear? What dare one hope? The spiritual flowering of the century, which in most of the countries of Europe had been so radiant, had suddenly been superseded by the rank spread of the revolutionary weed. Human nature's urge to self-destruction as an expression of its uttermost freedom gave place to horror at the atrocities and distortions of which society is capable in the attempt to create a paradise on earth by force, by means of institutions and laws. What had begun with elegant chatter turned to plebeian roaring and ended in a death-rattle. There followed a beneficial but momentous longing for order.

The peace treaties of Basel and Campo Formio brought about the dissolution of the first Coalition. Thanks to the genius of the young Field-Marshal Bonaparte, France had come off victorious; he had enabled the policy of 'natural frontiers', so much desired of kings, to gain the upper hand; nationalism was beginning to fashion the face of the earth. France had now only one enemy left,

4 The Château de Combourg today

5 Céleste, Madame de Chateaubriand

and that was England. In order to strike at her, Bonaparte started for Egypt and lost his fleet at Aboukir. He hurried home, leaving his army behind. The *coup d'état* that was to raise him to the rank of absolute ruler over France was near at hand. The *emigrés* in London watched these events with fluctuating feelings; they were beginning to feel proud of being Frenchmen, and the bonfires with which London celebrated the victory of Aboukir stirred their anger. England knew no such conflicting emotions; she had just quelled the revolt of Tippoo Sahib, and was now quietly and confidently preparing for a long war. She was not interested in the homesickness and mental confusion of the emigrant circle.

The Continent's one desire was for order. Order was the magic word of the moment, an attractive word, which at first hearing suggested nothing of the disorder it had wrought in the world, the amount of violence and oppression for which it had served as a pretext. Too many opinions had been rife in the last ten years of the century. The whole of public life had been ruled by conflicting opinions, philosophies and doctrines, and nobody had felt certain about any of them except the very few to whom it fell to decide between them. At the siege of Mayence—so graphically described by Goethe—when the French Revolutionary troops were forced to evacuate the town, those of the citizens who had been on good terms with them, and had thus incurred the accusation of being 'collaborators', went out with them to save their own skins. The furious populace were prepared to maltreat them, although they had been guaranteed safe conduct.

A particularly unpopular man was surrounded in front of the Duke of Weimar's residence as he was leaving the town with his possessions. When the mob became threatening, Goethe stepped in and saved the fugitive, shouting to the angry crowd: 'Neither your misfortune nor your hatred give you any rights in this matter!' Called to account by his friends for having succoured such a particularly objectionable individual, he declared that the open space in front of the Duke's house was 'sacrosanct'—and what would His Highness say 'if he could scarcely come at his own door over the wreckage caused by such unlawful proceedings?' Half in jest he pointed to the now empty space, and as his friends

G

still refused to be satisfied, he made his famous declaration: 'It's part of my nature; I would rather commit an injustice than tolerate disorder.'

The dictum was both fateful and ambiguous. The safe conduct covered everybody without exception, and that was a legal position he would not allow to be questioned; but law and justice are not always the same thing. The anger of the multitude may be just, and yet offend the law, and here he had acted on behalf of justice. At the same time he had been horror-struck by the mass excitement, the excess of emotion, always distasteful to him as an incentive to public action.

The dictum was ominous because it could be taken to mean that men must put up with injustice if they wanted order. The people of those years, who had been through so much terror and upheaval, were weary; they were disinclined to weigh the dangerous alternatives, and were prepared to pay any price for order. The *emigré* in London could not fully realize the difficulty of wiping out the Revolution. He judged the state of the world less by French conditions than by English ones, which seemed to him orderly and just at the same time. What a pity that this country, which was still giving shelter to so many fugitives, should be at war with France! Whose victory ought he to wish for? No honest and honour-loving Frenchman must tolerate the misfortune of his country for a moment, even if he belonged to a class that had been deprived of its rights. Was there not a figure appearing, whose radiance promised honour and glory—and not one alone? All at once, in the France that had seemed delivered up to the rabble, a host of brilliant warriors had appeared, capable of restoring order by the sword throughout their province and raising the standard of honour again: not Bonaparte alone, but Moreau, Pichegru, Bernadotte and Masséna! The constantly increasing importance of the sword in the public life of France was a great temptation to those who were thirsting for security; but the sword is only a tool, not an institution. The grandest victories and bravest generals could not solve the question as to what foundation men should build their lives upon, in order to regain their senses and find peace.

Chateaubriand would have liked to return home; but what would the France he was yearning for look like, how would it receive him? His valiant friend Fontanes, so wordly wise and with such a flair for success, had gone on ahead and was telling his friends about the young man who was coming to maturity among the *emigrés*, and was a hope for French literature. Who was François-René de Chateaubriand? Nobody seemed to remember him; but in a few years' time he would be the best known writer of his country and of his epoch.

For the moment he was intent on composing a work that was to bear more or less the title: *Of the Christian Religion in relation to Poetry*. This awkward and restrictive description gave no hint of the dynamic of the final work, which was to embrace every sphere of life. But by October of that year he offered the half-finished book to a publisher under the title: *The poetical and moral beauties of the Christian religion and its superiority to all other cults in the world*. A long-winded, tentative title for the book of which he was one day to assert that it had opened to the French people the churches the Revolution had closed! But the spirit of his undertaking had obviously grown bolder. He would undertake no more research, establish no further association of ideas, but fight for an Institution, and help it to triumph by his literary skill. Christianity was to be recognized afresh as a spirit; it was to throw off its mourning hue and restore a long-lost order, not only to men's souls but to the whole organism of society.

What had made him turn to religion in this way, for its own sake and as a stimulus to his poetic creation? He had gone into exile as a disciple of the Philosophers, and neither poverty nor suffering had driven him to seek consolation in the faith of his mother and sisters. Old Malesherbes, whose mortal remains had long since been mouldering in a common grave, had certainly never counselled piety—it was out of fashion in the free-thinking society of his day. In the *Essay on Revolutions* the not very deep-seated but studied scepticism of the eighteenth century is still perceptible, though it is not always easy to see whether the author is attacking the Church in particular or religion in general. He had in fact been strangely little influenced by the religious atmosphere in which he had grown up—for though his father was a 'philosopher', and went to church only by way of fulfilling his duty as a man of property, the women of the family, especially his mother and Julie, were of a nun-like piety.

According to some of his friends his conversion had been a sudden one; almost overnight divine voices had shaken him out of his indifference to a true practice of the faith. Others suggested that his mother's death had contributed to it. He had loved his mother, although even at Combourg she was in the habit of spending as much as three hours daily on her knees in the chapel, which might well have intimidated rather than attracted him as a boy. Now she had died in the odour of saintliness. His sister Julie, whose imprisonment during the Reign of Terror had robbed her, if not of her beauty, at least of her love of life, told him the sad news in a letter, and added 'If you knew how many tears your errors had cost our venerable mother, how deplorable they must appear to anybody not merely sensible but devout, it would perhaps open your eyes and help you to give up writing'.

Hardly an encouraging letter to a budding author! Julie was an imperative creature; like all Chateaubriands she went to extremes. She hid her fine shoulders from sight, stopped wearing jewellery, and threw her good poems in the fire, along with her laces and ribbons. In spite of her bad health, the result of her imprisonment, she slept on a board and lived on bread and water. Her piety knew no bounds; she was standing even then on the threshold of eternity, and her letter had a ring of the other world about it.

What Chateaubriand experienced at the age of thirty-one might certainly be termed a conversion, but it was no heaven-sent revelation of the cardinal truths of Christianity: 'I confess that I did not undergo any great supernatural illumination. My conviction came from my heart. I wept and believed.' An honest declaration. He was returning to the faith of his fathers, influenced by the appeals and prayers of his womenfolk from beyond the grave. The emotional experience had its roots in loyalty—loyalty to his family, his arms and his tradition. He was a believer out of chivalry, as he was to be a Legitimist and a servant of kings out of chivalry; the religious impulse had comparatively little to do with it. Nor had the emotional reaction to the book itself, when it appeared, much to do with a return to religion. The Christian virtues were extolled by the author, but not made the basis of social life. The man who said 'If somebody gives you a slap in the face, give him back four, at once, never mind on which cheek' had little inclination to preach Christian humility. He wrote his book in full awareness that he was doing more for society than for the teaching of Christ.

Christianity, to him, was a restraining, formative, organizing force; it could afford men the order they longed for, and protect them from their passions. By means of fantasies, portraits, descriptions and examples (the latter developed into independent novels such as *Atala* and *René*), he gave a significance to Christianity that the Church could not but accept, must even welcome: the beauty of divinely inspired art and thought, the beauty of religious practice and ceremony, the glory of souls entirely merged in God. The Church was passing through a period of dire necessity, and hailed with joy such a poetical presentation of Christianity as a cultural value of the highest order, clearly recognizing though it must have done, that all this amounted merely to marginal illustration: these conceptions of harmony and order had little to do with the theological core, and if carried to extremes might lead to the conclusion that a man or a society could be a Catholic without being sincerely Christian.

At that time, however, Rome was engaged in hard power-political struggles, and was not over-particular in the choice of its allies; the Church could not afford to withdraw into the sphere of pure faith and defend it with strict consistency or she would scarcely have tolerated Chateaubriand's idea of a cultural Christianity; she would have asserted that the binding force of dogmatic truth had no need of the wonderful illustrations of the Christian spirit which the author was so eloquent in enumerating. But while his pen travelled over the pages, day after day, and the sheets grew full and the finger of time neared the end of the seventeen-hundreds, Chateaubriand felt not only a Christian who had found himself again, not merely a Catholic who had realized afresh his duty of loyalty to the Church, but a Frenchman, that is

to say a member of a country that had always been known as the
eldest daughter of the Church, and had faithfully preserved her
Christianity 'with a minimum of religion'. France, which had
produced so many marvellous saints, had lived nevertheless from
the very first close to the frontiers of dogma and the cardinal
truths of Christianity. The idea of vicarious salvation had enabled
her not to transgress these frontiers: salvation through the cumula-
tive effect of good works, through the devotion of the saints, and
the ever-renewed sacrifice of the Son of Man. Chateaubriand's
great work presents religion simply as a way of life—the most
beautiful, the grandest and most stable way of life of all time and
all peoples—with such almost provocative insistence that its
appeal would never be silenced again, but would one day force
Rome to call a halt. This, however, was still in the womb of time.

Chateaubriand was carried along by his work as if by a stream;
he wrote of the sacraments, the life of the cloister, processions,
penances, the mystery of the Mass; he undertook, though with
insufficient equipment, an apologetic that was theologically highly
controvertible, but gave a lively picture, in impressions and
images, of the author's own personality. He could not know that
he was creating a religious style which was to endure for more
than a century, and weary people to such an extent that even the
original would become an object of disgust. In the third part of his
work, however, treating of the fine arts and literature, he set
standards and introduced elements that would henceforth be
inalienable from aesthetic criticism. History was forcing its way
into the scene of worldly affairs, a sense of time was making itself
felt with a surprising effect of depth. Though it aroused much
satirical comment and gave birth to tasteless imitations, Chateaubriand's preoccupation with historical places, ruins, graveyards
and funeral monuments created a new and enduring relation to the
passage of time. He organized the past, albeit for the moment
under its Christian aspect alone; he established the pre-eminence
of the seventeenth century, and dissolved its apparent unity with
the eighteenth. He shattered the omnipotence of the century that
was just coming to a close.

There must have been odd, almost fantastical publishers in

those days. Although the book was not yet half finished, the publisher Dulau, who had settled in London, was already hard at work printing it as fast as the author brought it to him. A few fragments of it were handed round or read aloud, and their success was astonishing; people felt stirred by some force they could not define. The Chevalier de Panat wrote to the author 'My God, how interesting that reading was, for which I have to thank your courtesy this morning! Our religion has had great and illustrious Fathers among its defenders, and these athletes have wielded all the weapons of reasoning with great force. Unbelief was conquered, but that was not enough. It remained to display all the magic of this wonderful religion, to show how well suited it is to the human heart, and what marvels it offers to the imagination. It is no longer the school theologian, but the great painter and the sensitive man that open up a new horizon.' This, in the style of a man of the world in the year 1799, was a very good intimation of what the world might look for from *The Spirit of Christianity*.

FROM CLOVIS TO ROBESPIERRE

Chateaubriand would have liked to confide in his friend Fontanes and ask his opinion of the new book of which he entertained such high hopes. He was determined to undertake nothing further as a writer without the advice of this discerning, disinterested friend. But correspondence with Paris was difficult, Fontanes himself seemed suddenly to have misgivings about exchanging news with the *emigrés* in London. Then, on November 9th, came the thunderclap. General Bonaparte had ventured the *coup d'état*: with the help of his devoted troops he had overthrown the Directory and made himself master of France. The reign of order that everyone had been longing for after his own fashion was actually there; it appeared settled, and was taking on a golden hue in the light of a power without equal. The authority of the State was restored. If the shadow of violence was not yet banished, at least the law was beginning to recover its majesty.

At a later date, pampered generations might condemn this *coup d'état* as an attack on the achievements of the Revolution. But for the moment Bonaparte appeared as the man destined to deliver the country from the necessity of humbling itself before the Bourbons—lately overthrown with such shouts of triumph—and to establish firmly all the elements of the Revolution worthy of survival. The country was undoubtedly impoverished, but its institutions had made a gigantic stride forward; it was now the most modern country in the world, and the First Consul had every intention of maintaining it in this position. The establishment of the new governmental apparatus must be hurried up. To his new Minister of Finance he said 'Look sharp, get yourself sworn in as quickly as possible, we haven't much time!' This was only too true, for there was only 137,000 francs left in the Treasury. The Constitution drawn up by the hesitant Siéyès was dismissed as rubbish by the General, and rapidly altered in a few bold strokes. 'All for the people, nothing by the people,' was his dictum. 'We have finished the romance of the Revolution, now we must start on its history, and only pay attention to what it is possible and realistic to achieve on the basis of its principles.' On Christmas Day the Consuls took office; the government manifesto concluded with the words: 'Citizens, the Revolution is over.'

Work could begin; it looked overwhelming. Bonaparte himself declared 'Everything is only in the germ, there is no lack of elements, but nothing is in its right place'. This was very euphemistically expressed, for most of the 'elements' were lacking. Reports from the provinces, which were pouring into the office of the Minister of Police, Fouché, showed a terrible picture. The misery of the population contrasted with the revolting luxury of speculators, often easily identifiable as corrupt politicians. In the south the arid agricultural soil was turning boggy, on the west coast the harbours were silting up; whole streets were becoming dilapidated, villages without number were standing deserted. In many parts of the country the excesses of the robber bands were assuming a threatening shape. These robbers were for the most part merely degenerate *Chouans*, former peasants loyal to the monarchy, whose houses and farms had been burnt down. They were now roaming hopelessly about the country. Industry and trade were at a standstill, especially in Paris, Lyons and Marseilles. The

armies were unprovisioned, living entirely at the expense of the
conquered countries. But Bonaparte was not in the least discouraged; he set to work everywhere at once, imbuing his administration and the country at large with the conviction that the
bad times were over for ever. He lived in a delirium of activity.
Later on he said of this period of his youth 'At that time I foresaw
what I could become. I saw the world flying past beneath me as if
I were borne by the wind.' But he was standing firmly on the
ground.

The ground was no longer shaking. France had changed, it is
true, but the abyss that separated her from her past was beginning
to close. The new ruler had appropriated the Revolution without
disavowing the things that had given the country its dignity and
historic greatness. From the Frankish King Clovis to the Robespierre of the Committee of Public Safety, he felt solidarity with
them all, so he declared. The unity of France was restored, not
only historically but morally. 'All men of talent are welcome.'
Was that not a challenge to all those that had so far stood aloof to
return to their homeland and co-operate in its restoration?
Fontanes understood the signal at once; he overcame the distrust
Fouché had always entertained of him by writing a letter to
Bonaparte, saying 'History has sufficiently taught you that the
great leaders of armies have been friends of art, and especially of
writers whose souls are sensitive, whose voice is grateful, and
who have always fought against oppression and evil'.

This fine phrase, modestly but unambiguously drawing attention to the rights of the cultured classes in the State, recurred to the
First Consul's memory when he was looking for somebody to
pronounce a eulogy of Washington at a State ceremony. The
leader of the United States had just died, and Bonaparte thought it
important that this first hero of a great young Republic, from
which the French Revolution had learnt so much, should be
fittingly celebrated in Paris. He had obviously read an essay that
Fontanes had published on the great American, and decided that
it sounded the right note for an oration that must be fair to every
political opinion. Fontanes had known the subject of the oration
intimately, his style possessed the modern verve while retaining

its classicism. A touch of aristocratic stiffness would not be amiss at that moment, when the old republicans in Paris were beginning to murmur. What might at another time have appeared all-too correct would in this case commend itself.

Fontanes delivered the oration and fulfilled his thorny task with so much elegance that Bonaparte was quite enchanted, and praised him as a 'most useful man'. After keeping so carefully in the background he had come to the fore at a single stroke, and had taken the first step in his brilliant career.

He at once renewed communication with Chateaubriand, advising him to return, and transfer his activities to the capital, the only place where real opportunities were to be found. The intellectual field had been almost deserted during the last ten years; the neglected soil needed to be fructified by those artists and thinkers that had taken the spiritual treasure of France with them into exile and preserved it there. The young writer longed to follow the suggestion, although he now had no place of his own in France, and hardly any relations left. His brother had been executed, his mother was dead, his sister Julie had followed her, his sister Lucile, once so near and dear to him, had lost touch with him and was married to an unknown Monsieur de Caud. What of his hastily wedded wife? He had only spent a few months in her company, and had seen nothing of her for eight years. He could scarcely remember her features.

The company of French *emigrés* was gradually breaking up. They had quarrelled sedulously among themselves, but helped one another too. A common feeling had grown up among them, born of their familiarity with English life and institutions. Some there were that had still learnt nothing, and still did not realize that the world had changed. Had it changed for the better or the worse? In any case it was different.

VII

FAME AND WOMEN

THE ASSASSINS ARE IN OUR MIDST

On a May evening of the year 1800 a gentleman landed at Calais, whose passport declared him to be Jean-David de la Sagne, born in Neuchâtel, Switzerland. A very surly member of the harbour police examined the document, which had been drawn up by the German Ambassador in London, and allowed the traveller to pass. According to the passport he was aged thirty-two, height medium, eyes grey, hair brown, special characteristics none. It did not mention that he was broad-shouldered and stocky, but with a certain elastic slenderness of limb that suited the almost unhealthy delicacy of his features. His face had the pallor of the century, strikingly intensified by the shock of ruffled hair and the bitterness of the mouth. His baggage was slender, the most conspicuous part of it was the bundle of papers he kept somewhat anxiously stuffed under one arm.

He surveyed with keen attention the activity on the quay at which his ship had just tied up. There were a great many soldiers about, and a number of naval ratings; the officers, he thought, had a rather theatrical appearance, with their enormous plumed hats, their wide tricolour sashes, their heavy sabres dragging along the cobble pavement. Everything was a bit loud and exaggerated. The ladies were dressed like Greek goddesses, very *decolletées*, but with their faces half hidden under huge coal-scuttle bonnets. The men's clothes were very tight-fitting; their neck-cloths reached to their ears, heavy watch-chains dangled from their fobs, hung with all sorts of trinkets. The affectation with which they peered at the world through their lorgnettes contrasted strangely with the heavy, knobbed stick they carried in the other hand. In London, thought the newcomer in retrospect, everything was simpler, more subdued, more relaxed. On the other hand the women here were better-looking, and if appearances were not deceitful, more approachable.

Our Swiss, of course, was Chateaubriand, but as his name had not yet been struck off the list of the *emigrés*, and he did not want to be held up by this lengthy procedure, he had obtained a false passport so as to be able at last to re-enter his own country—or, as it was the fashion to call it nowadays, his *patrie*, his fatherland. His departure had been almost a flight, so impatient had he grown. He had interrupted the printing of his book *The Spirit of Christianity*, taken the finished sheets with him, torn out of the huge manuscript of his prose epic *The Natchez* the two complete pieces *Atala* and *René*, and packed the remainder in a trunk that he left with some friends. He started on his journey with few possessions, but the mass of paper he carried with him was an element of immortality. The little sailing ship took four hours to carry him over the Channel—a short time in which to relegate seven years of banishment finally to the past. France and her poet were reunited; both had altered, yet both had become conscious of their fundamental unalterability. Both had ripened, for both had greatly suffered.

With a swelling heart René surveyed the country from the road along which his post-chaise was trundling towards Paris. Everything looked poverty-stricken, badly tended and dilapidated; the villages were dirty and deserted, the peasants were wearing wooden shoes, their women, bent double, were toiling in the fields, their faces tanned by the sun, strands of hair hanging from under their ragged kerchiefs. On every hand he saw half-ruined houses looking, from a distance, like the remains of a conflagration. The châteaux were nearly all destroyed, the fine avenues leading up to them had long since been felled, the parks were overgrown, lean cattle were grazing on the rank lawns. The once familiar sound of church bells had been silenced, the statues of the saints on the façades of the churches beheaded or daubed with paint, many of the old wayside crosses hacked down. The walls alongside the road still bore inscriptions dating from the

Reign of Terror, 'Liberty, Equality, Fraternity or Death'. Attempts had been made to efface the word 'Death' with chalk, but it kept reappearing under the onslaught of rain and sun; a skull and crossbones had often been added. The roads were in a terrible state, either the carriage rattled and rocked through a cloud of dust, or it laboured through bottomless mud.

Shortly before reaching Paris René alighted at the country house of some acquaintances, whence he was to be fetched by Fontanes. The two friends met with emotion, and as they walked towards Paris René wondered anxiously how the capital would receive the fugitive that had been absent so long, and was now striding through the city gates at Fontanes' side, on foot and under a false name. He looked eagerly at the city within whose walls Terror had raged for ten long years. What had happened here had shaken the entire globe. Must not the signs of blood and fear be clinging to every stone? Signs of poverty and disorder were abundantly visible at any rate. Here too he saw half-effaced inscriptions and revolutionary watchwords, many a shop window displayed a notice-board warning customers not to use the old-fashioned mode of address, 'for here we honour one another by "thou" and the title of "citizen"'. The houses were in bad repair, the plaster had fallen off the walls, many windows were boarded up, the street paving was damaged. The home-comer, deep in his gloomy thoughts as he walked down the Champs Elysées with his companion, was surprised all at once to hear the sound of music and see people dancing among the clumps of trees now green in their spring foliage. It was Sunday afternoon, the people seemed quite cheerful in spite of their shabby clothes and unkempt appearance. The Place Louis XV, now renamed Place de la Concorde, lay wide and empty, it had 'the ruined, melancholy, deserted look of an ancient amphitheatre'. Here the guillotine had stood, here the King's head had fallen, here René's brother had been executed, here all those people René had known and re-spected had been constrained to die. No blood was to be seen, the dust of time had covered everything, the tireless feet of people coming and going day after day had trodden everything away.

The Sunday quiet, the closed shops, the scanty traffic lent the hour the sad solemnity of a Good Friday.

Was this a home-coming? At least his exile was over. All the people round him spoke his native tongue; present events and conditions were a part of him, and affected him personally. He took possession of his modest lodging in the Rue de Lille with some hesitation, anxiously entering into conversation for the first time with neighbours and strangers. Did they perhaps recognize him as an aristocrat, a Count? Had he ended by acquiring an English accent? A stay of so many years in England was not to be wiped out from one day to another. He was no longer used to being asked how he was, and having his hand shaken. The noisy behaviour of the Parisians, their gesticulation, their loud voices intimidated him. He could not get used to the dirty staircases and tavern tables. People had a way of staring you in the face, starting conversation with you, and if they were feeling cheerful, giving you good-natured digs in the ribs that got on your nerves. Perhaps these very people who seized him by the lapel of his coat when they spoke to him were former assassins that had once stood round the guillotine, roaring applause at each head that fell.

Restless and distressed, René roamed the streets. In the ancient squares the statues of the kings had long been removed from their pedestals, the walls that had once enclosed peaceful cloisters had been pulled down, in the gardens of the Palais-Royal people were sitting about under the trees, watching the jugglers and hawkers. Refreshments were being sold on all sides with a lot of shouting. The days were growing warm, and he would have been glad of a glass of wine, but he had not a sou in his pocket. A sort of dancing frenzy appeared to have seized the townspeople; dance music could be heard issuing from every tavern cellar, at every street corner there were couples dancing to the sound of fiddles and flutes. He watched these people in astonishment, he could not rid himself of the thought that these shabby, carefree creatures were the same that had made world history only a little while ago. So these were the 'giants', who with their rioting and shouting and brawling had dealt the death-blow to one era and brought another to birth. The solitary walker could not tear his eyes from this spectacle of a life so constantly renewed and yet forever the same.

He had so much to forget and so much to learn. Being always alone, he talked to himself a great deal, and he did it in English. The long years in America and England had almost disaccustomed him—the great renewer of French style—from the daily use of his native tongue. Expressions of surprise, pleasure and annoyance came to his lips in English; when he counted, he did it in that language. But none of this lessened his consciousness of being a Frenchman. Whatever reproaches he might prefer against his nation, which had robbed him of so much, he was proud of it at bottom. Things that had seemed strange to him at first began to appear as advantages: the affability, 'the charming, easy, lively intercourse between mind and mind, the absence of arrogance and prejudice', the unforced equality, the taste for witty repartee, the quick understanding of every situation—all this was beginning to give him pleasure; he could put it to the credit side of his account, as it were, and however divided his feelings might be, he was glad to be not merely a Frenchman but a Parisian. 'One has only to be settled in our midst for a few months to realize that Paris is the only place to live in.'

So far, so good, but there was another side to the picture. With the lively flair for contemporary tendencies, which was part of his genius, he sooon discovered that 'the late Robespierre', although publicly condemned, still had many adherents among the lower classes. Of the gospel that he and his friend Saint-Just had preached, often in very obscure terms, a sediment remained in which the most peculiar flowers sprouted. The so-called Conspiracy of the Equals, attempted three years earlier, was not yet forgotten. Its leader, Gracchus Babeuf, had been executed, but there were factions and cliques that still honoured him because he had died for the equality of property and for 'Communism'. A fire had broken out with Robespierre, the significance of which nobody understood; it still smouldered, it would set the 'social question' alight again later on. Those who cherished the memory of Robespierre were not in themselves very important people: René found they were mostly doorkeepers and others of the lower middle classes, who visibly regretted the bloody theatre of the guillotine and talked with a sort of nostalgia of the days when they cut off the heads of women 'who had necks as white as chicken meat'. In his eyes the men selling roast potatoes in the street were doubtless the 'September assassins' who had taken part in the massacre of prisoners in Paris. The inhabitants of the various quarters of the capital were now very mixed, many had left the streets they lived in during the Reign of Terror and buried themselves elsewhere, for fear of being recognized as former Terrorists. Others, who had managed to enrich themselves without getting blood on their hands, had acquired the finest houses of the nobility sold by the State as 'national property'. These people were now firmly in the saddle, a new upper class was beginning to form, which was anything but diffident. The hunt for the 'contaminated', the day of accusations, disavowals and sordid purges was yet to come.

NAPOLEON HAS A USE FOR HIM

The returned exile sat writing in his little room on the ground floor in the Rue de Lille, buried in manuscripts and printed sheets of his work on the Spirit of Christianity. He had now as good as decided to introduce the two self-contained tales, *René* and *Atala*, into this new work, as evidence of the power of religious feeling. But the more he considered these two pieces, the more he felt inclined to publish at least one of them in the near future—the moving story of the beautiful Indian maid Atala and the love that bound her to Chactas. The feeling for nature that pervaded it, and the entirely new literary style, might enable him to capture the public by a sort of surprise attack. He had realized long ago that literature was to be his destiny, but impatience to begin his career by affording the new society a completely novel sensation seized him now like a fever. With the artist's instinct for careful craftsmanship he combined the artist's urge to attack the public with a kind of fury, shrinking from no stratagem or violence that could further his conquest. This double nature of the artist, at once responsible and dangerous, conscientious and unscrupulous,

was apparent in a wider sense as well, for he was writing a
book intended to re-establish an order of society founded on
Christianity, capable of withstanding the turmoil of political
events, and at the same time he was calling into play the anarchical
side of his personality that would brook no restraint where art
was concerned, but with the voice of the poet, the eternal
magician, would call up the tempest to lay everything waste.

His brain was in a fever, but he lacked the commonest necessaries of life. Though not actually starving, his means would not
suffice to turn the shabby home-comer into a Parisian. His
family, with whom he had just renewed contact by letter, were
hardly in better case, and could not possibly contribute to his
support. His beloved sister Lucile had been widowed after a brief,
unhappy married life, and was herself in want. As for his own
marriage, he preferred not to be reminded of it. He chose to think
of poor Céleste as his 'widow', and far from calling her to rejoin
him, was content to leave her in the charming but very provincial little town of Fougères, where she was living on the
modest remains of her fortune, quietly and piously, but not
without a secret grudge against her gypsy of a husband.

Once again he was obliged to appeal to Fontanes' faithful,
understanding friendship. He wrote to him 'Do me two kind-
nesses: first give me an introduction to a doctor, and then see if
you can lend me twenty-five louis. I have unsatisfactory news of
my family, and don't know how to manage till my next bit of
luck turns up. It's hard lines having to worry about my keep
while I am engaged on the work of the Lord. Just and lovely
Revolution! They have sold everything. I am now as I came
from my mother's womb, for even my shirts are not French;
they are the fruit of another country's generosity. Help me out
of my dilemma, therefore, if you can. I can live on twenty-five
louis until publication decides my fate'.

Fontanes helped. He helped more than his friend expected,
for he was engaged in finding a publisher for the book that was
nearing completion. In this he was not acting solely out of
admiration for the author's great talent; he was a generous creature
always ready to help, but he had a great deal of worldly wisdom

H

and adaptability; he never neglected the practical side of life for
literature, and had a shrewd instinct for power. His critical sense
allowed him no illusions about his own literary talent; he knew
he was better suited to be an intermediary than a creator, better at
appraising intellectual values than at originating them. He saw
in Chateaubriand's work a peculiarly apt means of preparing
public opinion for the restoration of the Church in France. He
was convinced that the First Consul would sanction religion at
least as a principle of order, and would re-establish public worship
if he felt he could now afford to abandon the kernel of revolutionary ideas.

Fontanes was not indulging in empty speculations in this
respect. Ever since the victory of Marengo, which had elevated
him to a fresh peak of fame, Bonaparte's visions of social regeneration had been assuming firmer outlines. The old royalists
were much mistaken if they thought the First Consul looked upon
himself as the sword-bearer of a future Louis XVIII and was
secretly in favour of some kind of restoration; on the other hand,
in spite of the many former Jacobins in his entourage, such as
Fouché, Grégoire and Carnot, he had no intention of introducing another period of revolution. The Talleyrands, Roederers
and Bourriennes that were trying to incite him to dictatorship
recognized the signs of the times, and it says much for Fontanes'
political instinct that he should have considered the re-establishment of public worship as not only possible but probable.
Consolidation was in full swing, but it might well be wrecked
by the religious question if this was not taken into consideration
in the stabilization of society. It was a purely practical question,
and he lent his support to Chateaubriand's work because by
means of its artistic qualities and its enthusiasm it could make
the 'beauty of Christianity' a public concern at a single stroke.

Fontanes wrote to Napoleon's brother Lucien 'Without public
worship there can be no government. Next to a victorious army
I know of no better confederates than the men that guide the
consciences of others in the name of God. So far as I know,
victorious conquerers have never fallen out with the priests.
These can be held in check and made use of at the same time.

One may laugh at the augurs, but it is pleasant to eat up the consecrated chickens with them. So thought Cicero and Pompey and even Caesar, who had himself appointed High Priest. These men belong to your family, which has inherited them and must imitate them in everything.'

He could afford to adopt this frivolous tone with Lucien, for he had attached himself closely to him, and had induced him, as Minister of the Interior, to appoint him Chief Censor of the theatre and of literature. Lucien was still a powerful man at that time; everyone knew that without him the *coup d'état* of the 18th Brumaire would have failed. Such was the bland, harmless Fontanes! He knew how to steer his bark by favourable winds. It was rumoured that he was carrying on an intimate friendship with one of Bonaparte's sisters, the temperamental, clever Elisa Bacciochi, and could do a great deal for his friends with her assistance. His opportunism was not repugnant, since it was pursued with discretion and was profitable to his closest friends. Chateaubriand could count on being soon struck off the list of the *emigrés*, and in addition a publisher had been found for his book, for who could refuse anything to the Censor?

Napoleon was, in effect, much preoccupied with the question as to whether he could establish his autocracy without allowing religious institutions to be revived. The problem interested him solely from the point of view of political expediency; he regarded religion as a moral, not a spiritual, and still less a theological phenomenon. He was clear as to the social principles of his age and the character of post-revolutionary France. However discontented the veterans of the Revolution might be, France was basically Christian and Catholic. When he received the clergy of Mayence he told them that 'no society can exist without a morality, and there is no good morality without religion. Only religion, therefore, can give the State firm and lasting support. Society without religion is like a ship without a compass. France has learnt from its misfortunes and opened its eyes at last. It has realized that the Catholic religion is the only anchor that will hold in a storm.' He was even more explicit with certain royalist emissaries, who besought him to restore religion. He replied in an imperious tone 'I shall restore religion, but for my own sake, not yours'. Fontanes had discovered how the wind lay: Napoleon was in need of Chateaubriand's work.

PAULINE DE BEAUMONT

While the great work was being printed, its author could hardly restrain his impatience to appear before the public. He decided, therefore, to publish his little love story *Atala* in a separate form. He simply could not wait any longer; he had been at work on the manuscript for years—in the vineyards of the Moselle, devastated by war, by camp fires in the American forests, in the English parsonage, in his London garret—it was high time he made his public appearance. He had, as always, a keen sense of the critical moment. The evening before the work was to appear he said to a friend with whom he was dining in the Champs Elysées, 'My fate will be decided tomorrow. I shall either be a poor devil, or I shall be exalted to the skies'. The book appeared, and in a few days, everybody was reading it. There had not been such a literary success for years. 'With the publication of *Atala*,' said the author, 'the noise I have made in the world began. My personal life came to an end, my public career was started.'

After so much military success, a literary success seemed a miracle. People were famished, so to speak. In a few weeks the book was circulating not only in France but throughout Europe. At the annual fairs the touching story of the love between the two children of the wilderness and the death of the beautiful Atala, was sung by ballad-singers; everywhere, in all the inns, cafés, and reading rooms the coloured engravings with which the book was illustrated were displayed. In the waxwork show run by a German of the name of Curtius in the Palais-Royal, Chactas and Peter Aubry were shown carrying Atala's lovely corpse to the grave. Parodies and imitations sprang up at once; in the suburban theatres the amorous 'savages' appeared in feathered finery. Enthusiasm, mockery and distaste were expressed by critics and readers, nobody remained indifferent. 'All this commotion only served to increase the stir my appearance had made. I became the fashion. My head was turned; I had never yet tasted the pleasures of self-conceit and I was almost intoxicated. I was in love with fame as with a woman, a first love.' Suddenly everybody wanted to know him, everybody wanted to boast that he was a friend of theirs. Young women, especially, still capable of weeping over romances, crowded round him. 'I was buried,' he says, 'under a mountain of perfumed notes.'

The days of loneliness were over. Before he knew it, the writer who had become famous overnight was the centre of a little circle, which actually included the noted scholar Joseph Joubert. Wherever this disinguished, courteous man appeared there was sure to be good conversation. He was so cultured, and devoted so much time to reading, that he seldom had much leisure for writing anything himself, and his critical powers so far exceeded his imagination that he rarely contrived to finish a book, but what he had to say was all the more incisive. Elegant and wealthy, spending both time and money judiciously, he was born to attract important people and become a part of their *entourage*. He loved books, not only for themselves but for their bindings; his library was worth seeing, consisting as it did entirely of books he had read with attention and covered all over with manuscript notes. One of his lady friends once said of him that he looked like a soul that had found a body by chance and was getting on with it as well as he could. He was convinced that he suffered from all sorts of ailments, which forced him to live today on milk, next month on nothing but raw beef, and the month after to swear by young turnips. No Apollo, therefore, to rob women of their senses, but the personification of friendship, untiring, and incapable of refusing any claim upon his generosity. 'I am like the Aeolian harp,' he said, 'which gives out a few beautiful sounds, but can never complete a melody'. A charming and apt comparison, for the wind to which this harp vibrated was the life of his friends.

Nobody could have been made more deeply aware of this than Chateaubriand, who was soon moved to describe him, in an equally delightful fashion, as 'an egoist who only thinks of others'. Joubert had been among the first to read *Atala* and to voice his delight at the opening pages. He saw the imperfections and mannerisms of the work, but he recognized the new note: 'This savage enchants me. We shall have to purge him of Rousseau, Ossian, the fogs of the Thames, ancient and modern revolutions, and leave him the Cross, the sunsets over the ocean and the American savannahs. Then you will see what a poet we shall have to cleanse us from the remains of the Directory, as Epimenides once cleansed the city of Athens from the plague by means of rites and verses.' The verdict of this *esprit fort* put an end to the hesitation of the fashionable world, and gained Chateaubriand genuine admirers. He knew now where he was welcome.

When people did not meet at Joubert's, they gathered at the Countess de Beaumont's, at her little apartment in the Rue Neuve du Luxembourg (now the Rue Cambon), elegantly furnished with the few family relics saved from the Revolution. Pauline de Beaumont was in poor health, she could not bear bright light or noise of any kind, and the company that frequented her little drawing-room was accustomed to dim lighting and muted conversation. The happiness of being together again in freedom after so many years of restraint and fear gave the little circle of friends a quiet gaiety. Madame de Staël, who was dying to meet the new celebrity, burst into the room one evening 'like a whirlwind', and dispelled the quiet with a flood of witty questions, without waiting for the answers. The gifted daughter of the Finance Minister, Necker, whose dismissal by Louis XVI had sounded a drum-beat in the overture to the Revolution, was engaged in a war with Napoleon—an underground war so far—in which she showed more composure than the great man himself. She still admired him, but she warned him against dictatorship, although he had long been a dictator.

She had just published a treatise *On Literature in relation to Social Institutions,* in which she declared that literature, and the things of the mind in general, had only one danger to fear, and that was despotism. Napoleon glanced at the book, an unwieldy volume of nearly seven hundred pages, and shrugged his shoulders; but he could see what she was driving at. He had the authoress kept under close observation by Fouché's men, otherwise she was free to do as she liked. In reality, however, Germaine de Staël was seeking persecution; she had had the wit to realize that Napoleon's enmity would render her immortal. For the moment, however, she was holding her aggressive impulses in check, because Benjamin Constant, the great love of her life, was still a member of the Tribunate created by the First Consul.

Germaine, at that time, was still a beautiful woman; she was about thirty-five years old, and what she lacked in sweetness was made up for by the charm and force of her expression. She dressed a trifle too conspicuously, and some people wondered whether the big, brightly-coloured turban framing her fine head was kept on all night. There was something about her that excited sarcasm, though nobody doubted that she was the greatest woman of her time, and not merely a political genius but also a literary one. She spoke very loudly and forcibly, perpetually seizing some object or other to whirl it round, or thump the arm of her chair with it. She talked with equal authority on every subject of political and intellectual life, and on the rare occasions when she found herself in a dilemma would simply declare 'I understand everything that is worth understanding. What I don't understand doesn't exist'.

Germaine fired off her impetuous questions at the Vicomte de Chateaubriand, who seemed very shy and said very little. She observed him closely as he stood by the fireplace, leaning against the mantelpiece. He was certainly no all-conquering manly beauty. 'Monsieur de Chateaubriand is small and rather badly built,' a woman she knew had lately told her, 'there is nothing amiable about him.' He was decidedly short, and his head was set too low between his broad shoulders, but the head itself was magnificent with its wild mane of hair and the flashing eyes that expressed audacity and melancholy at the same time. His voice was soft and varied in tone, his smile was irresistible and was soon to become famous.

It was untrue to say he was not amiable, he could, on the contrary, display a seductiveness that came near to offending disinterested spectators; but in the absence of any special occasion

for this he remained rather taciturn and even at times a trifle too
solemn. Germaine de Staël was too busy to make a frequent
appearance in this simple circle, as yet undisturbed by the fiery
breath of the demon of power. The friends kept to themselves,
and Pauline de Beaumont could lie on her sofa listening to their
conversation and watching the young writer. She believed she was
admiring genius, she believed she was only listening to the voice
that was reading passages from *The Spirit of Christianity* with so
much expression. But she had already confided this to her diary:
'Monsieur de Chateaubriand's style gives me a sort of amorous
shiver. He plays the piano on all my fibres.' Joubert was fully
aware of what was happening. He had not the right to be jealous,
but the current flowing between Pauline and René, which
suddenly made itself felt in the quiet room under the dim lamp-
light, filled his valetudinary, chilly soul with a tinge of envy. He
heard Chateaubriand reading the sentence: 'Arise with speed, ye
longed-for storms . . .', and saw Pauline's eyes fixed on the
reader's face. Such a surrender would never fall to his share, but
neither would he be forced to lower his eyes for shame under a
glance of unconcealed desire. His instinct was for moderation
and good taste—qualities that involve much renunciation and
much happiness.

Pauline de Beaumont was the daughter of the Montmorin who
had been a minister under the late king, and had been murdered
by the mob during the September massacres. She was living at
that time with her mother and sisters, half hidden among relations
in Passy, when one day the ruffians carried off the rest of the
family to prison. They left her alone. 'Not worth while', they said,
for Pauline was coughing up blood, to all appearance mortally ill.
She fled into the country and lodged in a peasant's hut not far
from Joubert's country house, and a friendship sprang up between
them that saved her life. Joubert took care of her, and felt ade-
quately rewarded if he could sit by her bed and read aloud to her.
He was delighted by her intelligence, but the sensual desires with
which she approached life distressed him. He wrote in his diary
'As to Madame de Beaumont. Her senses all directed outwards.
Nothing inwards. Too naked.'

In the pleasure-seeking days of the Directory she surrendered
to the intoxication that seized those women that had escaped.
'She is a true Frenchwoman' somebody said of her at that time,
'all or nothing.' She took too much rather than too little from the
life that she felt threatened by her lung trouble. Pleasure and ill-
health had now left their mark on her face, she was 'more of a
Muse than a Grace', but her femininity with its mingling of keen
intelligence gave her appearance a charm that Chateaubriand
could not withstand. Did he love her? In the society of that decade
the love relationships of the upper classes played a strangely public
role. The entourage always knew everything about the fervour of
these liaisons, but nothing of their actual intimacy. People had no
scruple about displaying their attachment and presenting it in a
romantic light; but of their emotions, their embraces, their tears
of passion nothing was known, so that the exact nature of
many a famous love-story of those years is still a mystery
today, in spite of all the letters, notes and other evidence still
extant.

Pauline, with her 'senses all directed outwards', and René,
suddenly emerging from years of solitude, renunciation and
suffering into the blinding light of life, denied themselves nothing.
But René had no intention of being merely this woman's lover,
he wished to assume the guise of her protector and friend, to
associate his importance as a writer with a woman of the world
who could further his aspirations in the Parisian society that was
slowly forming. In Paris, where women were so favoured, and
allowed such an important place, literature was inseparable from
feminine influence. Not that the woman's verdict was decisive, but
she possessed the art of disseminating the verdict of a qualified
judge by slipping it into conversation. The coin was minted by
connoisseurs, but put into circulation by women. The stable
basis of fame was laid down by critics such as Fontanes and
Joubert; fashion, which gave it wings, was unthinkable without
the co-operation of clever, charming women like Pauline.
René very soon discovered this connection, amounting almost
to a law, and acted in accordance with it for the rest of his
life.

More confederates appeared, the circle of friends grew wider, Germaine de Staël turned up from time to time. Men of such great importance as Molé, Bonald and Pasquier enjoyed the evening talks and allowed themselves to be influenced by Pauline's zeal for Chateaubriand's success. *The Spirit of Christianity* was nearly finished. 'There is a new Pascal among us', whispered Pauline to her friends, because René happened to be fond of quoting this saying of the great thinker: 'There are two qualities in the truths of our religion, a beauty that makes it lovable and a holy majesty that makes it venerable'—a saying that hardly preserves its full significance out of the original context. Chateaubriand intended it to underline the fact that his own work was concerned with the cultural rather than the theological side of religion. Pascal could hardly be worse interpreted, but nobody knew much about that great genius in those days, they were content to regard his works as a mixture of science and edifying piety. This alleged mixture would have described Chateaubriand's work at that time, substituting poesy and beauty for science. As usual, he was on the hunt for 'evidence', piling up documents and source-books. Pauline helped him in this, delving in histories of the saints and missionary archives for edifying quotations with which to embellish his work.

She was happy, for now she was not merely his mistress but his fellow-worker. For a time they retired to the country and lived in a little house situated between a village and some fields. When night fell they sat together in the doorway looking at the sky. She showed him the constellations and taught him their names. René was serene and cheerful, he had never been so light-hearted and carefree. It gave him no qualms, as a married man, to be writing a work on Christianity in which the sacrament of marriage was extolled, under the same roof with his mistress. Friend Joubert did consider the adventure a little shocking, but he could never bring himself to judge Pauline severely. He helped them, therefore, with books and advice, while warning them against an excess of quotations: 'Can you imagine music being interrupted by the reading of some authority for the melody! As a prose writer Chateaubriand has no equal; thanks to the

force of his thought and his expressions his prose is both music
and verse. Let him ply his craft and enchant us.'

POETRY AND FOREIGN POLITICS

The book was finished and the lovers returned to Paris; Pauline
was more cheerful than she had ever been, though her cough was
often terrible to hear. There could be no doubt that her health
was steadily worsening, but she would not admit it. With her hair
cut short *à la* Titus she would go out of doors of an evening in a
thin cotton frock, and when her friends told her she was risking
her life she merely said 'What does it matter?' The worse she
became, the greater was her longing to live, to enjoy her love and
to be of use to her beloved. René's name was now erased from the
list of the *emigrés*, and he had thus recovered full rights of citizen-
ship. He saw a good deal of the First Consul's brother and sister,
Lucien and Elisa, and persuaded them to show the great man a
few sheets of the book. The Consul had a look at them and made
some notes in the margin. His interest was awakened, and René
was soon to know why. This was the year 1802; the Concordat
was promulgated on April 18th and the Catholic religion had its
rights restored to it. *The Spirit of Christianity* was published on
April 14th, and on the 18th a solemn *Te Deum* was sung in the
cathedral of Notre-Dame to celebrate the restoration of religion.
All the bells of Paris found their tongues again and filled the air
with their clamour. At the entrance to the cathedral the Papal
Legate, the Archbishop of Paris and thirty bishops stood awaiting
the First Consul. He appeared in the red velvet coat in which
Ingres painted him, with a canopy held over him. Some of the
generals accompanying him had not been inside a church since
their childhood, and murmured against the religious ceremony.
'We've got the old clerical mummery back again', they said, but
a sharp glance from Napoleon reduced them to silence. There
was great rejoicing in the streets, because now that peace had
also been concluded with England, everybody was hoping for a
period of quiet and freedom from care. On the same day Napoleon
published in the *Moniteur* a proclamation on the subject of the

Concordat, and below it was an article by Fontanes on Chateaubriand's book.

The success of the book, the publication of which, owing to the coincidence of events, had the effect of a ministerial pronouncement, or at least an official event, was indescribable. It was as if the bells had been ringing out the author's fame and the bishops had appeared at his call. Napoleon's action and his book assumed a connection, not only in the eyes of the public but in his own mind, which almost suggested they had been prepared in common. In his excited imagination a sort of lightning revelation occurred: *Napoleon and I*. This day saw the birth of his political ambition: he had re-opened the churches to the French, he and Napoleon had put an end to the long period of enforced paganism and achieved a political exploit together. From now onwards his life would be ruled by the conviction that it was his task to assist the temporal power, in whatever hands it might be, with his intellectual gifts. All the mistakes to be made in his lifetime by rulers and governments he ascribed henceforth to the circumstance that he had not been consulted in time. The necessity of uniting power with intellect became a guiding principle in his life. Intellect, he decided, must take a hand in the exercise of power, but it must never be the other way round. His artistic sensibility must be protected from tutelage and even the intrusive goodwill of those in power.

In the matter of politics Chateaubriand was no dreamer, he might rather be called a political dilettante. But is not every real politician a dilettante, a man, that is, whose mind works from the core of the general consciousness, while making clever—and cautious—use of the experts? All that Chateaubriand undertook politically was well thought out, sensible and useful. In later years he proved a good administrative leader, not himself concerned with details, but able to inspire those whose business was with details, without putting a finger in the pie. He was a perfect diplomat, but his relationship to the highest representative of power, from the day of the Concordat onwards, would always have a tinge of mysticism about it, and procure him, for that reason, hardly anything but disappointment. In the *Mercure*, published by Fontanes, he made an attempt to define the political position of the man of letters. 'People assert that writers are not capable of the conduct of affairs. How strange that the genius required to write *The Spirit of the Laws* should not suffice to run a ministerial office!'

Eternal misunderstanding ever since the far-off days when intellect and power were separated! The intellectual thirsting for action, whose position has become so important that politics can no longer overlook him, since his name would be an ornament to them, thrusts himself into foreign politics because these have still preserved a faint aura of world-wideness and romance. When Chateaubriand was later offered the Ministry of Education he refused it with indignation; he wanted the Ministry of Foreign Affairs, and was to obtain it. Victor Hugo, when the Second Republic wished to appoint him Minister of Education, burst out with equal indignation: 'You offer me the Ministry of Children. I want the Ministry of Foreign Affairs. From there one can keep a watch on Europe!' The Rulers, however, took more or less the opposite view, though it was not so much on the score of incompetence that they would have nothing to do with the Intellectuals, as because of their tiresome tendency to draw attention to the intellectual background of political affairs. As if those affairs were not sufficiently complicated already! Even as First Consul, Napoleon said of Chateaubriand 'People that write, and have attained a literary reputation, are tempted to look upon themselves as the centre of everything.' Louis XVIII's verdict was even harsher: 'Beware of ever letting a writer meddle with your affairs; he will spoil everything. Those people are no good.'

But no stricture of this kind could disconcert the man that had just proved a stabilizer of society and a revivifier of France. The conjunction of the hour had convinced him that his office as a writer gave him a mysterious priestly power, without which no durable temporary authority was possible. Henceforward there would be two Chateaubriands, the Enchanter, whose fascinating personality would be fatally attractive to women—a simple, amiable creature whom Goethe had referred to as a 'nice lad'— and the Great Man who, with his hand tucked into the opening of his waistcoat, fixes his solemn gaze far away over the heads of other men, and seems to be sighing: 'If you only knew what a burden I have to bear!' His sudden fame had not actually spoilt him, his character was not simple enough for that, but it had precipitated him into the march of events. He burdened himself with a responsibility that was not within his province, losing sight of the knife-edged boundary line that must always separate the poet from action. As his success increased his unrest grew stronger; he wrote to Fontanes 'I can't come to see you this morning, I'm snowed under by business. I can only tell you that the auguries are favourable. Yesterday, for one thing, the publisher had orders for a thousand livres' worth. Yesterday, too, I saw the Great Men; they appear to be in a good mood. Protect me boldly, therefore, dear friend; remember you can send me to Rome'.

Convinced that he had laid the Church's daughter, France, in her lap again, he longed to go to Rome, the focus of Christianity, whose gratitude he might then enjoy on the spot. He hoped in this way to attain to higher politics and bring his hidden light from under the bushel. But everything depended on Napoleon, whom he had only once met, at an evening party given by Lucien. The company had been brilliant, the conversation full of wit, the guests in festive attire suggestive of Court dress. Chateaubriand, who was given to shyness, and assumed a misanthropic expression if people failed to compete for his attention, was standing lost among the expensively dressed crowd when Napoleon suddenly, almost at a bound, strode up to him—not to draw him into conversation but to address him, without greeting or compliment, as though he were resuming an interrupted conversation. He talked of religious subjects, described the Muslims at prayer, as he had often seen them in Egypt, went on to Christianity without giving the talk any personal turn, broke off and passed on. Chateaubriand was impressed by his boyish appearance, he noticed the almost tender smile, reminding him of some marble bust of the antique, and admired the fine shape of his eyes; but he could not escape a feeling of awe, and was reminded of the passage in the Book of Job: 'Then a spirit passed before my face; the hair of my flesh stood up: It stood still, but I could not discern the form thereof: an image was before mine eyes, there was silence, and I heard a voice. . . .'

After this meeting Chateaubriand felt certain that he had been selected 'for Rome'. But Bonaparte had already chosen his mother's half-brother, Cardinal Fesch, for the post of Ambassador, and felt no great enthusiasm for the Breton nobleman: 'I will try him out first in a second-class appointment, and if he stands the test I will promote him.' Things did not move, however, the desired appointment failed to materialize. Napoleon, no doubt, had forgotten the writer again; there were such a lot of people and so many tasks to be dealt with in those short months when he was not engaged in any war. His time was taken up with a whirl of work and reform; discussing the *Code Civil* day after day with the Council of State, composed of the 'fifty least stupid Frenchmen'; founding the Legion of Honour, calling the *Banque de France* to life, building harbours, organizing education, promulgating decrees that 'opened all careers to talent', drafting drill books and field service regulations, abolishing the last remains of local self-government and establishing the rigidly centralized system of Prefectures. France was content, and allowed herself to be involved in this youthful creative urge: the days of Henri IV had come again, or so it seemed.

Chateaubriand might not have waited so impatiently to be employed if he had not, like so many opponents of the Revolution, fallen into the error of thinking the new ruler must be at a loss for suitable men from which to form an upper class. But no revolution has ever been wrecked by the problem of personnel. However many high administrative officials, generals, bishops, ambassadors and scholars had been beheaded or if they had survived the Terror, were standing sullenly aside, the new era could draw freely upon its store, it could easily find the men it needed, and appeared to have no lack of talent. Chateaubriand alternated between exaggerated pretensions and despondency. He wrote to Madame de Staël 'There is nothing here but meanness, intrigues, party spirit and cliques. There is nothing honourable left but quietness and invisibility. I'm hesitating between absolute retirement in some remote province and fresh emigration'. Nevertheless he thought it useful to send the Pope his book with a reverential dedication, and when in March 1803 a new edition appeared it had Napoleon's name on the title-page, with a dedication that lacked nothing of courtly flourish.

The diplomatic mission must surely follow, for Bonaparte himself declared—possibly with a mocking though gracious smile —that he 'had never been better praised' than in this dedication. Pauline, who was burning with ambition for her lover and believed him capable of fulfilling the greatest tasks in the State, began to look forward to René's fresh success, but at the same time to tremble at the thought of separation. If he was really sent to Rome, could he, would he take her with him? After all, he was married. Should the extoller of the holy sacraments, who had even inserted a 'Praise of Virginity' in his book, present himself with his mistress at the seat of the Church? René had just made a tour of the provinces and allowed himself to be acclaimed wherever he went, but he had also visited his 'widow', poor Céleste, his rightful wife, wedded to him before God, and discovered to his relief that she was by no means as bitter and offended as he had reason to fear. That she allowed herself to be deceived by his book as to the extent of his virtue may be doubted, for she was shrewd and her judgement was incorruptible; she knew he had not the slightest pretension to be a saint or a Father of the Church. But she was almost without means, and a man hoping to appear as a diplomat at the Vatican must at least see to it that his wife does not suffer want. She had had plenty of time to think about this strange husband, whom she hardly knew except from hearsay; many rumours had reached her, and she knew she would never be able to keep him if she did not make up her mind to tolerate his bad qualities, his inconstancy and vanity. He had promised to set up house with her in the near future, and would have taken her with him now, he said, had he not been so entirely at a loss for the money the double fare would cost him.

So Céleste was appeased for the time being. Pauline canvassed Paris in the interest of René's career, tiring herself out with begging expeditions on his behalf. She sang his praises almost to tactlessness, and procured friends and confederates for him. René

was too sensitive a man not to be irked by this display of zeal, due
in part to Pauline's fevered condition, but he could not help being
the Enchanter, the spell-binder whose words and glances set every
feminine heart a-flutter; no sooner was he in the presence of a
woman than he began to radiate this charm without really intending to. Like all too seductive men he often found himself in
embarrassing situations that were not without their slightly comic
side: he could not bear that a woman should remain indifferent to
him, but as soon as she began to yield he felt his liberty threatened
and his success a burden. He was really no Don Juan, still less a
thoughtless seducer, and yet his conquests always had that tinge
of the ridiculous that is the fate of the too successful man. His
power of attraction had first declared itself with the triumph of
Atala; the boundless emotions of the characters were unthinkingly
attributed to the author himself. Every feminine reader came to the
dangerous conclusion that the man who had written this would
understand her too. Madame Hamelin, who was later to play a
part in his life, described the effect of the *Spirit of Christianity*, a
work intended to further the spirit of piety, in these words: 'Not
a woman in Paris slept that night. People tore copies of the book
from one another, or stole them. Then what an awakening, what a
cackling, what a flutter! "What!" we all exclaimed, "Is
Christianity like that? It's exquisite! Who is the man that has
revealed it to us in this fashion?" '

The Enchanter—to whom the name would cling forever,
though his good sense might at times be offended by it—the
Enchanter employed no artifice, no tricks, his natural manner was
enough to suggest the fulfilment of all their dreams: most wonderful understanding, most chivalrous intimacy, intoxication, adoration, flights to the stars . . . in short, the unattainable. His speech,
his melancholy, his expressive glances and the dark background
of his conversation promised in some honourable and yet incomprehensible, ambiguous way the satisfaction of all that women
hope for from life. Each of them had hitherto hoped in vain, each
had been tempted to bury her aspirations for ever, and content
herself with the commonplace uniformity of existence. Then the
poet appeared, in an aura of fame, an atmosphere of sadness; their

eyes met, the half-buried feelings revived and were bedewed with fresh hope.

WHO PAYS FOR THE MARBLE?

Poor women? But the happiness and peace of mind of the En-chanter himself were equally endangered. He made no promises, it is true, but his whole being was a promise; he demanded nothing, but all his fibres trembled with desire; he never attempted to bend a woman's will, but every woman was to accuse him of having subjugated her in spite of her resistance. The life of the Well Beloved was an exhausting alternation between vows and scenes, blissful laughter and despairing tears. The question today was: How shall I win her? Tomorrow it was: How shall I get rid of her? Madame de Boigne, never one of his 'ladies', describes his relation to women with a caustic pen: 'Except for the fact that he throws their life overboard, he is prepared to make that life pleasant for them. Now and then he may even feel inclined to make sacrifices for the person that loves him, but this goes too much against the grain for him to keep it up.' She gives some examples of this, and goes on: 'I could add many names to this list, for Monsieur de Chateaubriand has always found it very easy to get himself adored without troubling his head about the pain he is causing.' This was not a kindly description, nor was it a fair one. Of course no man can be held guiltless of the effect he has on women; even when he does not seduce them but contents himself with being seductive, he is not without responsibility. René was no commonplace breaker of hearts, but he was standing on the threshold of a century in which women panted for the fulfilment of their dreams. They had been silent and obedient, they had resigned themselves to the extinction of earthly sunshine, like Chateaubriand's mother, to whom her husband hardly ever addressed a word from one year's end to another, and who found consolation on her knees before the altar. Now their souls and senses were beginning to unfold, and the chorus of languishing women sang in irresistible strains. Chateaubriand's relations with women were therefore more than mere adventures; there was something inherent in his nature, for good or evil, that throws light not only on the artist, not only on the feminine heart, but on the period itself.

One of the most beautiful and ingenuous letters he received after the publication of *Atala* came from Delphine de Custine, a charming young woman of one of the first families of France, whose husband had fallen a victim to the guillotine. She had defended her father-in-law, General de Custine, the conqueror of Mayence, with great courage though without success, before the revolutionary tribunal, and was then imprisoned herself. In the former Carmelite convent, where she shared a cell with Josephine de Beauharnais and gave up hope of ever seeing the light of freedom again, she entered upon the series of her violent love affairs and, 'to the knowledge and before the eyes of Josephine', enjoyed the embraces of General de Beauharnais before he was forced to mount the scaffold. When he was taken away to be executed Delphine behaved so desperately, wailing and screaming so horribly for her love, that the whole prison was in an uproar. Only Josephine remained passive; her marriage ties had been loosened long ago, and though it was a bitter trial to lose the father of her two children, Eugène and Hortense, she had enough restraint not to vie with her husband's mistress in despair.

Should one not forgive the women of that time a great deal? They had lost everything, they were young, the husbands they had just married had been torn from them, their parents and brothers led away to death; the houses they had grown up in were burnt down; they were driven out of the homes they had just set up for themselves, arrested in their turn and thrown into prison. At any moment a fist might rap at the door of their cell and drag them away; day by day the company of their fellow prisoners grew smaller. Life would end tomorrow. Wasn't the world itself coming to an end? Wasn't this Revolution the beginning of universal destruction? Life would never be the same again, never would one's eyes rest on blossoming gardens and blue distances, there would never be any more fine clothes, nor smiling faces with lovelorn eyes reflecting the light of candles. There would be no more reckoning demanded, no doing or leaving undone would be brought to book. Sensual passion, therefore, could be resolutely and ruthlessly enjoyed to the uttermost.

Delphine's husband had been executed soon after her father-in-law; her two children had been left behind, at home, with the old maid Nanette; but Delphine herself had been spared. Whose protective hand was it that helped her to survive until the 9th Thermidor and thus regain her liberty? Among the men that had arrested her was a former journeyman mason of the name of Gérôme, who had been hopelessly vanquished by her delicate, sensitive face. He constituted himself the Marquise's guardian angel, stealing into the office of the Public Prosecutor Fouquier-Tinville to destroy her *dossier* so that her case should never be proceeded with, taking her with him more than once on pretended domiciliary visits so that she could see her children, procuring a thousand favours for her without ever letting her know who her mysterious benefactor was. When he learnt from Nanette that the children were suffering want, he sent her a sum of money every week, but she had to promise never to reveal his name. After the death of Robespierre he was forced to go into hiding as a fugitive terrorist, but even then he contrived to send money regularly for the children's support, till one day Nanette let the secret out. Delphine then helped him in her turn and got him smuggled out of France. He succeeded in reaching America and making a fortune there.

Delphine had never been loved so selflessly, and would never again know such devotion—a devotion that hoped for no reward and chose to remain concealed. What would not the ex-journeyman-mason have given for one of the promising glances the young woman was so lavish with! In the twilight of death all barriers are obliterated, and the Marquise de Custine would bestow many more caresses before the world returned to its everyday road. After the reaction of Thermidor, did she not bewitch the mighty Fouché, that stony austere man, with her blond grace, the softness of her skin and her languishing glance? At any rate he helped her to recover a considerable part of her sequestrated fortune. Her beauty easily withstood events and time; she was as fresh and lovely today as when her mother's lover, the gallant

Chevalier de Boufflers who was Governor of Senegal and wrote such witty letters from there, christened her admiringly 'Queen of the Roses'.

Delphine did not withstand the Enchanter for long, or perhaps it would be truer to say that he could not bring himself to avoid this tempting danger. Once again he found himself murmuring 'Arise, ye longed-for storms . . .', and Pauline was soon aware that her adored poet was absent-minded and had less time for her than of old. The hectic spots on her cheeks burned more fiercely, but she concealed her grief and was careful not to give vent to any complaints or reproaches, for she knew that René was one of those men whom the monotony of feminine suffering plunges into profound boredom. It was in his nature always to love a little less than he was loved. Although he had no wish to give pain, he had not imagination enough to realize the pain he was causing. So long as there were no tears to be seen, all was well; as soon as he saw them he fled. Without deserting Pauline, without forgoing the blessing of her active friendship, he let himself be intoxicated by the enfolding passion that Delphine offered him. Both women knew he would soon be leaving for Rome, for his appointment as Secretary to the Embassy under Cardinal Fesch had been confirmed. Elisa Bacciochi had been somewhat insistent with her brother Napoleon, otherwise the great man might have forgotten this insignificant affair. René saw the appointment on a larger scale; he wrote later 'I entered politics through religion. *The Spirit of Christianity* opened the door to me'. Fontanes was requested to thank Elisa: 'Tell the best of all women, the most generous of protectresses, that my heart is full of gratitude and that I have the same reverent love for her that one feels for the angels. . . .'

When one enlists in the service of the State one must learn to obey. Chateaubriand's departure for Rome could not be put off any longer, though it was not easy to free himself from two pairs of arms. To Delphine he wrote 'You cannot imagine what I have suffered since yesterday. I was supposed to start today. . . . Believe me, I am half demented, and I think I shall end by resigning. The thought of leaving you is killing me'. With Pauline there were tears and vows; the poor woman was more ill than ever, and had secretly resolved to follow him so as to be near him when she died. She was brave, and let him go. This time too his pockets were empty; although his books had lost none of their popularity, he had borrowed so much from his publisher already that the latter could not advance anything more. Who was to help? Fontanes, of course; he was daily becoming more influential, and could arrange details of this kind without any trouble. He sent him a note: 'The Cardinal says that only six months' salary can be advanced; that makes six thousand francs. Plus my travelling expenses. Do your best to see that Talleyrand behaves generously.' He was given nine thousand francs, and set out at last on his journey.

As he habitually lived only in two phases of time, the present and the future, and discounted the wearisome journey through the intervening hours and days, as he always anticipated the future and was actually in Rome already, as he had scored all his triumphs there and might just as well have remained at home, as he regretted not having taken Delphine with him and was relieved that she had not accompanied him, as he longed for Pauline's care of him and yet was glad to have escaped from her, as he behaved in fact towards time, space and human laws after the manner of a true artist, he enjoyed the journey, shed a few farewell tears, and looked towards the future full of high expectation.

He embraced Rome with all his senses, with his entire capacity for realizing greatness and transience. The Pope received him two days after his arrival. This was Pius VII, who still had much trouble and annoyance in store for him from the government that had sent him the poet. The Ruler of Christianity took him by the hand, called him 'my dear Chateaubriand' and pointed to his visitor's great work, which lay open beside him and which he had just been reading—like all the eminent personages of this world when a man of letters comes to visit them. Everywhere he went he was spendidly received; Roman society took an interest in him, he was surrounded by distinguished men and beautiful women. 'It's a sort of frenzy', he wrote to Pauline, who decided there and then not to delay her journey much longer.

Chateaubriand disported himself heedlessly in the rush of this new existence, quite overlooking the fact that he was a dependent, subject to definite service regulations. He paid a visit to the King of Sardinia, whom the French Republic had robbed of the greater part of his State, and who, since Sardinia had become too small and desolate for his comfort, was living in Rome, and surrounding himself, in the shadow of the Papal Court, with *emigrés* and enemies of France. The Ambassador flew into a rage over this *faux pas*, and reminded his First Secretary of the limits of his office. When Chateaubriand proceeded to deal directly with the Curia and, without asking leave of the Ambassador, presented French visitors to the Pope, the Cardinal, who was not very magnanimous and had no sense of humour, lost patience altogether and banished the self-willed Vicomte to the passport division, where he could do no harm. Making out passports is no very exciting occupation; it does not lead one to the centre of world affairs; but the documents were at least readable, for the author's handwriting had been influenced by his long stay in England—it was large, round and upright. The room in which he worked was under the roof; it was so infested with fleas when he first entered it that his white trousers were immediately covered with black specks. When there was nothing else to do he looked out of the garret window and responded to the gay signals of the Roman laundresses in the house opposite.

His diplomatic career did not look very promising. The mighty city of Rome was there to delight his soul daily with its monuments and ruins, but his desire for action found no satisfaction. The incident of the King of Sardinia had not gone unnoticed; Cardinal Fesch had complained to Paris. René, on his side, had sent a note direct to Napoleon, through Elisa, in which he expressed himself critically on the subject of his Chief. Poor Pauline tried to repair the damage, but Napoleon's verdict on this undisciplined civil servant was unshakable. She persuaded Fontanes to write a fatherly letter to René: '. . . Statesmen may sometimes flatter great writers, but they do not like them.' The reply was not exactly a docile one: 'I shall regret all my life having engaged in this imbroglio. The briefest follies are the best. I'm counting on you to get me out of this dilemma. I must add that now I am here, I can see plainly that a post as Secretary to the Embassy is too circumscribed for me.' Fontanes could only shake his head over this difficult *protégé*, who only a few weeks earlier had been talking of himself as the 'ruler of Rome'. But he knew that a severe trial awaited the young man. Pauline had left for Rome, but at the sacrifice of her last remaining strength.

The sick woman had no illusions either as to her condition or her friend's character, but she loved him, and as she was doomed to die she was determined to die beside her last and greatest love. In the shadow of the approaching end her words and actions assumed a sublime simplicity, she commanded respect and admiration by her composure. 'I'm coughing less,' she said, 'but I think that is to allow me to die without noise.' Somebody who saw her at that time said 'Her cheerful spirit was like the slender flame, the glowing breath of an ember that is nearly extinguished'. René fetched her from Florence, and kissed her emaciated hands with emotion. He hired a little house for her in Rome, not far from the Spanish Steps, and did not stir from her side again. His egoism, his obsession with himself seemed to have left him. Grief transformed his nature for the duration of this drama and gave him an unaccustomed sincerity. The nearness of death made people overlook the irregularity of the union; the Pope sent Pauline tokens of favour, even Cardinal Fesch showed the best side of himself and relinquished his secretary entirely to the dying woman. The end came quickly. On one of the last days of October René took her out once more into the open air. She seated herself on a block of stone in the Colosseum and let her gaze wander over the ruins, which were overgrown with bright-coloured foliage, then stood up again with difficulty, saying 'Come, I feel cold'. The carriage took her home and she went to bed.

Awaiting death, her great consolation was the violence of his grief. She knew, of course, that he enjoyed great tragical emotions, but she shut her eyes to his weaknesses and saw only his suffering. Would he weep for Delphine in the same way? Delphine was alive and healthy, with her abundant golden locks she snuggled softly against life, and would still be there when she, Pauline, had crumbled to dust. But at this hour his sobs were for her alone, and this made her happy. She had shed so many tears over him, over his naïve egoism, his badly concealed delight in the blonde Marquise, his incapacity to remain faithful to herself even in the worst days, that she was glad to be affected by his farewell grief. She was dying in the consciousness that her beloved would mourn her in all sincerity.

He mourned her, but he took care that his mourning should not go unnoticed. He was more of an artist than he knew, and already fast in the grip of artistic creativeness, to which the deepest emotions serve as material. He loved death as the highest symbol of human metamorphosis, leading mortal man to the uttermost limits of his potentialities. Pauline's death was undoubtedly a bitter loss to him, but her lifeless body communicated to him that profound peace that emanates from the perishableness of all flesh. Pauline was healed, her new condition led the poet to love shadows and ashes even more devoutly than before. Given back to earth, she belonged to him more than in the moments when he had held her in his arms. No reproach would rise from that grave, such as he had often read in her eyes during her lifetime. He had a wonderful monument erected to her, in white marble, for which he composed the epitaph. Needless to say, a beautiful epitaph, on which he had worked as long as on a page of a book. He fostered his grief by every means, so that it might be his tragedy for a good long time, and win him the respectful silence and the esteem of his contemporaries. He was fully aware of the effect of his mourning on his surroundings. 'You can't imagine,' he wrote to Paris, 'how much affection and respect my grief and my behaviour on this occasion have procured me!' Even Joubert shed tears over his grief-laden letters, and declared 'You can't help loving the good lad when you read what he has written; you feel she would have given ten years of her life to be mourned like this'.

Rome appeared to him now in an altered light; he was more than ever susceptible to the grandiose traces of decay and the melancholy of the sunset light that history cast upon these ruins. 'I recognized neither the trees nor the buildings nor the sky. I wandered about the Campagna, among the waterfalls and the

aqueducts, as I had done among the forest trees of the New
World.' He was not going to remain here; he had enjoyed all the
emotions, raptures and pains the place could afford him, his diplomatic activity—if it could be so called—bored him. The feelings
he expressed in his celebrated letter to Fontanes on the Roman
Campagna were those of farewell. The letter was not written as a
communication, but with a literary intention. It is one of the finest
things he ever wrote, and created quite a school. Not only did
Germaine de Staël make repeated attempts to emulate the style in
her descriptions of Italy, but it had a great influence on French
painting; the effect of the style is even discernible in Corot's work.
'There is nothing to beat him in prose', Sainte-Beuve affirmed
categorically in later years. René's genius had crossed yet another
threshold, as a gift of Pauline's from beyond the grave. Grief had
touched him; the desire to give his grief a worthy frame, the need
to add the mystery of a death to his own life had opened new
channels to his powers of expression. Who shall ever measure the
cleavage inherent in what is called the artistic gift? A death is
mourned and almost enjoyed, a tomb is erected, and in its shade
blossoms a poetic fulfilment.

As usual when he wanted to make a change in his life, Chateaubriand importuned his friends, especially Fontanes, with letters.
Fontanes had meanwhile become a great figure in the State, he
was President of the Legislative Body, and on solemn occasions
walked immediately behind the First Consul. He saw an opportunity of doing something for his friend in Rome. The Swiss
Canton of Valais had just become an independent republic, a
vassal state, that is, created by Napoleon in order to secure the
Alpine passes into Piedmont. He intended to send a *Chargé
d'Affaires* to the little capital, Sion, and had no objection to
Chateaubriand's taking up the appointment. It was a little post,
but an independent one, or so René fancied, and he wrote to
Fontanes 'If I am appointed I shall obey the orders of the Consul
and respect the wishes of my friends. I shall go to the Valais. But
in any case I must be released from Rome; I'm dying here'. Alive
enough, however, to add 'I can only laugh for pity when I hear
fools crying out that I only know how to write books. As if it was

nothing, to be able to write books that get read! Putting four good
ideas together needs more organization and skill than signing all
the passports in the world and giving a diplomatic dinner'.

His hopes of keeping pace with Napoleon's triumphal progress
were small at the moment. The mighty figure was beginning to
blot out his horizon, and he would have to make the best of it.
The notion of Empire was in the air; in Paris it was easy to discern
that the period of the Consulate was nearing its end and that the
days of the Republic were numbered. The Royalists, on whom
many people may still have pinned their hopes, were beginning to
resign, or else to attempt desperate stratagems. Conspiracies,
outrages and plots were discovered and frustrated every day.
'The air is full of daggers', said Fouché; but it was not to be so
much longer. Chateaubriand was soon to learn how actively and
self-sufficiently the new régime was behaving. Fontanes, whose
dress-coat was now covered with gold embroidery, took him to
see Talleyrand. The Minister for Foreign Affairs received the new
Chargé d'Affaires very kindly, and assured him that the Catholic
Valais was delighted to see the famous author of *The Spirit of
Christianity* in its midst.

As usual he obtained a considerable advance on his salary, and
busied himself first of all with his private affairs. He had to visit
his friends, to embrace the adorable Delphine and reassure her as
to the permanence of his feelings, which she appeared to doubt.
Madame de Staël, who had written him such a sympathetic letter
at Pauline's death ('My dear Francis'), had once more been forced
to leave Paris; she was wandering about Germany and exciting
unrest and altercation in Weimar, where she visited the great men
of Germany. What a pity she was not in Paris! She was such a
helpful creature, she would throw her friends into the water for
the pleasure of pulling them out again. René must find his way
through the political situation without her admirable advice. As
regards his personal situation, Fontanes was seeing to it that his
relations with his 'widow' should at last be put on a proper
footing. Céleste was now thirty, and having suffered from smallpox had certainly not improved in looks; but her wit had become
even sharper, and if her husband imagined that she might not

please his friends, he was mistaken. Her youth was over, it is true, but her sarcasm had retained all its freshness. It did not take her long, once she was in Paris and established in the same flat with her husband, to see her position very clearly. René would always escape her, but she would make sure that the aura of unreality that always clings to the breakers of hearts should not fade. On her own behalf, meanwhile, she had won the friendship of both Fontanes and Joubert.

There was of course no money in the house. Talleyrand had forked out twelve thousand francs, but heaven knows how this not inconsiderable sum had disappeared. Agreed, there were debts to be settled—poor Pauline's marble monument to begin with, which had cost no less than nine thousand francs and was not yet all paid for. As Delphine de Custine was a very wealthy woman, René hit upon the impossible idea of borrowing a certain sum from her. Delphine was indignant at being involved in the cost of René's pompous mourning for a rival. He was no less indignant that she should reward his 'confidence' in her with so little understanding. This engendered a certain amount of irritation between the lovers —as they still were—and furnished Delphine's talent for scenes, weeping, quarrelling, and tempestuous reconciliations, with plenty of material. What was to become of her if he moved into the Valais? She felt so unsupported, so exposed to every breath of wind, so hungry for affection. He, for his part, was preoccupied with his future mission, for this remote town of Sion was to be only a stage in his career. He had also to get used to the idea of living henceforth under the same roof with his wife.

On March 19th he attended a great reception in the Tuileries for the purpose of taking his *congé*. Napoleon, who entered the room accompanied by Murat, looked pale and distraught he stared grimly in front of him, and seemed not to see his guests. He took no notice of the newly appointed *Chargé d'Affaires*, and went on into another room; whereupon René, glad to escape the irksome ceremony, left the Palace in all haste. Two days later he heard a town crier shouting the latest news: 'Verdict of the court-martial sitting in Vincennes: Louis-Antoine-Henri de Bourbon, born August 2, 1772 in Chantilly, is condemned to death.' He could not believe his ears. What! The Duke of Enghien, grandson of Prince Condé, son of the Duke of Bourbon, executed in Vincennes? What crime had he committed? How had he come to Paris, anyway? Hadn't he been living as a fugitive in the Baden village of Ettenheim? He could not take it in. He hurried home and shouted to his wife 'The Duke of Enghien has just been shot'.

What had induced Napoleon to have this young man arrested on foreign soil and shot under cover of night? 'This news,' says René, 'altered my life, as it did Napoleon's.' So that was the reconciliation with the past, the regard for the law they had been promised! With lightning rapidity his ideas fell into shape: Here was an opportunity to detach himself from this man; now was the time to destroy the fatal dedication in the third edition of the *Spirit of Christianity*; now he, the Breton Vicomte, servant of the fleur-de-lys and defender of the faith, could dedicate himself once more entirely to the tradition of his fathers. But he saw further than this, he realized that this challenging transgression of the law, amounting to murder, had caused internal injury to Napoleon's authority and tainted it with a form of original sin from which it would always suffer. No power on earth would ever absolve the great potentate from this bloody deed; a secret sickness would infect his greatest triumphs because he had begun his rule by a crime against humanity.

Chateaubriand did not hesitate for an instant. He sent his resignation to Talleyrand on the spot, making his wife's health his excuse, and quitted the diplomatic service. In spite of its moderate form it must have been obvious to everybody that the letter was a refusal, not to say a challenge. How would the mighty one take it? Fontanes feared the worst, he saw his friend arrested and shot in his turn. They expected the police at any moment, but nothing happened. Napoleon, taking note of the resignation, merely remarked 'That's all right'. Chateaubriand was the hero of the day to his friends; but Talleyrand, on being asked if he intended to follow the writer's example, replied 'If Napoleon commits a crime, that is no reason why I should commit a folly'.

VIII

<hr>

THE QUICK AND THE DEAD

EXECUTION UNDER COVER OF NIGHT

WHAT had happened? The air was certainly full of daggers, Fouché had not exaggerated. Napoleon had no desire to be poinarded. He had only escaped by the skin of his teeth from the terrible gunpowder attempt on Christmas Eve in the year 1800. The following months had been quiet because the young Dictator's successes had dazzled the world, and the adherents of the old régime still thought it possible that he would recall the Bourbons to the country once he had re-established a state of order. These foolish hopes were soon disappointed; it became ever more obvious that Napoleon was forcing his way to autocracy and taking steps to erect a stable throne for himself. Those who had fought for the royal fleur-de-lys ever since the first days of the Revolution became more and more discouraged. The revolts of the loyalist peasants, the Chouans, in the Vendée and in Brittany, died down. Their provinces had long been laid waste by the republican troops, the villages had been burnt down, the churches destroyed, and the survivors were living in the woods and among the ruins. Of their leaders, who at the height of the insurrection had raised and commanded whole armies, those still alive were leading the life of outlaws, contenting themselves with highway robbery, attacking mail-coaches and other state vehicles. Their one hope was that some prince of the royal house would appear in their midst and lead them, or at least serve as a banner to which the rebels might flock again.

But the grandees among the London *emigrés* had no intention of taking such a risk. Ten thousand peasants had fallen in the royal cause, but neither the man that now called himself Louis

XVIII nor his brother the Comte d'Artois paid much attention to the cry for help that reached them from the ranks of the Chouans. They left the whole affair more or less to the English government, which—when the political situation made it expedient—sent a frigate with arms and money to the French coast, but mostly showed as little regard for the poor devils as the princes themselves. The indifference of these high-ranking *emigrés* was repellent; heartlessly and arrogantly they refused to receive the emissaries of the Chouans if they happened to bear bourgeois names, or if their clothing showed traces of the bush war and left somewhat to be desired. When at last a short-lived peace occurred between France and England, a plan was seriously discussed in London for deporting the entire 'Chouannerie' to Canada.

Among the few rebels that were determined not to give up the cause of the Bourbons but to go on fighting for it was the thirty-three-year-old Breton Georges Cadoudal, a simple clerk of the court, but a lion for courage and enterprise. This gigantic man, who could snap a gun barrel with his hands, concealed in his huge frame a pious soul and a fanatical belief in the cause of royalty, which in return took very little interest in him. He made a last attempt to bring about a *coup d'état,* the plan being to go to Paris and kidnap the First Consul. The conspiracy was to consist of only a handful of people, some twenty men, who were to establish themselves in Paris without delay and make all arrangements. This part of the undertaking met with no difficulty, in spite of the increasing vigilance of the police, though Georges had to exercise the greatest care on account of his huge stature. He got in touch with General Pichegru, the conqueror of Holland, who had been banished to Cayenne by the Directory and had escaped to London. Contact was also made with the popular victor of Hohenlinden, General Moreau, who had been dismissed by Napoleon and was nursing his idleness and his rancour in Paris. Uniforms had been procured, so that the conspirators, disguised as Consulate Guards, could overpower Napoleon and carry him off to the coast. The figure-head of the conspiracy was the 'Prince'. A member of the Royal Family was to enter France secretly and take over power at the critical juncture. Georges was convinced of the watertightness of his plans; he was a tried conspirator, circumspect, wary and brave. The Bourbons having pledged their word that they would send one of themselves, he could not doubt the success of his foolhardy plan. 'I swear to you,' he said to a fellow conspirator, 'on my word of honour, that you will see the Comte d'Artois, the Duc d'Angoulême, the Duc de Berry, the Duc d'Enghien, General Pichegru, Moreau and all of us, you and me, here, sword in hand, or I am no honourable man!'

However, the 'Prince' did not turn up, the conspiracy was betrayed, Georges was arrested in the streets of Paris and sent to prison after he had shot a gendarme. At his first examination he was reproached with this shooting because the gendarme had a wife and children. 'Then you'd better have me arrested by a bachelor next time!' he retorted. But there was no next time; Georges was executed, the conspiracy had failed. It was said that Georges was the only person Napoleon was ever afraid of. Now he was dead; but who was the 'Prince' that was to have entered the country so secretly? Napoleon never seriously believed that the young Duc d'Enghien had been the leading character in the conspiracy, but he was determined to strike a blow that would rob all royalists for ever of the courage to conspire against him. He wanted to dig a blood-filled trench between himself and the Restoration.

When Réal, the Prefect of Police, entered the First Consul's study in the Tuileries on the evening of March 10, 1804, he found Napoleon lying at full length on a map on the floor, studying the line of the Rhine from Freiburg to Basel. 'Look here, monsieur le Conseiller d'Etat, you never told me that the Duc d'Enghien was living only four miles from our frontiers and weaving plots against us.' The remark was not pure invention; Georges, who was still in prison, and aware that he was doomed, had not allowed a word to be wrung from him as to the identity of the 'Prince' he had been expecting, but rumours had been gathered, according to which it might have been Enghien. Whether Napoleon attached any credit to these rumours or not, he tapped his finger on the map at the spot that showed the Baden village of Ettenheim. The young duke had been living there for three years, weaving a love idyll with a young Princesse de Rohan who had followed him into exile, going hunting, and otherwise doing no harm to a fly. Ettenheim is not far from the Rhine, which forms the frontier at that point. 'Am I a dog,' queried Napoleon imperiously, 'to be killed in the street while my murderers go free? They're after my life, are they? Good; an eye for an eye. . . . I'll find a way of putting an end to these conspiracies . . . the head of the culprit shall compensate me. . . .' Then, referring to the Bourbons, in whom he saw the leaders of these machinations against his person, he exclaimed 'My blood is as good as theirs!'

Réal was aghast; the atmosphere had been very sinister all these weeks. The imprisonment of Georges Cadoudal had removed the chief danger, but it had also shown how widespread had been the conspirators' plans. Pichegru, Moreau—had not Bernadotte and Macdonald been mentioned too? Fouché was only too glad not to be Minister of Police at this juncture. He rubbed his hands, for he knew more than Napoleon, and was glad to be able to keep his knowledge to himself. It was incontestable that George's attempt pointed to a fresh, perhaps final, wave of resistance to Napoleon. Napoleon seized the moment with sure instinct: something must be done at once! As there existed a few reasons, however uncertain, for suspecting Enghien, son of the Duc de Bourbon and grandson of Prince Condé, he should be the victim whose blood would divide the old age from the new.

A Council was held that night at the Tuileries, in which Caulaincourt and Talleyrand took part. At break of day some hundreds of French dragoons and gendarmes invaded the territory of the Margrave of Baden and surrounded the house in Ettenheim where the Duke was residing. He was just dressing to go shooting when the troops broke into the house. He and his attendants were taken to the brickworks, where General Ordener, in command of the enterprise, was awaiting him. By midday they were across the Rhine, on French soil, which the young Prince had not trodden for fifteen years. They were taken on foot to the next village, the prisoner marching between the horses of the dragoons, followed by his dog, which had refused to leave him; he was wearing his

K

green hunting suit, with a gay feather in his hat. In Strasburg the night was spent in the citadel; next morning they drove out of the city gates in a travelling carriage. An Alsatian officer of the name of Petermann sat beside the prisoner and chatted with him. They surveyed the landscape, spread out in the austere beauty of early spring and growing gradually misty. Enghien was untroubled, he hoped to be allowed to speak to the First Consul as soon as he reached Paris. 'A quarter of an hour's talk with him, and everything will be all right,' he thought.

No time was lost on the journey; meals were eaten in the carriage, the prisoner slept a little, talked to his dog lying next to him on the seat of the carriage and chatted with Petermann as best he could. Finally, at midday on March 20th, they reached the gates of Paris. A courier appeared and led the carriage across the city, so rapidly that the young man had scarcely time to recognize the streets and squares; then, suddenly, they came to a halt before a fine palace, the courtyard of which was surrounded by classical columns. This was the residence of the Minister for Foreign Affairs, Talleyrand. The Duke was about to alight, but he was asked to remain in the carriage. The postillions stayed in the saddle, a fine rain fell without ceasing. They waited in this way for an hour, till a man appeared and gave an order in a low voice. The carriage started off again, along the Seine this time, over the old Pont-Neuf, past the Hôtel de Ville and through a wide square where the Bastille had once stood. The prisoner looked attentively at the streets, the squares and the buildings. Some he recognized, many had altered, but it was still the old, enchanting Paris. All at once they were out of the town on an endless high road.

The ancient Castle of Vincennes was a gloomy, fortress-like building with an enormous tower, thick walls, and a moat long since dried-up. Here Enghien was lodged; he was tired by the long journey and fell asleep at once. But while he and his dog slept peacefully, the Governor of the Castle sent for three picks and shovels. What did he want with these tools on a cold, foggy night? Perhaps to have the huge manure-heap removed, which was lying in the moat and reached to the ground-floor windows? He could actually have enabled the prisoner to escape; but it was no concern of his, and he made haste to get back to bed, lest there should be more work for him. A clatter of hoofs and the rumble of carriage-wheels was heard turning into the roughly paved courtyard. It was Savary, commanding officer of the First Consul's Bodyguard, charged with the speedy execution of the whole business. The order, addressed to Murat, the Governor of Paris, read: 'Make it clear to the members of the Court-Martial that everything must be finished tonight. If the verdict is death, as I have no doubt it will be, arrange for the sentence to be carried out at once, and the condemned man buried in one of the courtyards of the fortress.' The officers of the Court-Martial arrived almost at the same time.

Lieutenant Noirot was sent to wake up the prisoner. Startled out of a deep sleep, he cried 'What do you want?'

'You are now to stand your trial.'

'What for?'

'To find out whether you intended to murder the First Consul.'

'No, seriously?' exclaimed the Duke.

He dressed in silence and followed the Lieutenant through the icy passages of the stronghold of Saint-Louis, down the steep spiral staircase, across the great courtyard, in the darkness of which the body of troops that had been silently drawn up could hardly be seen. The Court was assembled in Governor Sarel's drawing-room under the presidency of General Hulin, the 'Conqueror of the Bastille'. Savary was standing by the fireplace, warming his back.

The Duke declared his innocence; he spoke in measured accents, but with decision. He had had nothing to do with Cadoudal's conspiracy, he knew neither Pichegru nor Dumouriez, and was not in touch with any enemy of the Republic. Yes, certainly, he had fought against the Revolution in his grand-father's army. It was also true that he was in receipt of a small pension from the British government, which represented his entire income. He signed the report, and was conducted back to his room. The tribunal conferred for a few minutes only; sentence of death was passed unanimously and the verdict drawn up, leaving a blank space where the law under which sentence had been passed should have been referred to, because it was not known.

While this was going on, the gardener, who had been wakened hours before, was sent to the moat to dig a grave there; pick and shovel were at hand. The man had begun to remove a heap of rubbish from the moat the day before; he went on working at the same place, digging out the grave. While he was at work, with a little lantern holding three candles beside him, soldiers began to appear in the darkness; the gardener heard rather than saw them. A detachment of grenadiers marched in single file beside the walls, behind them a troop of cuirassiers with the heavy tread of dismounted cavalry. They formed an open square round the gardener, who was feverishly hurrying to finish his task, with the sweat of exhaustion and terror on his brow.

Harel went to fetch the condemned man, who whistled his dog and followed him. Another journey along passages, down stairs and through small courtyards, lighted by a flickering torch. Suddenly they went down a steep flight of steps, at the bottom of which the dark moat yawned like an abyss. Enghien recoiled: 'Where are you taking me?' And as Harel did not answer, he went on 'If I am to be buried alive in a dungeon, I would rather die on the spot'. Harel steadied his voice and said 'Please follow me, and summon up all your courage'.

Now they were in the moat, between high walls dripping with damp. The condemned man, still followed by his dog, noticed a party of grenadiers standing in the pouring rain, armed with muskets. An adjutant stepped up to him and read him the death sentence by the light of a torch. He listened in silence, without stirring, then he called out 'Has anybody a pair of scissors?' One of the soldiers had a little pair about him; they were handed to the Duke, who cut off a lock of his hair and wound it round one of his rings; he added a letter to this, which he had written that evening, and begged the adjutant to have the whole conveyed to the Princesse de Rohan. Now he was ready; his dog pressed close to his leg, and he tried in vain to push it away with his foot. The salvo crashed, echoing a hundredfold from the narrow walls; heavy smoke rose slowly through the dripping darkness. Two soldiers threw the body of the victim into the grave. It was three in the morning and still raining.

THE QUEEN OF THE ROSES

This was the drama, the fateful issue of which induced Chateaubriand to leave the retinue of the Great Man whose hands were now stained with blood, and go over to the camp of those who would have nothing to do with the new State. The next step to be taken was not merely to stand aside but to work for the return of the Bourbons. But René had not got so far as yet, he was not even sure whether Napoleon had seen a declaration of war in this not very important resignation. He still had friends among the Dictator's entourage; Fontanes was basking in the new sun of grace, and the 'adorable Elisa' was still there too. She had given her brother a grateful smile when he teased her with 'Confess you were horribly afraid for your friend!' Fouché was indulgently inclined, thanks to Delphine's intercession. Neither Molé nor Pasquier, who had surrendered entirely to the new régime, thought of breaking with Chateaubriand. Fanatical differences of opinion, capable of separating old friends, were unheard of. 'During the Empire,' wrote Madame de Chateaubriand 'people of opposite opinions could mix with one another without tearing one another's eyes out. That was impossible under the Bourbons.'

The couple were now living in the Rue de Miromesnil, almost in the country, that is. Cornfields spread before their door, the old Parc Monceau with its tall trees and overgrown fields afforded Chateaubriand his daily walks.

However, one cannot live on dreams, and as usual the couple had not a sou. The advance he had received from Talleyrand on his appointment as *Chargé d'Affaires* he had at once repaid to the authorities—otherwise his solemn resignation would have made no impression on anybody—and now there was only a trifle left between them and actual want. But even when they were in cash the splendour did not last long. Neither of them had the smallest talent for economizing, and Chateaubriand would wonder all his life where the receipts, advances and royalties he had yesterday could have gone. 'The money that household devoured without ever presenting an appearance suitable to their social position,' said Madame de Boigne, 'is a fresh proof of the disadavantages of disorder. As a matter of fact Monsieur de Chateaubriand himself confesses that nothing would bore him more than to be living on a regular income. He likes to acquire riches and spend them, feel the pinch of want, squander the housekeeping money on whims and fancies, give up his post to feel still more distressed, surrender an appointment where he had twenty-five horses in the stable, and enjoy the pleasure of refusing an invitation under the pretext that he cannot afford a cab to take him there. In short, he wants to experience every sort of sensation for the sake of ridding himself of his boredom, for that is really and truly the great secret of his life.'

Now that Céleste had decided to shut both eyes to her husband's infidelity, and his affairs with his 'ladies' no longer made her jealous so much as anxious for the health of his soul; as she teased him but never made scenes, and as he ended by being amused at her little sarcasms and spiteful remarks, they were living quite amicably together. Of course she could not give him the 'poetry' he needed for his daily sustenance, and he looked for it elsewhere. He visited Delphine de Custine at her Château Fervacques in Normandy, where one of the guest chambers was furnished with Henri IV's enormous bed, and played the Enchanter more than ever. He had to take a certain amount of trouble, for Delphine had a fatal leaning towards dramatic reproaches and scenes, all harping on the one subject—that he did not love her enough, for if he did, he would make this and that sacrifice for her sake. He pacified her, smiling, and called her his 'Crosspatch'—a somewhat surprising nickname for the 'Queen of the Roses.' She understood no better than other women that reproaches, complaints and threats will tire an admirer, who under more pacific treatment might perhaps get used to the monotony of constancy. She actually went so far as to threaten suicide, and seized a sporting gun—unloaded, as it happened—'to send a bullet through her heart'. She declared she did not want to sleep any more, 'for fear of not thinking of her love', upon which a more worldly-wise woman friend advised her to love him a bit less, so as to be able to love him always.

The perpetual scolding did not prevent him from writing her delightful letters: 'I left your owl castle really most regretfully. It wouldn't do for me to visit it too often, for I believe I should get too much used to it. Try and leave it soon and come back among the living. Remember that in Paris you would be my neighbour, and could visit me as often as you liked . . . I am yours for life.' He liked going into the country, and was made welcome there. He enjoyed staying with Joubert, who had a fine estate in Burgundy. Jouberg had made friends with Céleste, and often had her to stay. Joubert's younger brother describes one of these visits: 'I shall never forget how happy we were for those six weeks, when we had those guests. We worked the whole morning, and then spent the afternoon on the hills and in the meadows. We played all sorts of high-spirited games, suitable to the gaiety of a younger age. Any serious person, knowing Chateaubriand only from his books, and seeing the author of *The Spirit of Christianity* enjoying these childish games, quite forgetful of himself, would first have been astonished, and would then have decided that this man of genius must also be a kindly creature at heart.'

Napoleon's coronation as Emperor was an event that promised to consolidate the relations of political power in France for a long while. Chateaubriand had gone over to the Opposition, but he had neither opportunity nor inclination to use his influence. 'I'm planning to retire completely. The clock that never tells the same hour twice will soon be striking my thirty-fourth year. I suppose I have got to languish as long again in this world. I hope it will all be over quickly; all that troubles me today will matter little to me when the curtain has fallen.'

The recipient of this letter would certainly have smiled at the young man's ideas if he had not known that René had sustained a great loss at that time. Lucile, the sister he loved above everything in the world, had just died. Her unhappy, mutilated life had come to a sinister end. Her youthful exaltation, her susceptibility and her pessimism had developed into persecution mania and melancholia. As she had no means of her own and had used up her last reserves, her brother had installed her in a Home run by nuns, whence she wrote him heartbreaking letters: 'God can now afflict me only through you. I thank Him for the precious, good, dear gift he made me in your person, and for maintaining my life without a stain. Those are all the treasures I have. As an emblem of my life I could take the moon in a cloud, with the motto: Often darkened, never stained.' And this: 'Good day, my friend; what is the colour of your thoughts this morning? Nothing can compare with the thought of death, which rids us of the future. Ever since yesterday I have been quite pleased with my state of mind. I take no heed either of my sadness or the inner decay that I feel. I have released myself. Go on being kind to me as you have always been, that will be charitable of you at this time.'

Often darkened, never stained! Lucile, the pale guardian angel of René's early days, who had stimulated his imagination and perhaps even brought the germ of artistry within him to life, his theatrical and yet serious sister, was definitely obsessed by the idea of purity. She had married an elderly man, but the marriage had never been consummated. She had been engaged to a friend of her brother's, the poet Chênedollé, but years before, during the emigration, he had been married in church to a French-woman, and all attempts to have this marriage annulled were unsuccessful. The growing dimness of her mind became un-equivocal: 'My brother, do not let yourself be wearied by my letters and my existence; I cannot collect my thoughts any more. You will soon be delivered from all the trouble I cause you.' He was absent from Paris when she died; she had probably com-mitted suicide, for the place of her burial is not recorded in any church register.

René's grief was genuine, but as so often, owing to his habit of describing his feelings more clearly than their cause, he laid himself open to the suspicion of always relating every stroke of fate, every drama, to himself. His first word would always be 'I'. This time too he wrote 'You see that I'm born to every kind of suffering.' But he really was almost stunned with grief. Lucile had left her lodgings on the eve of her death; nobody knew where she had died and been buried. René left nothing undone, but 'Lucile was unknown, and had no friends, only Madame de Beaumont's old servant knew her. He followed the forsaken coffin alone, and was dead himself when at last I was able to return to Paris. My sister was buried among the poor. In what grave-yard was she laid, in what motionless waters of an ocean of the dead was she sunk?' And he added the wonderful sentence 'God will have recognized my sister, and she, who cared so little for the earth, was not meant to leave any trace upon it'. We may believe him when he says 'Those are the actual, the only events of my real life. When I lost my sister, what did I care about the thousands of soldiers falling on the field of battle, the collapse of thrones and the alteration of the face of the world?'

Lucile's 'tyrannical moods' had made it all the greater trial to have her near them, because Madame Chateaubriand, too, found the situation intolerably painful, and was often nearly driven to desperation. Céleste was a very natural person, she was frightened by Lucile's emotionalism, which prevented her from ever engaging in any normal conversation. René himself found the intense admiration for him that she always displayed getting more and more on his nerves. He could stand a good deal of feminine adoration, but Lucile's rapture over every word he said or wrote was so morbid and clamorous that he avoided her as much as he could. This was no doubt why he considered an indisposition of his wife's a sufficient excuse for not hastening to her during the last days of her life. Now that she was dead and not a trace of her could be found, his sisterly star—often darkened, never stained—shone forth with the quiet light of remembrance of the foreboding days of their childhood.

THE JOURNEY TO JERUSALEM

Chateaubriand remained in Paris for a time, writing; but he had vast travel plans: 'I was longing to throw myself into a new ocean and swim across it.' His desire was no longer for a quiet hermitage in the forest, but for distant lands, sea voyages, signs of antique greatness and holy places. He wanted to see Athens and seize the spirit of antiquity in its haunted ruins; but he wanted even more to visit Jerusalem and bow down before the Holy Sepulchre. He would be the second of his name to do so, the first having trodden the sacred soil as a Crusader, and as the author of the now world-renowned work in praise of Christianity, he thought he owed this visit to himself and to his admirers. He began making preparations for the journey, the most important being to procure the necessary money. The famous writer had no intention of travelling on the cheap and enduring privations. For all his talk of the 'pilgrimage' he had set his heart upon, he wanted to travel, not in the ascetic guise of a pilgrim, but in the style of a *grand seigneur*. His coffers were fairly empty, they contained, as he said, mainly mortgages on his castles in the air. But his lady admirers did not fail him. The celebrated Frau von Krüdener, who was in such high favour at the Russian Court, was able to rouse the enthusiasm of Tsar Alexander's wife for Chateaubriand's travel plans, and it seems probable that the 40,000 francs that suddenly filled the travelling chest to overflowing were contributed by this romantic Tsarina, who liked to fancy herself reflected in René's pessimistic prose.

What would Delphine say to this lengthy separation? (His wife was hardly consulted). Would she try to hinder René's departure by tears and scenes? Well, there was no hurry, especially as he had begun writing a new book, to which he was giving the provisional title of *The Martyrs of Diocletian*, later shortened to *The Martyrs*. A Roman officer, Eudorus, who is a Christian, meets the pagan priestess Velléda in the Celtic forests. Both she and the other female character in the book, Cymodocéa, are virgins— the one from virtue, the other because of her vows. With Chateaubriand the conflict is always of the same nature; it is so in *Atala* and in the later novel *The last of the Abencérages*. Passion between the sexes comes up against the barriers of their faith; hence the sin, and hence the tragic solution by martyrdom and death.

Historical parallels were the great fashion of the day; in Tacitus and other writers of antiquity people read of the fate of tyrants in history. As Napoleon was admired, but at the same time hated as an usurper of the Throne, the law must be discovered by which Emperors rise, conquer and fall. Chateaubriand describes the Court and the retinue of a powerful ruler, and draws discreet parallels. Around Diocletian, too, there are Christians and 'Philosophers', that is pagans, fighting one another over their convictions. A certain alteration of style is apparent in the prose of this work; just as France, in her architecture, in the shape of her furniture, ornaments and table utensils, was going over to the pure Empire style more or less imposed by Napoleon, Chateaubriand's mode of writing was gaining in directness and clarity. What Prud'hon, Canova and Girodet had fashioned, what the posthumous poems of André Chénier exhaled, makes itself felt in his writing. He is still the first of the Romantics, but his work begins to show traces of the politically inspired style of the period of Austerlitz and Wagram.

Travelling plans, first sketches for the immense undertaking of his Memoirs—destined to be the greatest work of his life—interspersed with polite sparring matches with his wife and stormy altercations with Delphine on the theme of 'If you still loved me as you used to do . . .', nothing of all this could disturb his equanimity. He was busy with his dreams, so filled with the wonder of speech, so full of astonishment at the glorious things to be fashioned from words, so stirred by the mystery of creativeness, which could bring the most deeply hidden emotions into the clearest light, that he must often have appeared absent-minded, reserved and even cold to the outside world. The women whose emotions he stirred were not really in love with him, but with his soul, which promised the richest echo to their confused sensations. He attracted women that were not in harmony with themselves or the world; they expected everything of him, he was to lend a voice to all that they could not express for themselves. They were romantic creatures, in a word, stepping into his path and demanding to be understood, beautiful creatures with much experience of love, but still under some secret spell from which, as they believed, he alone could release them.

What lay hidden under this all-too-earthly love, the fulfilment of which was still unable to satisfy their uttermost desire? Though he was neither handsome nor aggressive, but as the Duchess of Arenberg wrote to Delphine 'really not good to love', women looked to him for the appeasement of a longing that can be expressed by embraces but lies far beyond them. For this reason he was nearly always the one to be wooed and allowing himself to be loved. His inconstancy was not due to the death of desire, but to the cruel fact that as a rule the women had soon fulfilled their role of releasing a fresh stream of creativeness in him. The storm of emotions they set loose in him had to be brought under control, and this was a matter for art rather than love. For art's sake too he needed solitude, and thus it always happened that the string-music set vibrating by a feminine touch went on playing alone.

Delphine was well aware that she was driving the man she loved ever further from her by her scenes and tears; he neither could nor would make any concessions, and became thoroughly bored by her complaints. His eyes had long been fixed on another face. Natalie de Noailles had often been one of the party at Fervacques, and had thus become acquainted with Chateaubriand under Delphine's own roof. She was beautiful and elegant, with a very romantic past. A well-known portrait shows her in hunting costume, wearing a grey top hat with a turned-up brim on her luxuriant hair, a coat with fur collar and cuffs, and the lace trimming of her bodice just visible. She is shouldering a little sporting gun inlaid with silver. Molé has given a full description of her: 'She was an Armida, her charm exceeded even her beauty. Whether speaking or singing, the magic of her voice was irresistible. She had an almost supernatural capacity for learning, with more adaptability than talent. Able to transform herself to suit the nature of whomsoever she wished to seduce, she could strike any note at will. At eighteen she had the innocence and naïvety of my own age. With Count Melzi she had the wit, brilliance and softness of an Aspasia; with the blind classicist Portalis she interpreted Virgil. With Chateaubriand she amused herself by surpassing him in his inclination for adventure and imitating him in indescribable disorder and fantasy. Her coquetry amounted to a mania. She could not bear the idea that a man's eyes might rest on her with indifference. At table I often detected her in the act of scrutinizing the faces of the servants waiting on us, for the effect she was making on them.'

She and Chateaubriand met at a time when he was seeking the outlines of one of his characters. He was looking for a creature whose features he could lend to the beautiful heathen, Cymodocéa, of his *Martyrs*. 'A shade, whom I had long named Cymodocéa, shaped itself indistinctly in my brain, but no feature had yet established itself. As soon as I had a glimpse of her I shut myself up with her as I always do with the daughters of my fancy. Before they issue from the dream state and approach the shores of Lethe they undergo many changes of form. If I create them out of love, I release them out of love again, and the one beloved apparition I then bring to light is the fruit of a thousand inconstancies.' Thus Natalie's appearance became an artistic necessity to the writer; she enabled his restless fancy to connect the dream figure with an earthly image at last.

Natalie's history, like Pauline's and Delphine's, was determined from the start by the Reign of Terror. Death waiting outside the prison door was the fundamental reality of their youth. At the age of sixteen Natalie had married the handsome Charles de Noailles, who emigrated very early, leaving his young wife pregnant. She was thrown into prison with the whole of her family and that of her husband. Delicate as she was, she became the guardian angel of all these Noailles, Labordes and Mouchys. She waited like a maid on her husband's grandmother, the aged Maréchale de Mouchy, and exhausted herself in the service of these old, pampered people, who contrived to maintain their aristocractic composure in the midst of their miseries. Her father was executed, and so was her grandmother; every day the jailer dragged one or other of the party to death under the guillotine. When the prison doors flew open on the 9th Thermidor she had only one thought, to go to England and rejoin her husband, with whom she felt more in love than ever. She did eventually succeed in reaching London and finding her husband. But he had become entangled in a love affair with a well-known lady of the English Court, and he established his wife and little daughter in the country, in Norfolk, so as to remain unhampered in London. He ended by begging his friend Vintimille to go to Norfolk and keep his wife captive there by his seductive charm.

The affair points a moral: Vintimille succeeded in seducing Natalie, but as a punishment for his co-operation in this iniquitous scheme, he fell passionately in love with the doubly deceived victim. One evening he confessed the intrigue to which he had lent himself. Natalie, who had believed in him, was shattered by the blow. Half out of her senses she fled next day back to France, leaving behind her a much relieved husband and a lover who would forever be fettered to her. She lived for a time with her mother in Paris. Life had begun again in the capital; the Directory had no taste for austerity; laxity and disorder reigned in the new society, and the beautiful Natalie appears not to have denied herself many of the frivolous pleasures of the time. 'I'm really unfortunate,' she is reported to have declared, 'No sooner do I fall in love with a man than another turns up, who pleases me better still.' 'Her choice,' says the severe Madame de Boigne, 'was as shameless in quality as in number. She had fallen into such depths of disorderliness that her liaison with Monsieur de Chateaubriand was almost a rehabilitation.'

Although this new conquest took up much of his time, it was not enough to make him happy. Céleste and Delphine were no doubt jealous of their new rival, and Natalie was hurt because he often made his wife a pretext for not visiting her, and because Delphine was still of sufficient importance to him to have to be consoled; but the most tormented by jealousy of them all at that moment was Chateaubriand himself, the object of his discordant emotions being Napoleon. Half admiring, half embittered, he watched the irresistibly increasing lustre of the Emperor, his victories, of which France was beginning to be proud, his power, born of sagacity and energy, to which Europe was bowing. René's relation to the Emperor had always had a strongly personal tinge. Not only did he measure himself by him, and consider him the only permissible model for his own urge to greatness, but he saw in him the worthiest material for his art: 'My admiration for Napoleon has always been great and sincere, even when I have attacked him most sharply.' He felt himself in some hardly explicable sense tied to the great man's star. His self-esteem made him seek someone of equal birth with himself, and in his constant preoccupation with himself and the origin of the different elements of which his nature was compounded, he always came up against Napoleon as the only mortal besides himself who had entered life according to some entirely personal law.

This was not due to megalomania but to his ineradicable conviction of the uniqueness of every outstanding existence, conforming to no historical or social precedent. Even before the Revolution, so he thought, their two careers had had points of contact: 'I was then, like Bonaparte, a slender lieutenant, entirely unknown. He and I arose out of the darkness at the same time, I to seek a name in solitude, he to seek fame among men.' He measured the force of Napoleon's personality by the mediocrity that possessed France after his day, and nobody in France, no historian, no writer, not even Stendhal or Balzac, has done such justice to Napoleon as he. Nobody has described him so magnificently as this Breton Vicomte and romantic writer, who had dedicated his life to the Bourbon cause, and fought literary battles against the 'Usurper' with a passionate force exceeded only by Madame de Staël.

This purely apparent inconsequence throws a little light on Chateaubriand's power of attraction. His convictions and principles were not founded on knowledge but on the impulses of his heart. Loyalty to ancestral symbols and an ever lively sense of honour did not prevent him from being bewitched by this great personality. There was no party spirit in him, however violently he might take sides. He had the courage to say that Napoleon had stirred up something in people which was greater than they; and it was his readiness to recognize a spiritual influence of this nature, and to proclaim it, that bound people to him, especially those women who did not understand themselves, but were happy when they felt themselves understood. He had, of course, to keep this mental conflict with Napoleon to himself; he could not confess to anybody that he felt jealous, that he was following this star's orbit with a feeling of envy, and that his own unobtrusive existence was

being driven completely into the shade by the loud *furioso* of the
Imperial victory march. His honour commanded him to stand
aside, his prudence advised him not to repeat the semi-homage he
had attempted in the dedication to the third edition of the *Spirit of
Christianity*. He realized with discomfort that there was no room
for him in the present situation, and he started, therefore, on his
long journey. Greece, Egypt, Jerusalem, all these must eventually
be useful to his literary projects, for the term 'local colour' was of
his invention, and he made a habit of incorporating the cities and
landscapes he had visited in the scenery of his fiction. He intended
to return via Spain and meet Natalie there, to listen with her to the
nocturnal voices of the Moorish fountains. From the Holy
Sepulchre he was to hasten to a most unholy but wonderful
rendezvous, let Napoleon conquer the rest of the world meanwhile.

The parting from Delphine at Fervacques proved easy, for she
was shrewd enough to realize that she ought to have had the
patience to retain him by forbearance and a little irony. Now that
it was too late she accorded him a few restful days in her company,
desisting from reproaches and behaving as an understanding
friend. He left her house, therefore, with a feeling of enormous
relief, with the almost murderous cheerfulness that a man may
experience when he has at last separated from a woman he no
longer loves, and is meanwhile sure of a new love. She wrote to a
woman friend: 'This dream of Greece has become a reality; he has
gone to fulfil his own wishes and destroy mine. Our last fortnight
was perfect, but now everything is over.'

The Enchanter started on his travels, planning to meet Natalie
de Noailles in Granada on the way back. She looked forward
with pleasure to driving along strange roads, visiting strange cities
and seeing strange faces. Her former seducer, Monsieur de
Vintimille, the victim of the frivolous intrigue and of his own
boundless passion for her, had just died in Naples. She had always
refused to see him again, and it was rumoured in Paris that the
unfortunate man had killed himself out of grief. Whether this was
true or not, the drama enacted in Norfolk had come to people's
ears, and Natalie, whose heart had never been healed of the wound

inflicted by her husband, longed to get away, to avoid the pitying or malicious glances of her acquaintances and escape from their gossip. She was not in a cheerful mood, therefore: 'One must find things to do, otherwise one's brain would go soft with all the painful thoughts that keep coming back. When the spirit has once been wounded, the mind gives way, and it would be a thousand times better to die.' René, on the other hand, was imperturbable; he did not conceal the fact, writing of it later, that the whole journey was merely a détour to Granada: 'Did I visit the tomb of Christ as a penitent? I was preoccupied by one thought alone. I counted the moments impatiently. On board my ship I kept my eyes on the evening star and begged it for favourable winds and fame, for the sake of being loved. I hoped to find these in Sparta, in Memphis and in Carthage, and bring them to the Alhambra.'

The journey lasted a year; it is fully described in his book *Journey from Paris to Jerusalem,* although, following his usual system of working, the description was afterwards completed by the fruits of his reading and other additions. His departure did not lack certain comical touches. His wife travelled with him as far as Venice, and was not sparing of ironical remarks on his suite. He had loaded his magnificent travelling coach with arms, powder and shot, in readiness for every adventure. His servant Julien— who actually kept a very prosaic but reliable diary—was dressed as a sort of janissary, and was forced, to his sorrow, to wear baggy trousers and a blue turban. They had got no further than Lyons when one piece of his arsenal, an *espingole* (apparently a short-barrelled carbine, or blunderbuss) went off of its own accord. As the incident occurred just as they were crossing a bridge, Madame de Chateaubriand seized arms and ammunition with determination and flung them in the Rhône.

In Venice he embarked in the ship that was to convey him to Greece. Now he was quite the traveller of his earlier days, except that he knew the names of the constellations overhead, because Pauline had taught them to him. He enjoyed these nights of his voyage in the Mediterranean with an inexpressible sense of freedom. He was alone, he had recovered the masculine solitude that is the greatest happiness of the too-much-loved man. The night

L

and the sea, the rising sun and the wind filling the sails, all heralded a world full of fresh possibilities. But whereas he had once sought the wilderness, it was now a world burdened with history that allured him. 'I would like to sleep on the banks of the Eurota or the Jordan, if the heroic shades of the three hundred Spartans or the twelve sons of Jacob would haunt my sleep. But I would no longer strive to reach a soil untouched by the ploughshare. What I need now are old deserts that may suggest ancient Babylon to me if I choose, or the legions of Pharsalus, *grandia ossa,* fields whose furrows have something to teach me, and in which I, the man that I am, can find the blood, tears and sweat of mankind.'

Finding himself again, and meeting with man as such, is in fact, the meaning of his passion for history, and though he includes Homer, the Bible and Thucydides among the sources of his re-encounters, it is clear that he created an historical counter-world for himself out of this voyage, to help himself over the present, in which he could take no part, by means of a different, more profound form of actuality. Corfu, Sparta, Argos, Athens, Chios, Smyrna, Pergamon, Constantinople, Rhodes, Cyprus, Jaffa, Jerusalem, Alexandria, Cairo, Tunis and Spain, were roughly his stages. He travelled fast, a fleeting glance often sufficed him. He stayed only four or five days in Jerusalem itself, and of this short period many hours were spent on the ceremony in which the author of *The Spirit of Christianity* was received into the Order of the Holy Sepulchre. The experts acting as guides to the celebrated visitor in Argos and Athens, Jerusalem and Cairo, thought his haste somewhat offensive, and put it down to lack of interest. 'He is in the habit,' said one of them, 'no matter where he is, of leaving again two hours after his arrival.' He told the astonished scholars that in most cases a single glance was enough to confirm or correct the picture he had formed of the place. The statement was literally true; he was not coming as an investigator, nor even as a tourist, but with the explicit object of establishing the mysterious connection between vision and reality, from which the spark of inspiration springs. Byron spent only twenty-three days of his life in Rome, and yet wrote one of the finest and most perdurable descriptions of the Eternal City that we possess.

A great part of his journey led him through countries under Turkish rule. He does not conceal the fact that the Turks inspired him with horror, but assumes a tone that heralds the philhellenism of the next decades. Greece enslaved, and the Holy Places of Christendom under the feet of unbelievers draw moving complaints from him, many echoes of which are to be heard in the later Romantics. He refused no experience, and exposed himself to every shock that could result from contact with legend and the past. His appreciation of form was aroused most vividly by the sight of the Greek landscape and its antiquities. The pure light of the Parthenon taught him the secret of simple, calm artistic feeling: 'In this home of the Muses nature allows no deviation to appear; she leads the spirit back to the love of quiet, harmonious things.' And in another passage: 'When one has seen the monuments of Rome, those of France look clumsy in comparison; the monuments of Rome, however, look barbaric to me now that I have seen those of Greece.'

In the spring of 1807 he landed in Algeciras and travelled from there to Cadiz. Where was the longed-for meeting with Natalie—now, owing to her father-in-law's death, Duchess of Mouchy? The lovers took care to cover their tracks, writing deceptive letters and doing all they could to prevent their stay in Granada from becoming the subject of Paris gossip. Adrien de Montmorency declared later that he had found the interlaced signatures of the pair on a column in the Alhambra and discreetly effaced them. René is very cautious in his account, he merely declares that he has a wonderful recollection of 'those days of ecstasy, seduction and intoxication'. His tale *The Adventures of the Last of the Abencérages* describes the love of the noble Moor Aben Hamet for Blanca, the beautiful Christian, in whom he paints all Natalie's charms. He delayed the publication of this love story in Granada for nearly twenty years.

THE MOOD OF THE TYRANT

Chateaubriand had had a wonderful journey, and the Emperor was still there. But the adherents of the old Monarchy had not given up all hope. Where Chateaubriand suddenly found the means to purchase the newspaper *Le Mercure* for 20,000 francs, nobody knew. Nobody asked; but it was possible that the Royalists had dipped into their funds in order to give their cause a mouthpiece, and put it at the disposal of the most illustrious spokesman of Legitimism. The funds were there, they did not merely exist in the imagination of Fouché's police, but consisted of fine gold pieces, supplied for the most part by the English government. It was no pleasure to a Frenchman, even if he considered Napoleon's rule to be the regiment of the devil, to be carrying on propaganda with the money of a foreign power. Every attempt to weaken Napoleon militarily—since it did not destroy him—had the immediate result that war was waged with increased intensity, new recruits were levied and sent to the battlefields. But every Frenchman wanted his share in the glory of victory, in return for his share in the blood that was shed. Nobody wanted France to be defeated, even if the defeat of Napoleon was his fondest dream.

The problem was insoluble, it dominated conversation at home and in society. It made itself felt even among the upper class of the Emperor's creation, in which former Jacobins and veterans of the Revolution were opposed to the men who could not but be adversaries of Napoleon and yet had to support his rule 'lest worse should befall'. Fontanes was one of these; he had become 'Grand Master of the University', and had appointed Joubert and Bonald to high offices. Molé, Pasquier and many other figures of equal importance were serving the Emperor in all loyalty, and had the decency not to play a double game. The question that still busied everybody concerned the significance of the Revolution. Had it been a good or a bad thing? No imperial triumph could wash out this alternative, nor even solve it. It constituted an uncertainty that formed a bad foundation for the political shape of the Empire. Was Napoleon's power based on the ruins of the Revolution, or on its institutions? His refusal to give a clear answer constituted the ambiguity of the imperial régime.

Chateaubriand really had no choice. The execution of the Duc d'Enghien had shown him the road he must take in future. If he intended to wield his pen in the service of the Royal cause—and why otherwise should he have bought the *Mercure?*—he would have to content himself with allusions, veiled sarcasm, pertinent comparisons and artifices of that kind. He was not in the fortunate position of his friend Germaine de Staël, who had just published her *Corinne* and was living abroad, where she could express her opinions openly. Meanwhile her son was in Chambéry, waiting for the Emperor, who was on his way back to Paris from Milan. He begged an audience, to soften the great man's attitude towards his mother. Napoleon received him kindly, because it pleased him to see a son defending his mother. He said to the eighteen-year-old youth 'Your mother is not an evil-minded woman, she is intelligent, very intelligent, but she is not used to any form of subjection. If your mother were to be in Paris for six months I should be obliged to shut her up, either in a lunatic asylum or in prison. That would be a nuisance, because that sort of thing causes a stir, and injures me in the public eye. Tell your mother, therefore, that she cannot return to Paris so long as I am alive. She would start some tomfoolery or other, give parties and play tricks. She attaches no importance to such things, but I attach a great deal, I take everything seriously'. At parting he tweaked the young man's ear and said 'Your mother gave you a very ticklish task, which you have carried out very intelligently. I have enjoyed our conversation, but it won't help you'.

So the Emperor was not to be trifled with, and if one was actually living in Paris, where Germaine so longed to be, the opportunities for opposition were very limited. Natalie had by now become an aggressive Royalist, and was urging Chateaubriand to venture a word for the cause. Her brother had just published a book on Spain, the discussion of which gave René a chance to take the field against tyranny: 'When in the silence of subjection only the chains of the slaves and the voice of the denouncer are to be heard, when everything trembles before the tyrant, and it is just as dangerous to attract his favour as to earn his disfavour, then the historian enters the arena, entrusted with the vengeance of the nations. What did Nero's prosperity avail him? Tacitus had already been born in his kingdom.' He extolled the revolt of

Sertorius against Sulla: 'He was defeated, but he had probably never counted on succeeding. He consulted only his duty and the sacredness of the cause he was to defend alone. . . . No doubt the faint-hearted people of Sertorius's day thought it ridiculous for an unknown citizen to fight alone against the whole weight of Sulla. Fortunately posterity judges otherwise the deeds of men: cowardice and vice do not pronounce sentence on courage and virtue.'

The allusion was only too clear. Madame de Chateaubriand, whose judgement was never at fault, and who was fond of foretelling diaster, warned her husband. But he was thoroughly pleased with what he had done, and his success with the reading public justified him. 'One must have lived in those days,' he said later, 'to realize what an effect a single voice crying in the wilderness could produce.' But this number of the *Mercure* had hardly appeared when Napoleon defeated the entire Russian army at Friedland and signed the Treaty of Tilsit with the Tsar. The Emperor returned to Paris in a whirlwind of triumphal rejoicing. Probably he would never have heard of René's rebellious article if Cardinal Fesch, who had not forgotten his experience of René in Rome, had not taken care that he should be acquainted with the text. Napoleon allowed himeslf one of his carefully planned fits of rage, and shouted 'Chateaubriand must think I'm a fool and don't understand what he's driving at. I'll have him cut down with a sabre on the steps of the Tuileries!' Fontanes, who was present, interceded for the poor sinner: 'After all, Sire, his name is an ornament to your reign and it will be mentioned in time to come under your own. He is no conspirator, and can do you no harm, he has nothing but his talent. But that will make him immortal in the history of Napoleon's century. You can't wish people to say later on that Napoleon murdered him, or sent him to prison for ten years.'

The Emperor was not really out for Chateaubriand's blood, especially as the next number of the *Mercure* took a friendly tone towards the Government. But after this he was forced to resign control of the paper and sell it to two individuals nominated by the Government. The take-over proved a splendid stroke of business for him. 'It rained gold,' says Joubert. Obviously the Imperial Government paid a great deal more for the paper than it had cost Chateaubriand. Who knows whether the whole transaction may not have been an opportunity for Napoleon to play the part of Maecenas to a writer whose genius he admired, and whose opposition he did not take too tragically. In the end everybody was satisfied; the *Mercure* would henceforth only sing the praises of the Government; Chateaubriand had been sacrificed as the publisher of an article on 'the mood of the tyrant', but had earned so much money as a result that he could immediately purchase a country house on the outskirts of Paris. His life was taking exactly the direction he desired. As a victim to the good cause he sought solitude and withdrew from the world. But it was an idyllic solitude that awaited him.

IX

ENTIRELY WITHOUT NAPOLEON

THE VALLEY WITHOUT WOLVES

THE 'Wolves' Valley' (La Vallée aux Loups), to which Chateaubriand retired, was only a few hours distant from Paris, not far from Sceaux and Chatenay in a hilly country without much beauty, but peaceful and unspoilt. The condition of the house called for a great deal of repair and some alteration, and as progress proved very slow the couple settled in in November to superintend the work. The house was full of workmen who, after the fashion of their country sang, laughed and kept up a perpetual cheerful din. Two rooms had been made habitable to start with, and here they spent the first night, and saw the sun rise next morning 'with fewer cares than the Lord of the Tuileries'. René took great delight in playing the gardener and the artisan, probably getting in the way of the professionals. In a pair of heavy sabots he stumped about the freshly dug earth, planting the shrubs and young trees presented by his lady admirers for his new estate. These included cedars from Lebanon and Louisiana, a pine from Jerusalem, and other such treasures, the blue-stockings being determined to make the connection between their gifts and his literary work quite plain.

Hammering and painting went on in the house; a 'portico supported by two black marble columns and two caryatids in white marble' was added on, the garden wall was adorned with battlements and the gothic arches of the window-frames were intended to remind people that 'the owner of this residence had opened the churches again and blown the trumpet before the temple'. After a time he removed his study to an octagonal tower standing at a little distance from the house and hidden by trees. Nobody but the Master was to enter this tower, though it is an open question whether he did not permit some discreet lady's visit from time to time. His wife took note of everything and said nothing. Some time later she fitted up a chapel below the study, in the hope that this might deter the master of the house from any profanation of the tower. He accommodated himself politely to this communal life with his wife, although she was entirely incapable of providing him with domestic comfort. This difficult but sharp-sighted lady delighted in saying unpleasant things of other people, a tendency that was patently related to her piety. She preached suspicion of everybody, warned her husband perpetually against his friends, prepared him for the black ingratitude of the Bourbons, foretold the downfall of Napoleon (but prophesied that he would enjoy a long, undisturbed reign whenever she could annoy her company by so doing), accused the workmen of robbery and the gardener, Benjamin, of cheating. Benjamin was forever giving notice, but his master pacified him with 'My poor Benjamin, I don't pay the slightest attention to these torrents of words—and what haven't I to listen to all day long!'

It certainly cannot have been easy to live under the same roof with Chateaubriand as his wedded wife; but as it had been her wish, not his, she had perforce to exercise a degree of patience and resignation that might well account for her spiteful humour. She had friends, however, who enjoyed her sharp wit, and made allowances for the fact that she could not possibly be happy in her situation. The Joubert couple saw a great deal of her, and she was happy in the company of this intelligent man and his admirable wife. Her husband's lady friends caused her a great deal of pain, which vented itself in sarcasm. All these 'ladies' tried to win her favour, constantly sending her little presents and paying her other attentions. Céleste discovered, with malicious pleasure, that ever since Spain Delphine had ceased to play such an important part, and had been relegated to the rank of a 'bosom friend'. Natalie de Noailles, now Duchess de Mouchy, had assumed the first place, still delighting René by her beauty, and charming him yet more by her poetical moods and romantic melancholy. She had an increasing tendency to make scenes, however, but when she fainted and had everybody fussing round her, Chateaubriand did not stir; he went on quietly reading his book, being inured by now to these little dramas.

Despite Céleste's sarcasm at the expense of these women, it must be admitted that René had more than one real friend among them with great qualities of mind. Madame de Lévis and Madame de Bérenger cannot be dismissed offhand, still less the Duchess de Duras, who nursed a kind of unhappy love for him and took all her pleasure in doing him service. Born Claire de Kersaint, she was the daughter of an old Revolutionary who had sat in the Convention, but had been executed for disapproving of the September Massacres in the prisons. Claire was a radiant beauty, and intelligent to boot, but she cherished the sort of exaggerated admiration for Chateaubriand that can irritate even the most conceited of authors. She wooed his regard, and invited him to grand dinner-parties. He refused, of course: 'You are too kind, Madame, but I am really afraid of strangers. I am so shy, that I can never answer for my behaviour. However delighted I might be to spend all the time with you that you allowed me, I should be equally sorry to distress your guests by a long face and silence. Of an evening, especially, I am not of this world.'

Her devoted love touched him, however; he could not but admire her simple, generous nature, free from all artifice. He soon took to calling her his 'sister', and she was to play this honourable but thankless role until her death. Only once did she attempt to stray from this narrow path: she asked him if their friendship did not hurt Natalie's feelings, and elicited this reply: 'What folly, dear sister! Madame de Mouchy knows that I love her and that nothing can separate me from her. She is so sure of me that she neither forbids me to visit you nor to write to you, nor to go to Ussé (where Claire lived) with or without her. If she asked it of me, I should immediately obey her, as I have told you a hundred times. You have never found fault with that, you only like me the better for it. It was she that inspired the *Abencérages*; I am delighted to know it pleases you so much.' The letter is a masterpiece of cruelty; the line is sharply and definitively drawn: Claire is to understand, once for all, that she is, and is to remain, the good,

useful sister, while Natalie is not merely the beloved one but the
Muse. Posterity will adopt other standards, and place Claire above
all of Chateaubriand's 'ladies'.

The house in the Valley of Wolves was now in good condition,
and was beginning to excite the interest of the *literati* as the great
writer's place of refuge. Lamartine, still quite a young man at that
time, made a pilgrimage there with a friend, to take a peep at the
solitary genius. They hid for two whole days in a thick copse to
get a sight of him. At last the door opened: 'Out came a little man
in a black coat, with powerful shoulders, slender legs and a
distinguished head. He was followed by a cat, to which he threw
pieces of bread to make it jump about in the grass. Man and cat
disappeared at once in the shade of an avenue and the bushes hid
them from our sight.' One evening, while Chateaubriand was
away, Benjamin the gardener had some strange visitors. Two men,
one tall and elegant, the other small and simply dressed, begged
permission to look at the Wolves' Valley. Standing in front of the
door, the smaller of the two visitors folded his arms and said
'Chateaubriand is not to be pitied; I could be very happy here
myself'. They looked at the tower, went a little way through the
garden and took their leave. The gardener found a laurel sprig
stuck in the grass, with a new glove beside it. Was it the Emperor's
glove? Nobody would attach much importance to the story, had it
been recorded by Chateaubriand himself, but it is to be found in
his wife's diary.

It was the heyday of his unresting, effortless productivity. *The
Martyrs* and the *Journey from Paris to Jerusalem* had been completed, as well as the—unsuccessful—tragedy of *Moses,* and he
had started on his greatest work of all, the *Memoirs from beyond
the Grave*. Nevertheless he was glad when friends turned up and
dragged him away from his persistent writing. Madame de Boigne,
who was his neighbour for a time, writes: 'The home he had
created for himself was enchanting, and he was very fond of it.
We saw a good deal of one another, we often found him writing
in the drawing-room at a corner of a table, using an old split pen
that he could hardly thrust into the neck of a cheap ink-bottle.
When he caught sight of us going past the window he gave a shout

of joy, shoved his papers under the cushions of an old armchair, which he used as portfolio and secretaire, and came leaping towards us, as delighted as a schoolboy given a holiday.'

After visits of this kind he buried himself again in his documents and texts, working on several books at once, including the *Adventures of the Last of the Abencérages*, which he wrote to the end, although out of consideration for Natalie there could be no question of publishing it for the moment. He was busy, too, with his *Historical Studies*. He loved rummaging through old authorities and displaying his scholarship. His capacity for reading, and for discovering out-of-the-way passages suitable for quotation, was unlimited, and led him not seldom to overburden his own text. This is particularly noticeable in the *Journey from Paris to Jerusalem*, but *The Martyrs* suffers from it too, to say nothing of his actual historical writings.

Did he foresee that these were to rank as the best years of his life? It is unlikely, for although his ennui and his longing for death found little expression at that time—they were never entirely dormant—he was still tormented by the longing for action. He was never able to content himself entirely with his writing; some part of him always remained unfulfilled. His secret nostalgia was concerned with politics, but politics at that time owned only one master, Napoleon, and approach to him was obstructed. Even if he had attempted an approach, Napoleon would not have responded. He had said only lately to Metternich 'There are men that think themselves fit for everything because they possess one quality or one talent. Chateaubriand is one of these: he sides with the Opposition because I won't make use of him. He is the sort of man that argues in the void, but he had a great talent for dialectics. If he would make use of his talent in the direction one suggests to him, he might be useful. But he's not prepared to do that, so he can't be made use of. One must be able either to find one's own way entirely, or to submit to orders. He can do neither the one nor the other, and that makes him useless. He has offered to serve me a score of times, but as he demands that I submit to his fancies, which have always led him astray, I have refused his services.'

This ungenerous and cynical speech does little credit to the Emperor, for Chateaubriand had only once made an offer of his services, and that by way of the dedication of the *Spirit of Christianity*. Moreover, Napoleon still insisted that he had a high opinion of Chateaubriand's literary talent, and a very clear notion of his importance. When he visited the Salon in which the writer's portrait by Girodet was exhibited, he asked to see it. He stood for a long time contemplating the serious face framed in shaggy hair, the almost Napoleonic gesture of the hand thrust into the opening of the waistcoat, the whole arrogant but noble bearing—and ended by saying with his charming smile 'He looks like a conspirator that has just scrambled down the chimney'. There was no actual enmity in his feelings, at most a certain irony, which might sound to the ears of courtiers like a compliment.

As bad luck would have it, a cousin of René's, Armand de Chateaubriand, was arrested at that very time as a spy. The two of them had been close friends in their youth, and there were not many of their name left. René at once attempted to intervene. He remembered that Delphine, whom he had so sadly neglected, was a friend of Fouché, and he persuaded her to go with him to the Minister of Police. But the facts proved as unfavourable as possible. Armand, who was living in England, was one of the poor devils that had allowed themselves to be employed by the English government and the *emigré* princes in secret activities against the Napoleonic régime. Evidence was produced that under the orders of the London Government he had tried to procure a plan of the military harbour of Brest. Sentence of death was inevitable. René did all in his power to help, ended by begging an audience of the Emperor, and remained all that day and the following night in court dress, in case he should be summoned to the Tuileries. All in vain. Early next morning the executioner's cart drove out to the Plain of Grenelles; Chateaubriand arrived just in time to dip his handkerchief in the dead man's blood.

The many enemies he numbered among his so-called friends declared he was taking advantage of the incident to make himself conspicuous, that he was wrathful rather than grieved, and that he was trying to annoy the Emperor by wearing mourning for an

excessively long time. It was part of Chateaubriand's nature to
make an exhibition of the emotions aroused in him by every
stroke of fate, no matter how profound they might really be. In
his self-assumed role of counterpart to Napoleon he identified
himself with poor Armand, who had allowed himself to be mis-
used by unscrupulous people, and had now had to suffer a bitter,
but in no wise arbitrary, death. How could a writer always eager
for visible symbols forgo the blood-drenched handkerchief, the
mourning crêpe on his hat and the black suit? In any case Napoleon
paid little heed to these discreet demonstrations. He had just been
excommunicated by the Pope without injury to his spirits, and was
off to Austria to make up for his Aspern reverse by the victory of
Wagram.

WATCHING THE COMET

The Imperial Court was changing its appearance, it was becoming more solemn and majestic. The old 'regicide' Fouché had
been forced to hand over the Ministry of Police to Savary, the
Catholic dignitaries were coming to the fore, Fontanes had
become a member of the Senate, Pasquier had entered the Council
of State. Once again the French crown was born by a Hapsburg
Empress (the Emperor was careful not to let Marie-Louise be too
often reminded of the origins of the Empire.) The old nobility was
courted more than ever, and did not hold out much longer. Men of
letters too, so Napoleon decided, must have their place at Court,
to sing discreet praises of their lord and master, and convince the
world that he was no barbarian enemy of art. He forgot all his
earlier sarcasm on the subject of these unreliable creatures, and
advised his Minister of Police, who was to supervise public
opinion, to 'treat writers well; they have been prejudiced against
me, and told that I don't like them. This was done with evil intentions. If I hadn't so much to do, I should like to see more of
them. They are useful people whom one must treat with distinction, for they do honour to France.' The trouble with them
was, of course, that the useful ones among them were not easily
won over, and those that were glad to be harnessed had little to

contribute to the country's glory. Chateaubriand would have been extraordinarily useful to the Imperial Court; he belonged to the old nobility, had sung the praises of the Catholic religion, and was the most widely read author in France. His reputation had risen to a fresh peak in recent years; the *Martyrs* and the *Journey to Jerusalem* with their immense editions had proved that he was not, as his enemies had hoped, a man of a single book.

Napoleon was well aware that Chateaubriand's fame had only been increased by his aloof attitude. All the same he took pains to bring about a reconciliation, in the hope that he would at least allow himself to be distinguished without feeling obliged to make formal submission. He tried by every means to have the Academy's grand prize for literature awarded him. This was the opening of a literary-political comedy only possible in France. The Emperor's candidate, as Chateaubriand had paradoxically become, did not receive the prize; his old enemies, Abbé Morellet and Marie-Joseph Chénier, managed to prevent it; they submitted to no pressure, and produced a quantity of evidence that the work they were asked to select, *The Spirit of Christianity*, did not deserve this distinction and was even 'defective'. In short, the Emperor found himself up against not only the independent spirit of French writers but their love of intrigue, and was forced to admit that he could not shake the judgement of these gentlemen. He then tried to get round the Academy in another way, by 'recommending' the rejected writer for the next vacant seat in the Academy itself.

The affair remained in abeyance for the time being, but suddenly there occurred the death of Marie-Joseph Chénier, whose seat thus became vacant. Chateaubriand was to have it, such was the wish of the Emperor, and of Fontanes and other powerful friends. The deceased Chénier, brother to the great poet, had been a mediocre party bard; whoever followed him must, according to regulations, pronounce a euology on him. This prospect did not attract René. Fontanes was once more able to overcome his friend's misgivings, and so it came about that against his own will, but at the desire of the Emperor, whose antagonist he was, he was to solicit a seat in the Academy, which it did not want to give him.

The voting was not impressive, only twenty-three members were present, from whom he obtained thirteen votes only in the second round. The Emperor fancied he had half captured the great writer already, and rubbed his hands for joy at having 'played the Academy a trick', and added, 'I'll see if it isn't possible to give the new member some high appointment, such as the General Directorship of the Imperial Libraries'.

If only it hadn't been necessary to praise the wretched Marie-Joseph Chénier! A Jacobin, who had voted for the death of the King, and written revolutionary hymns of the cheapest sort for Robespierre, while his gifted brother ended his life under the guillotine as the last victim of the Terror! 'It doesn't really matter about praising Chénier,' said Fontanes, 'so long as you celebrate the Emperor, and I know you will do that out of sincere admiration in more than one respect.' But as so often happened, Chateaubriand upset all calculations. He was certainly conceited, and his ambition could be relied on; he was well aware that the Emperor wanted to win him over, and he was not averse from revealing a little of the admiration he felt for the great man. But his loyalty was so ingrained, and of such an almost atavistic ineradicability, that the eulogy turned out a veritable catastrophe. The Emperor came in for his meed of praise, but the condemnation of Chénier was so violent that it amounted to a condemnation of all the men and all the ideas connected with the Revolution. It was many years since such language had been heard, it was the accusatory harangue of an unshakable Legitimist against the enemies of the banished dynasty, of religion and the old traditions.

Napoleon, enraged, scored the text, which had been submitted to him for revision, through and through with cancellations, exclamation marks and furious scribblings. He was pleased with the incense lavished on himself, but he was not going to have 'the whole wrangle over the Revolution starting all over again'. He said to Ségur 'So the men of letters want to set France on fire. I've done everything I could to pacify the parties and re-establish peace. And now the ideologues want to reintroduce anarchy. How can people dare to talk of regicides in the Academy, when I that wear the crown, and ought to hate them most, eat at the

6 Madame de Custine

7 Madame de Beaumont

Right: Madame de Beaumont's tomb in Rome, raised to her memory by Chateaubriand

same table with them!' The manuscript was returned to the writer, who saw the traces of the Imperial reading with secret pride: 'The lion's claws had left their marks all over it, and it gave me an exasperated pleasure to imagine I felt them in my side.' The two great men were very near to each other at that moment, in spite of the incompatibility of their positions. 'I and Napoleon' held the balance with 'I and Chateaubriand.'

The problem of how Chateaubriand was now to take his place under the dome of the Institute proved insoluble. No euology, no seat! But those who tried to persuade him to make alterations did not know his Breton obstinacy. The Academy therefore left the date of the session at which he was to be received unsettled for the moment. 'I'm out of my difficulties for the time being,' he wrote, 'I have refused unequivocally to write another speech. I don't know whether they will strike me off the list. All that is certain is that I haven't the right to attend the session. I don't think anything will happen to me.'

Nothing did happen to him, either good or bad. He returned to his hermitage in the Wolves' Valley, enjoyed the success of his latest books, the *Martyrs* and the *Journey to Jerusalem*, and spun the threads of his 'main concern', as Goethe would have called his Memoirs, which were now beginning to assume a distinct shape. So he was not destined to play any public role? So long as the Emperor was in power—and he seemed more firmly established than ever—he would have to live on his dreams, without intruding into the world of action. But even the greatest literary success could be no consolation for this. He wandered at night, deep in thought, among his trees, gazing at the great comet of the year 1811: 'It was beautiful and sad, and trailed a long veil behind it like a queen.'

There were still plenty of 'ladies' to gather round him:
'After the reading, tea was brought in.
' "Monsieur de Chateaubriand, will you have some tea?"
' "Yes, please, I'd like some very much."
'There was an immediate echo all round the drawing-room:
' "My dear, he'd like some tea."
' "He wants tea!"

M

' "Give him tea!"

' "He's asking for tea!"

'And ten ladies bustled about to serve their idol.'

Madame de Boigne was certainly a very malicious chronicler. Moreover, she occasionally confused unusual words. Napoleon, in his attack on Chateaubriand, had spoken of ideologues, not idealists. But that does not excuse the sharpness of her sentence upon a great writer whose friend she declared herself to be: 'He (the Emperor) numbered Monsieur de Chateaubriand among the idealists, in which he was wrong. Chateaubriand had not the slightest sympathy with humanity. He was always preoccupied with himself alone, and sought to create a pedestal for himself, from which to rule over his century. Such a place was difficult to create alongside of Napoleon, but he worked at it without interruption. He was successful to this extent, that he could always create a little sphere for himself, of which he was the sun. When he deserted it, he was so painfully affected by the outer air that he became insufferably bad-tempered; but as long as he remained within it nobody could be more amiable than he, or distribute his rays with more charm. If only he had been content to be a writer, for which his uncommonly artistic temperament best suited him, one would have known none but his good, lovable impulses. But his ambition to be a statesman drew him into other spheres, where his badly received pretensions released a flood of evil passions in him. Chateaubriand had a subtle instinct for the situation of the moment. He had two or three principles, which he clothed according to each situation in such a way as to make them almost unrecognizable. With these he got himself out of every difficulty, and declared he was always consistent. This came all the easier to him in that his genial spirit was not restrained by any sort of moral consideration. He believed in nothing in the world except his talent—an altar to him, before which he was always on his knees.'

The description is so spiteful that one is inclined to look for some hidden reason. Madame de Boigne's analysis does unquestionably contain a grain of truth, but a clever woman who, as she herself confesses, shed tears when René read aloud from his tale of *The Last of the Abencérages*, at Madame de Ségur's, must have been secretly wounded in some way, to expose the writer so mercilessly. In her memoirs, which became famous later under the title *Tales of an Aunt*, she denies violently that she ever belonged to the circle of his female admirers. Perhaps Chateaubriand's way of ignoring any woman in whom he detected an internal resistance to his pretensions, had annoyed her more than she cared to admit. She refused to be reckoned among the circle of ladies at any price, which would be quite understandable in that case.

The ravishing Natalie seems not to have belonged to the circle any longer, or at any rate to have kept further away from it. Her moods, which at first seemed no more than romantic fantasies, and had held a certain attraction for her admirer, gradually developed into distortions of fact that could only be attributed to nervous disturbances. René was no doubt a man born to evoke scenes and bring feminine outbursts upon himself; he possessed the gift of remaining very quiet and amiable meanwhile and facilitating the reconciliation, which was usually of a tender nature. Was he fond of these scenes? Did he count them among the 'longed-for-storms' that his hero and namesake called up? At any rate his experiences with poor Natalie must have far exceeded the measure of little vexations that a lover is prepared to accept. There were days when Natalie's lovely face stared at him with the grimace of insanity. He wrote to Claire de Duras, his selfless, discreet confidante, 'In the Rue Cerutti (where Natalie lived) the storms have blown up again. Yesterday I was given my formal dismissal and I accepted it, for after all there are limits to everything. I don't know whether I shall ever be recalled; what is certain is that I've had enough of it.'

And later: 'Everything is the same in the Rue Cerutti. I've been recalled, but nothing is altered, nor can be altered any more. I've given everything I possessed, and there is not a trace left of all that formed part of the happiness and sorrow of my life. I fancy I may be the better off for this, although rather sadder. But time passes quickly, and carries me along with all my frailties and follies.'

But for Natalie de Noailles, Duchesse de Mouchy, time did not fly with the same speed, although—as her friends noticed with uneasiness—her pace on walks and in the street was becoming faster and faster till it almost amounted to a run. Since her rupture with Chateaubriand she had of course ceased to frequent the circle of the 'ladies'; she spent solitary days in her apartment, brooding, writing and painting. She was bored to a dangerous degree, because she wished to be bored; what was equally alarming, she had begun to neglect her appearance.

Adrien de Montmorency befriended her for a time, but his pious, sober temperament was soon at variance with her disturbing moods. Molé, who was not unused to consoling women that had separated from Chateaubriand, looked after her too for a few years. When Benjamin Constant's famous novel *Adolphe* appeared, he read some of it to her: 'One could see that she was affected by bitter memories, and concealed many secrets more oppressive than the despairing revelations of Constant's pen.' This wonderful creature, endowed with a thousand gifts, was slowly destroying herself, travelling about the country from hotel to hotel, from health resort to health resort, talking of nothing but her health, and of death, which she saw perpetually in front of her. She lived a few years in this state, until her fear of poison developed into persecution mania, and she had finally to be shut up, since her mental derangement could no longer be concealed.

Claire de Duras took upon herself a delicate task. She wrote to Chateaubriand (1817) telling him that Natalie's disease was incurable. He replied in a very typical way, as though the catastrophe had befallen himself rather than the poor woman: 'Oh my God! Poor Natalie! What a fate pursues me! Haven't I told you that everyone I have ever known and loved has gone mad, and that is how I shall end as well. What wouldn't I do and give to see Mouche happy! In spite of all the happiness she gave me I can do nothing for her. Dear Sister, what miserable, powerless things are our human friendships!' Yet the man that wrote this was to enjoy the most lasting and devoted friendship that has ever existed between man and woman, his friendship with Juliette Récamier.

Meanwhile the circle of 'ladies' was still in force—or rather, in his service. The Duchesse de Duras herself—the 'faithful sister' —the Duchesse de Lévis, Madame de Bérenger, formerly Duchesse de Chatillon, Madame de Montmorency, wife of Adrien, later Duc de Laval, and Madame Octave de Ségur formed a ring round the writer and shut him off from the outer world as much as he allowed them to. He allowed them to do a lot of things on his behalf because he knew the value of their friendship. The ladies were no blue-stockings, but all without exception very intelligent people, and great ladies into the bargain, high up on the social ladder, with an abundance of ideas, habits, prejudices, traditions and social forms in common with Chateaubriand, who never lost sight of the fact that he, too, was a Vicomte. Often referred to as 'the duchesses', they lived in great style, had been carefully brought up, and were used to mixing on an equal footing with important, highly-placed personalities. Besides which, they had time and capacity for a great deal of reading, a great deal of conversation and a great deal of hospitality. He did not disdain to make use of their influence, entrust them with a thousand little errands—often greater ones too—and allow them to provide and arrange many things in which he was not anxious to play a visible part.

Claire de Duras was particularly tireless in her efforts to please him and to use her feminine diplomacy in his interest; but he repaid all these benefactresses with genuine friendship. He showed them the best side of himself, and gave them to understand that a great writer prefers mixing with women rather than men, because women are more sensible, more tactful and less plagued by envy. Women were glad of his success, men were jealous of it; besides which they were slower in the uptake, and did not satisfy his sense of beauty. Madame de Boigne was probably not the only woman to ridicule and censure him, but of the 'ladies' not one has left a censorious, disappointed or even merely cold reference to him.

It must be said, however, that he was not the man for friendly intimacy. It gave him no satisfaction to open his heart and become confidential; nobody could boast of having penetrated to his inner self; all the expressions of sadness and ennui that he let fall were always clothed in a general form. His thoughts were constantly occupied with tombs, ruins and other witnesses to human decay, but he appeared to be entrenching himself behind these things so as not to have to talk about his own state of mind. 'I am enjoying complete freedom, and ask for nothing but solitude and peace. The passion now ruling my heart, after so many others, is for my garden. When one grows old one must have something to talk about, good or bad.' Claire de Duras behaved like the majority of women in such cases; for all her cleverness, she did not realize the great mental benefit his retirement offered him; she thought he ought to 'mix with people', so as not to lose touch with 'life'. He explained to her gently that life did indeed consist of human beings, but not necessarily of intercourse with them, and that he bore the highest form of reality within himself.

His retirement may also have been due in part to his eternal lack of money. Where his not inconsiderable receipts as an author disappeared to, nobody knew, least of all his wife, who, though admittedly a very virtuous person, had hardly any more sense of order than himself. Both of them dispensed charity on a grand scale, and for those wishing to inaugurate collections, or even merely to beg, the Chateaubriands' house was a lucrative address. The couple themselves seldom lacked superfluities, but necessaries often. Claire de Duras was a reliable support here too. She was the only one of the 'ladies' that Madame de Chateaubriand treated in a friendly manner, and she was able to take the money affairs of the household in hand as well. She not seldom contributed a thousand francs out of her own pocket; at other times she founded a sort of joint-stock company, to which various friends contributed a certain sum, to be covered by the rights of René's next book. Claire's name always headed the list of these 'shareholders', but Adrien de Montmorency took shares, and so did the Comte de Tocqueville, whose son, the future author of *Democracy in America*, was then just seven years old. A few of the 'ladies' also took part in this not very lucrative business, as did the author's two nephews: 'If my nephews contribute four thousand francs, I can easily find another two thousand among my own family.

There would then be a further six thousand to raise from you and other friends. That shouldn't be difficult. In that way I should have twelve thousand francs a year and could live like a grand gentleman.'

He was now forty-four years old, and considered himself an aged man, or at least so he declared: 'My forehead is growing bald, I'm beginning to babble, I'm bored with myself. The fever will seize me, and one morning I shall be carried off to Chatenay. Who will remember me? Can you say, dear sister? A few old books that I shall leave behind, and that nobody reads, will provoke a little controversy after my departure; some people will say they are worthless, and as dead as myself; others will declare there's something in the rubbish; they'll close the book and go off to dine, dance, weep.'

But the controversy started in his lifetime. His enormous literary successes provoked not only imitations and parodies but refutations and personal polemics. His youthful *Essay on Revolutions* was dug up by antagonists in order to demonstrate that the illustrious defender of Christianity had once attacked religion after the manner of the 'Philosophers'. To vindicate himself, he wanted to have the whole book reissued; but the Censor forbade it. This made him so angry that he openly attacked the Imperial institutions; upon which his friend Prefect Pasquier was ordered to banish him for a few days to Dieppe. A peculiar form of disciplinary punishment! René went off to the coast and remained obediently—under police observation, that is—for a short time in the little fishing town, only too delighted to see the sea once more. It was still summer, but the sea gave a hint of autumnal storms to come. It was the year 1812, Napoleon had long ago crossed the Niemen, he had entered the deserted town of Smolensk, and was now facing the great city of Moscow. The towers and domes of this strangely silent city lay spread out before him under a pale September sun.

THE RETURN OF THE LILIES

The golden and gilded glory of the Imperial era was slowly

fading. France's pride in the victories was counterbalanced, bit by bit, by the huge expense of blood and treasure. Even those Frenchmen that considered themselves enemies of the Emperor had so far thought it quite natural that French troops should invade one country after another and plunder it. Most of them had even nursed a secret conviction that this system of exploitation must actually benefit these foreign countries, simply because it was carried out by the French. There was a time when they thought the Spanish, who let themselves be hacked to pieces rather than submit to the charm of the French soldiery, must be simply mad. Only very slowly did the idea dawn on them that foreign rule, whether exercised by Napoleon or anyone else, was a hated burden on the nations. French pride was injured: 'What! They don't want us—us the most glorious and irresistible of mankind?' The revelation was a bitter one, and the blame for this incomprehensible change in world opinion was laid on Napoleon, whose luck was beginning to desert him.

This time the Allies were determined to pursue the struggle until the Emperor was overthrown. Out of the ruins of the *Grande Armée,* which had perished in the snows of the Russian steppes ('they were mostly foreigners!' he had said by way of excuse), Napoleon had formed fresh units and replenished them with eighteen-year-old recruits, whom he inspired, as usual, with his dynamic force. He defeated the Russians and the Prussians, but he had come up against such an entirely new fighting spirit that he was alarmed. Something new had come over the world; it was seizing the nations; the soil on which the victor of forty battles had erected monuments to his uniqueness, had begun to quake. The Austrians joined the Allies; in October 1813 the Emperor was defeated at Leipzig and forced to retreat.

While France was awaiting the entry of the Allied troops, Chateaubriand started to write. He thought it urgent to prepare the country for the end of the régime and the return of the Bourbons. A generation was growing up, which no longer knew anything of the old dynasty. The twenty-year-olds hardly even knew the name of the illustrious family that had ruled France for centuries, and whose last crowned head had fallen to the guillotine of the Revolution. Chateaubriand had no illusions on the score of the present representatives of the dynasty; he knew their weaknesses, their lack of realism and their arrogance, which forbade them to face the reality of the last twenty years of French history. He saw quite clearly that they had neither the will nor the capacity to bring about an appeasement in the country. He knew, too, that there was nothing in his own personality to inspire the future king with the slightest liking for him, in spite of which he yielded to the upsurge of a loyalty founded on inherited emotions rather than on mature consideration.

His famous essay, completed while Napoleon was still in power, is entitled *From Buonaparte to the Bourbons*. The part concerned with the Bourbons is peculiarly reserved; the author does not attempt to suggest the return of the King and the régime connected with him as the ideal solution: he refrains from representing legitimate monarchy as an institution axiomatically superior to all others; he contents himself with the statement: 'Only the Bourbons can cope with our unfortunate situation today, they are the only physicians that can heal our wounds.' And further: 'Their mere presence will suffice to revive the condition of order, the principle of which they represent.' He treats Napoleon mercilessly, he has not a good word to say for him: nothing in this attack on a great man nearing ruin would suggest that in a few years' time the author would write the finest and fairest pages about him that French literature possesses. The mere spelling—Buonaparte—augurs a not very magnanimous treatment of the adversary to whom he had once dedicated *The Spirit of Christianity*. 'Absurd in administration, criminal in politics—how did he, this foreigner, contrive to seduce the French?' He ended, nevertheless, on a conciliatory note: 'Frenchmen, Friends, Companions in misfortune, let us forget our quarrels. Let the cry that can save us be heard on every side, the cry that our fathers sounded in misfortune as in victory, which shall be for us the signal of peace and happiness: Long live the King!'

It is the first of the many political diatribes with which Chateaubriand intervened in contemporary events, but it is certainly not the most attractive. The reminder of Napoleon's foreign origins was more worthy of a narrow-minded Breton aristocrat than of a great critic of his times. And another characteristic of the author comes to light in the essay, namely his contempt for the masses. Speaking of the Revolution, he refers scornfully to the populace of the capital as the kings of their epoch, and thus describes their appearance on the stage of the Revolution: 'Then out of their hiding-places appeared all these half-naked kings, filthy, stupefied by poverty, disfigured and emaciated by their labour, with no virtue save their shamelessness and their pride in their rags.' This comparison of the poor to a rabble is repellent, and shows that Chateaubriand had never asked himself how it came about that in a rich country like France, at the outbreak of the Revolution, that is to say still under the Monarchy, people could go about in rags. It was still a far cry to the slogan 'On your knees to the worker!', that he was to hear before he died, but in any case he would always regard the masses as a force hostile to his nature and to his existence. The emergence of the machine age strengthened this feeling in him; he forsaw that 'Every individual will be a mere bee, a wheel in a machine, an atom in an organized material'.

It was the last winter under the sign of the Imperial Eagle. The Chateaubriands had rented an apartment in the newly-built Rue de Rivoli, with a view of the Tuileries and its gardens. The street was far from being completed; the Arcades were up, but there were as yet only a few houses behind them, separated from one another by pleasant gardens. The polemical essay was ready, but Napoleon's police were still active, and the manuscript had to be kept carefully hidden. At night René laid it under his pillow; during the day Madame de Chateaubriand concealed the compromising package in the pocket of one of her numerous petticoats. The text was taken to the printer piecemeal, and at a time when the distant thunder of cannon could already be heard in the capital, it was printed sheet by sheet in the utmost secrecy. But events outstripped it: the gunfire came even nearer; through the city gates, in utter confusion, poured a flood of fugitives, Russian prisoners and wounded French soldiers. The recruits enlisted in the provinces marched in endless columns through the capital at night, on their way to the front; along the outer boulevards the baggage wagons and the heavy guns of the artillery rolled through the darkness.

The war was approaching the barriers of the city gates, the legendary Cossacks could be seen on their little lean horses, with their long lances, swarming up and disappearing again as if they were playing a game. The Prussians appeared on Montmartre; the first shells burst on the Boulevard du Temple, Maréchal Moncey despatched some of the National Guard to the barrier of Clichy, where they fought valiantly and suffered grievous losses. The last heoes of all were the hundred and fifty Polytechnic students, hardly more than boys, posted as gunners in the old-fashioned fortifications of Vincennes. They were entirely surrounded by the enemy, and refused to surrender. The huge Russian grenadiers flung their arms round the powder-blackened lads, some of them wounded, 'and restored them, bleeding, to their mothers, with cries of victory and admiration'. On the day of the capitulation, while the victors began their entry into the capital, the essay *From Buonaparte to the Bourbons* made its appearance with the sub-title 'Of the necessity of attaching ourselves to our legitimate princes for the salvation of France and of Europe'.

From the Butte de Chaumont the victors looked down on the great city; they could as yet see little of the scattered engagements, and they took a long look at the life below them, which appeared to be going on untroubled. The Tsar was in the best of humours, and drew the attention of the gloomily gazing King of Prussia to the Parisian ladies promenading the streets, all carefully dressed and adorned. While the guns still thundered at the barriers, the womenfolk were taking their daily exercise, armed with their fans and parasols. In the afternoon the population streamed in vast crowds to the suburbs to catch a glimpse of the odd-looking foreigners taking possession of the 'Capital of the World'. Would these monarchs avenge themselves, and make the French suffer for all the Emperor and his troops had done to them? Parisian opinion on the subject was much divided; people were not yet sure whether they should stick to their tricolour

cockade or provide themselves with the white badge of the
Bourbons. They were all of them soon agreed that the victorious
enemy would feel much honoured at being allowed to ride
through the streets of Paris, and, as Béranger said, 'present
himself to Clovis's city, hat in hand'. The Parisians were not
disappointed in their expectation.

Hesitation was short-lived. When King Louis XVIII entered
Paris in May, the population could not rummage out enough white
material to display their loyal enthusiasm with flags, banners,
kerchiefs, ribbons and rosettes. 'Even white petticoats were cut
up to make cockades,' wrote Madame de Chateaubriand, who
could not find words to express her bitter contempt of the
vacillating Parisians' inconstancy. Chateaubriand himself watched
the drama of the reversal with mixed feelings; he had sought the
Emperor's downfall, but he could not be blind to the fact that the
fallen Emperor had taken all sense of greatness with him into exile.

He was present at the King's entry, and took particular notice
of the troops lining the route. His new Majesty having refused to
be received by foreign troops, although they alone had restored
him to the throne, a regiment of the Old Guard, the flower of
Napoleon's army, had been drawn up. 'I do not think,' writes
Chateaubriand, 'that human faces can ever before have expressed
anything so terrible or so threatening. These battle-scarred grenadiers, conquerors of Europe, smelling of fire and gunpowder, these
men that had been robbed of their leader, were forced—since they
were under the control of an army of Russians, Austrians and
Prussians in Napoleon's occupied capital—to salute an old king,
an invalid of time, not war. Some of them wriggled their scalps
till their bearskins fell over their eyes, others drew down the
corners of their mouths in furious disdain, and others showed
their teeth through their moustaches like tigers. When they
presented arms they did it with a furious jerk, and the clatter of
the weapons made one shiver. One must admit that no men have
ever before been exposed to such a trial and suffered such torture.
At the rear of the column rode a young hussar with a bared sabre
in his hand, which with a convulsive movement of fury he
seemed to be swinging in a dance. He was pale, his eyes were

rolling in their sockets, he kept alternately opening and shutting his mouth, gnashing his teeth and suppressing cries of which only the first sound was audible. He caught sight of a Russian officer, and the look he threw him cannot be described. When the King's carriage drove past he made his horse rear, and there could be no doubt that he was attempting to fling himself upon the King.'

REACTIONARIES AMONG THEMSELVES

Restoration: the term signified merely the re-establishment of the old dynasty. The fact that many people took it to mean the re-establishment of former conditions as well, gives this period, which began with the entry of Louis XVIII into Paris, an atmosphere of ambiguity. It was a time of disappointment, revenge, purges that violated the dignity of public life, and much stupidity, but it was also a time in which great things were accomplished; it brought genuine piety to a fresh birth, helped the arts to prosper, and enriched political thought by an unavoidable preoccupation with constitutional ideas. People were not happy in those days; they enjoyed, it is true, more external peace than ever before, they benefited by a distinct decline in warfare, and were no longer burdened with military undertakings, the object of which had no place in their lives; but conditions had degenerated, so to speak, overnight. Pride in being Frenchmen shrivelled up, the external signs of national triumph grew pale, national pride, the exploitation of which had served Napoleon so well, had nothing left to feed on. The general population, which had been obliged to make great sacrifices under the Empire, had been psychologically pampered. There would be no more of that; the effrontery of the ruling class would no longer be moderated by the system of promotion. It was Chateaubriand's fate to play a leading part— to be obliged to do so—in this contradictory and most unpleasant era. He had both admired and opposed the great usurper, but the mediocre Bourbons, whom he did not love, and whose personal characters he found highly displeasing, he served with devotion and loyalty. This was the flaw in his political life; he was entirely consumed by the conflict, it made such demands on him that his literary career may be said to have come to an end with the beginning of the Restoration.

The Restoration was interrupted by the mad, sad adventure of the Hundred Days. Napoleon came back to France, as if he had left something behind and wanted to fetch it. But he discovered that he had gone too far. The French do not care to have great men intruding in their affairs too thoroughly or for too long. They will gladly accept the benefit to their *amour-propre*, but they are sensitive to any affront to their human sense of proportion. Just as the Bourbons reached back into the past for the anointing oil in the sacred ampulla of Rheims, Napoleon attempted to re-invoke the spirit of the Revolution and of *La Patrie en danger*, but this interruption of the Restoration, as will be seen, could not last long. For the moment, the Bourbons did not stir a finger to win over the people, they were content disdainfully to ignore everything that had happened since 1789, from the storming of the Bastille to the Emperor's victories. Talleyrand, the shrewdest of all the men that had turned their backs on Napoleon's cause at the right moment, and prepared the Restoration, declared that the Bourbons 'had forgotten nothing and learnt nothing'. Tsar Alexander was of the same opinion, he confided to Caulaincourt that the Bourbons 'had not improved and were incapable of improving'.

The Court actually behaved worse than the King, who though a lazy man, was undoubtedly an intelligent one. They could not understand why the new form of government should be so minutely discussed and debated. 'I can't see the use of all this pother,' drawled one of them, 'surely it would be enough to decree that everything is to be the same as before 1792!' The atmosphere of the Court soon determined that of Society. 'The rabble must sweat blood!' shouted the King's favourite, the Duc de Blacas. He and his kind did not realize to what extent the 'rabble' had attained a sense of dignity since the Revolution, that was independent of material conditions. The 'rabble' had not fared well during the Revolution or under Napoleon, but public affairs had come within reach of the individual; he felt a certain responsibility for them, and referred them to his own life not only in a material, but also in a moral sense. The Revolution had developed in the Frenchman a sensitive pride in his power of judgement. Nothing angered him more than to be taken by those in power for a gullible fool, prepared to swallow every false theory and every palliative. He was well aware that public life could not be carried on without lies, and was even prepared to concede their usual privileges to the ruling class, but this derisive sufferance ceased as soon as he discovered that people were reckoning on his gullibility.

Chateaubriand had no illusions as to what the future held in store; Talleyrand, not himself, was lord of the hour, lodging Tsar Alexander in his private palace and discussing with him the manner in which France was to be ruled in future. Chateaubriand was convinced that his essay *From Buonaparte to the Bourbons* had done more to bring the King back to the throne than an army of a hundred thousand men. The essay did find an important echo, the influential *Journal des Débats* constantly referred to it, and called the author 'the Tacitus of today'. That the men at the head of affairs, who were discussing the destiny of the country, were of the same opinion, may be doubted. Chateaubriand was granted an audience of the Tsar, in whose hands lay the most important decisions of the moment, but in the *salon* in which he was left to wait he found a writer of the name of Etienne, one of whose plays Alexander had seen the evening before. The Tsar appeared, said a few kind words to Etienne about his play, and then turned to Chateaubriand, saying that he had not yet found time to read his essay, adding that 'writers should content themselves with amusing the public, and not play with politics', and leaving the room before Chateaubriand could open his mouth.

The King's brother, the Comte d'Artois, later Charles X, had entered the city ahead of the King and been met by a number of noblemen on horseback, Chateaubriand among them. Artois, very distinguished and elegant in appearance, but without the intelligence of his gout-ridden brother, and arrogant to an almost comical degree, had paid the author a few compliments on his essay, and then hurried off to Talleyrand's house, to dine there with Caulaincourt. Think of it! At last one of the 'Princes' had come, for whom so many brave men had sacrificed their happiness and their life, and with whom did he eat his first meal? With the old Royalist, with the honourable remains of the Chouannerie? No, indeed, but with Talleyrand the apostate Christian, the ex-Bishop of Autun, and with Caulaincourt, who had taken part in the plot to kidnap the Duc d'Enghein, and was still loyal to the Emperor!

While Chateaubriand, as he tells us, was waiting in the street under the windows of Talleyrand's palace to be called up and asked for his advice, the future Charles X was receiving the detested Fouché, whose days every sensible man now believed to be counted. Napoleon's Prefect of Police, Pasquier, remained in office, the valiant Fontanes, who had after all been one of the great dignitaries of the Empire, was appointed Grand Master of the University. To the Comte d'Artois, whom he waited upon on this occasion, he said 'Monseigneur, we have been through some hard times', which was certainly the most diplomatic remark possible at that moment. Artois could not contradict him, and looked kindly at him with his somewhat prominent eyes.

'As for us poor devils of Legitimists,' grumbled Chateaubriand, 'we were not admitted anywhere. We were not considered of any value. At one moment people said publicly that we should do better to go to bed, at another we were recommended not to shout "Vive le roi!" too loudly, because other people had already been given the job.' To be able to attend the first Reception at Court, he had to get the *Journal des Débats* to send him there as a reporter. He was loyal enough to describe the King as a figure that commanded respect. Other eye-witnesses were less merciful; they referred to the undignified swarm of people that had just discovered their royalist hearts and wanted to be at hand when the first signs of favour began to rain down. Marshals Mormont and Ney were particularly surrounded; they were legendary figures, and badly needed because nobody could be sure of the army.

The King was quiet, rather bored, and in ill health as well. His legs were so swollen that he could only use them with difficulty; he had clothed them in gaiters of red velvet. A spectator, less respectful than Chateaubriand, said 'The King looks like

8 Chateaubriand's house in the Vallée aux Loups.

9 Madame Récamier

something between an old woman and a eunuch'. The description appears to have been a good one, but the 'helpless old man', as he called himself, had more than this to his credit; he possessed tact, dignity, and an ineradicable consciousness of his 'divine rights'. This was all the more remarkable in that he was obliged, as a constitutional monarch, to rule through a Constitution. He accepted the 'Charter' without conviction, but he had such a keen sense of what was possible and necessary at any given moment that he merely opposed a dissenting gesture to the pressure of irreconcilable courtiers such as the Duc de Blacas. These people wanted the strictest discipline imposed on all who had not emi-grated 'in those days', but the King was shrewder than these die-hards. He was not without arrogance himself, though this was mitigated by his perpetual fatigue, but he made no secret of it that the 'Ultras', as the advocates of the old absolutism were called, irritated him. The Constitution was unavoidable, for—alas, alas— the world had greatly changed.

The reactionary claims with which the King was perpetually plagued could not, therefore, be fulfilled, but insolence afforded some compensation. Not a day passed without the narrow-minded effrontery of the Court and nobility leading to incidents. Their class had waited two decades for the Restoration—often in ad-verse circumstances—dreaming hourly of the day when they would come into their rights again. Now the day had arrived, and they were asked to be considerate, to shut one eye, spare people's feelings, and even tolerate talk of the 'glorious Eagles' and the 'achievements of the Revolution!' No wonder, then, if clashes and wrangles were the order of the day. Only when they were quite among themselves, in certain aristocratic drawing-rooms and private circles, could they entertain one another with the ab-solutely inexhaustible subject of their relations, and picture to themselves how the 'rabble' would have to sweat blood if things were properly ordered.

Strict Legitimist though he was, Chateaubriand could not but shake his head over the behaviour of the Court. His aim was to re-establish the 'moral unity' of the country. His authority was great, as he realized with satisfaction when one day, in the *salon*

N

of Madame Récamier, who with her gentle grace was able to make friend and foe agree, he read aloud a fragment from his *Last of the Abencérages*. Society people of every description gathered round him to listen: hard-boiled reactionaries, just returned from England with the Princes to what was to them an unknown world, humiliated adherents of Napoleon, incorrigible Republicans, Russian officers, Prussian diplomats and Austrian Counts, all united by Juliette Récamier's conciliatory smile, listening to the author, who possessed such a masterly gift for reading his own prose. Everybody agreed, under Juliette's discreet leadership, that they had touched the intellectual core of France.

But Chateaubriand wanted to exert a political, not a literary influence. He was annoyed because he had not been called to the Committee for the elaboration of the Charter, in which Fontanes had the greatest say. When the list of newly created Peers of France appeared, he looked in vain for his own name. His wife shared his indignation at this contemptuous treatment of a man who had done so much for religion and for the Legitimist Party. 'It was hateful,' she writes, 'the way those men were treated that had suffered most for the cause of the Bourbons. When my husband saw that all the posts were being distributed, he thought he was entitled to know if he was also to be called upon to serve the masters to whom he had sacrificed fortune, honour and repose. Monsieur de Blacas refused every request.' Blacas was decidedly very narrow-minded, and ruthless to boot, for when it was pointed out to him that, now the *emigrés* were returning, Chateaubriand would have to emigrate in his turn if he was not provided with the means of living in France in a manner suitable to his importance, he retorted 'Then let him leave the country!' Madame de Chateaubriand referred to him ever after as 'that impudent valet'.

Fortunately there was Claire de Duras, the 'dear sister', whose husband had now been given an important post at Court. Claire, who considered it her life's work to protect Chateaubriand and give his political ambition opportunity to materialize, was distressed to discover that her offended friend and the no less offended Céleste were actually thinking of going to Switzerland. She resolved to act, and hurried off to Talleyrand, who was of course Minister for Foreign Affairs again. He listened with the politest attention to Claire's complaints of the neglect with which Chateaubriand had been treated, and exclaimed with well-simulated astonishment 'Good gracious! I supposed Monsieur de Chateaubriand hadn't been given anything because he didn't want anything!' The two of them then discussed what could be done for the great man. All ambassadorial posts had already been given away, except Constantinople and Sweden. Chateaubriand chose Sweden, and received his appointment from the hands of the King, who, well aware that the post was no brilliant one, added apologetically 'It's no more than a ring that I'm giving you'. He was no doubt glad to rid himself of the writer; as a dyed-in-grain man of the eighteenth century, a Voltairian imbued with classical scepticism, he could not but be bored with this Romantic, with his wild head of hair, his historical allusions and grandiose meta-phorical language.

The Constitution had been very hastily drawn up; several questions, among them the voting system, had been left open. Comte Beugnot wrote the preamble, which the King had not even read for lack of time when the whole thing came into force. The word 'Charter' had been chosen instead of 'Constitution', because it had its origin in the old régime, and thus implied that it re-presented 'a voluntary creation on the part of the King, by the free exercise of the royal authority'. It was at the same time a relatively modern instrument; it contained no axiomatic denial of liberty or equality, and guaranteed the people a share, albeit a limited one, in the government. The census of the electorate created a privileged class, as far as the right to vote was concerned, from which commoners without means were excluded. This meant that the Charter reduced the number of voters to 90,000, of which only 12,000 were eligible.

The Charter, which the King had agreed to with difficulty, had the misfortune to satisfy nobody. In the eyes of the 'Ultras' it was a fatal concession to the Revolution, while the self-styled In-dependents asserted that it did not go far enough. These formed the right and left wings of the Chamber, while in the middle sat the distinguished group of the Friends of the Constitution, who took the view that the Charter, provided it was loyally implemented, would be a reasonable solution.

Parties were thus formed, which fell upon one another with astonishing violence, and seemed disinclined for any reasonable co-operation. The internal peace of the country was therefore not ensured, and old Carnot, who had sent a friendly message from Antwerp on the return of the Bourbons, wrote a letter to the King in which he referred to the feeling in the country, and reminded him that public opinion was now a force that even the Crown could not afford to ignore. The letter became known through an indiscretion; an answer seemed urgently required, and the King was therefore glad when Chateaubriand composed a reply, which was less a reply than a summons to all Frenchmen to accept the Charter and achieve internal peace under its aegis.

It was an excellent document, one of the best political texts that Chateaubriand ever wrote. The King was very pleased with it, and felt thankful not to have to pay any further attention to Carnot's warnings. This success whetted the writer's appetite for a better appointment. Sweden? That was rather wide of the mark for a man that felt himself called to influence the course of events. He wrote to the ever helpful Claire 'The King was so pleased that he sent me thanks through the Chancellor and the Minister of Police. The former sent me word that the King wished to entrust me with something else. Do all you can, therefore, to enable me to stay here. It is clear now that I am about the only writer the public will listen to. Why should the government deprive itself of a weapon that is in its hands?' The King gave him the Cross of Saint-Louis, and appointed him colonel of cavalry, which gave him the right to wear a large sabre. But the pen was more useful, after all; he had now to reach unity: 'May love for King and country, may loyalty to the Constitution form the foundation of our convictions henceforth. It is true that we have lost a great deal through the Revolution, but have we not also gained a great deal? Shall twenty years count for nothing? Have so many heroic deeds, so much magnificent devotion no importance? Let us then cease to slander one another, let us set an example of courage and justice, as we have set an example of glory.'

This was obviously the right language at a critical moment. Chateaubriand's admission that the Revolution and the Napoleonic era had had some good in them showed his political sense, but it annoyed the Ultras. They rummaged in his past and dug up the *Essay on Revolutions,* while a certain Monsieur Bail wrote a pamphlet pointing to the existence of an edition of *The Spirit of Christianity* dedicated to Napoleon. Madame Bail, however, paid a visit to Chateaubriand to beg his pardon on her husband's behalf. She was very pretty, and did her best to make up for her husband's aspersions by a little infidelity. Chateaubriand was no monster; they parted good friends. But the incriminating quotations were now in circulation and had come to the ears of the King: there could be no question of a higher post for the moment. The author spent a few days in the Valley of Wolves, and gave himself up to his daydreams. To Claire he wrote 'So I'm to be Ambassador to Sweden! A pretty finale! Giving up everything—work, dreams and all. . . . Poor Valley! When shall I come back again? Perhaps never. . . . I should have done better to die the day the King entered Paris.'

THE FLIGHT TO GHENT

His journey was not to Sweden, however, nor even half so far. The atmosphere in France was so bad that the adherents of the Monarchy felt they had lost the first round of the game. Napoleon was in Elba, preparing to assault the French coast; he was accurately informed of the situation in the country, and fancied he could risk the great adventure. Fouché had prophesied that the spring would see the return of the swallows and of Bonaparte. Spring was near. Two days before the calendar marked its beginning the Emperor re-entered the Tuileries amid the frantic rejoicings of the Parisians. Holy Week had just begun.

The Royalist clear-out was tragi-comical and speedy. Madame de Talleyrand, Madame de Blacas and the Duchess of Orleans had not even time to pack a trunk. They were followed by a stream of travellers, all making for the Normandy coast and choking the roads to Rouen. The *diligences* for Brussels and Calais were booked up for days ahead. The banks worked day and night, sending specie and securities to England. Flight, and the saving of their possessions, was all that people thought of, except that they all tried to conceal their movements from the rest. The Court allowed no word of its plans to leak out while the carriages were being got ready for the King's departure. Chateaubriand was no wiser than the Duc de Richelieu. They met by chance in the Champs-Elysées. 'They're going behind our backs,' said the Duke, 'I'm on the look-out here, for I've no wish to be the only one to receive the Emperor at the Tuileries.'

Everybody wanted money. The funds of the various authorities were divided among them. Generals Dessoles and Maison hastened to propose war, but they demanded 200,000 francs each in gold pieces, for 'we must think of our families in this hazardous enterprise'. The ministers were ordered to join the flight of the King. 'All very well,' said the Minister for War, 'but running away costs money, especially if one has to leave everything in disorder in Paris.' Every member of the government was thereupon given a bill of exchange on the Treasury, which it was hardly possible to cash, since the Pay Office was already closed. Blacas was in such a hurry to be gone that he left in his desk at the Tuileries all the letters Talleyrand had written to him from Vienna. Worse still, Jaucourt, who had deputized for Talleyrand while he was in Vienna, forgot in his haste to put the original text of the secret military alliance with Russia in his portfolio.

In the general upheaval nobody thought of Chateaubriand, although he himself was firmly convinced that he was one of those 'who would be shot like dogs as soon as Napoleon arrived'. Only Claire de Duras, the useful sister, looked after his interests. She rushed to Vitrolles, Minister of the Court, and depicted the danger awaiting Chateaubriand if he were left behind. As Vitrolles' thoughts appeared to be elsewhere, and he was not really listening, she fell straight into a swoon, upon which the minister brought her round with the help of 12,000 francs, to allow the writer to leave with the King's retinue.

If it had not been for the women he would certainly not have got away, since he knew as little of the plans of the Court as the

Duc de Richelieu. But Céleste, always suspicious, has posted a manservant at the entrance gate of the Palace, who was to give the alarm if His Majesty should leave. He noticed nothing; but they had hardly gone to bed when a friend came round and told them the King had just started for Lille. This meant packing up at once and making frantic preparations for a journey of which the destination and duration were wrapped in obscurity. At four in the morning Céleste pushed her agitated husband into the travelling carriage. 'I was in such a rage,' he writes, 'that I did not know where I was going or what I was doing.'

In Lille they were met by news of Napoleon's triumphal entry into the Tuileries. The courtiers urged the King to proceed to England, but Louis contented himself with settling just beyond the frontier, in Ghent. Chateaubriand had only got as far as Brussels, where he found Richelieu lying smoking on the sofa of a shabby room at an inn. 'He referred to the Princes in the most brutal manner, and declared he would go to Russia and have nothing more to do with these people.' Not so Chateaubriand; he agreed with the Duke in principle, but when a courier came from Ghent to summon him to the King, he started at once, leaving the embittered Duke to his dismal thoughts. It might have been wiser not to show so much zeal, especially as he knew only too well that the King did not really like him, and that Blacas, the favourite, positively detested him. But he had learnt why he was needed in Ghent: Louis was forming an exile government, which was to be recognized by the whole of Europe. So the impatient writer, scenting the approach of power, must needs be on the spot.

The King formed a government—although at the moment there was actually nothing to govern—leaving out Talleyrand, who was lingering at the Congress of Vienna. Heaven knows why he offered Chateaubriand the Ministry of the Interior. The offer looked at first sight like the purest mockery, since the Minister of the Interior directs the administration of the country and gives directions to the Prefects, and this government did not rule over a foot of French soil. Nevertheless Chateaubriand accepted the offer, becoming not only Ambassador to Sweden but Minister of the Interior as well, and inhabiting two castles in the air at once.

In making this appointment the King had in mind, no doubt, that the new minister, who had proved such an incomparable propagandist with his polemics in favour of the Bourbons, would keep watch on public opinion, and see to it that in future old Carnot's warnings should be better heeded. Chateaubriand thus found himself for the first time personally nearer to the King, and he contrived to ingratiate himself with this cynical rather than formal personage by listening to him; for Louis took the greatest delight in telling spiteful stories about all and sundry, and as he could be very amusing, the upstart Minister of the Interior had no difficulty in delivering the expected applause.

In the King's study stood a circular conference table covered with green cloth; the Ministerial Council gathered round it, Baron Louis for Finance, the Napoleonic Duc de Feltre for War, Beugnot for the Navy, Blacas as Minister of the Court and Lally-Tollendal for Education. The last-mentioned usually held forth at length on the subject of his eminent forefathers who had once been Kings of Ireland, and mixed up the trial and execution of his father with those of Charles I and Louis XVI, while the King threw despairing glances to heaven and wiped the sweat from his brow with a large silk handkerchief. Things went royally in the evening; His Majesty received in great style, and so did his brother the Comte d'Artois, whose dinners were specially famous for the variety of the ice-creams and pastries. When the King drove out, he used a state coach with six horses; the town was full of troops, staff officers, reinforcements and recruits, for an army was being drawn up against Napoleon. Along the canal, heedless of the noisy coming and going, the anglers stood in a contemptuous row, taking no notice of the passage of the King of France. Even Wellington came hurrying now and then from near-by Brussels to raise the fighting spirit of the garrison. When the King met him he greeted him with a condescending nod.

Chateaubriand observed all this activity with a penetrating eye, and took notes that he later developed into a particularly delightful chapter of his Memoirs. He also drew up a long report 'The situation of France on May 15, 1815', which did not make much of a stir. Great and little folk were coming and going, the small Flemish town with its ancient citadel was living through great times. The Duchess of Angoulême arrived on her way to England. Wherever she appeared, discomfort spread through the company; even the King was afraid of her. This great lady, who in spite of appearances was not yet forty, had spent her childhood in the prison of the Temple and been forced to watch her parents, Louis XVI and Marie-Antoinette, being taken away to execution. A few years later she was exchanged between the Republic and Austria, and thus escaped the fate of the rest of her family. She was the Avenging Angel of the Restoration, the 'Survivor of the Temple'; both her mind and her outward appearance bore the stamp of the tragic circumstances of her life. When she strode past with her masculine gait, icily surveying people with eyes often reddened by weeping, as though she were looking at their hands for traces of the blood of her guillotined parents, even the most innocent person was overcome by a sense of guilt. Her perpetuated grief was the terror of everybody that came in contact with her; her thirst for revenge was inappeasable.

The news from Paris was contradictory: Napoleon had set a huge army in motion to meet the invasion of the English and the Prussians. . . . He was said to be trying to rule constitutionally, with the help of Benjamin Constant. . . . But it looked as if his belief in himself was failing. This latter was reported by Fouché, who had not for a moment believed in the success of the Imperial venture, and was keeping in close touch with the Court in Ghent. At a dinner-party given by the Comte d'Artois Chateaubriand, to his chagrin, heard these impenitent reactionaries singing the praises of Fouché, and acclaiming his traitorous activities at the Emperor's side. Without Fouché, they said, they would never succeed in entering the Tuileries again. Chateaubriand had once again the feeling of being on the wrong side.

On June 18, 1815, Chateaubriand left the town by the Brussels gate, to take a walk in the surrounding country. The day was too cool and cloudy for the time of year, but he longed for solitude and an opportunity for serious meditation. He followed the great high road, and paused for a moment in his stroll. He thought he had heard a distant rumble—perhaps of thunder?—

but nature seemed undisturbed. He listened, but heard only the cry of a moorhen in a reed-bed, then the striking of a village clock. As he was about to go on, the distant rumbling began again, at times hardly more than a quivering of the air, which seemed to be communicating itself to the soil of the wide plain, and then again louder. Not a thunderstorm? A different thunder? But where from? He leaned against a poplar at the edge of a hop-field, and listened with bated breath towards the south, in the direction of Brussels. As the wind increased, he could distinctly recognize artillery fire: 'This great battle, which had as yet no name, was the Battle of Waterloo!'

He stood there in the field, listening, hardly able to master his emotion: 'What was this struggle? Was it the final one? Was Napoleon there himself? Were they casting lots for the world, as they had done for the garment of Christ? Success or defeat for this or that army, what would be the outcome for the nations, liberty or slavery? What a lot of blood was being shed! Was not every sound that reached my ear the last sigh of a Frenchman? If the enemies of France were to triumph, would not that be the end of our glory? If Napoleon won, what would become of our liberty? Although a victory would mean perpetual exile for me, my country prevailed at that moment in my heart. My good wishes were for the oppressor of France, if only he could save our honour and rescue us from foreign rule.' This was the feeling in most French hearts next day. They wanted to see the last of the great disturber of the peace, whose flight from Elba had merely in-troduced a further period of blood sacrifice; but could they therefore wish for the defeat of France?

Brooding and shaken he stood here. No traveller came along the road; a few peasant women were quietly hoeing drills for vegetables in the distance, they appeared not have heard the guns. Suddenly the sound of hoofs was heard; Chateaubriand left his listening-post and stepped into the middle of the road to intercept the rider. It was a courier of the Duke of Berry's, coming from Alost with the report that Napoleon had won the battle and the Allies were in retreat.

Chateaubriand returned in haste to the town; the city gates

were about to be closed, because the head of Napoleon's cavalry was reported to have been seen. There was a general panic: carriages were being got ready, the Crown jewels were being stowed away; the King spent the night at the window, a prey to gloomy meditations. Was this nomadic life starting all over again? Must he leave his country once more? What had made it possible for the Usurper to re-enter the Tuileries? What errors had been committed, that the cause of the Bourbons should have been so soon deserted? They would have to manage better next time. But his musings were put an end to at daybreak, when a messenger arrived with a positive report of Napoleon's total defeat. The Battle of Waterloo was a great victory for the English and the Prussians. Once again foreign arms had freed the way to Paris for the Bourbon King. Rejoicing and mourning, revenge and miscalculation could begin afresh.

His Majesty set about his departure at once, to be in Paris at the first moment, where Fouché, thanks to whom the dethronement of the defeated Napoleon had been smoothly effected, had set up a provisional committee to supervise the affairs of government. The King was in a hurry; he did not want to leave the Allies time to meddle with the internal situation of the country, he wished, so to speak, to receive them from the Throne. Talleyrand, posting from Vienna in the hope of exerting his influence with the King on the future course of affairs before His Majesty reached Paris, was painfully surprised to learn that the Court had left Ghent already. He caught up with the travellers at Mons, 'in the bad humour of a king who thought his authority was being disregarded'. Chateaubriand, who was on his way to attend the King, suggested that the Minister should accompany him, but Talleyrand thought it wiser to appear in less haste, and said in a bored tone of voice 'I'm never in a hurry; tomorrow is another day'. When Chateaubriand was received by the King, this arrogant speech had just come to the latter's ears. 'He boasts,' said His Majesty, 'that he has placed the crown on my head for the second time.' Chateaubriand took the Minister's part, attributing his disinclination to ask for an immediate audience to the fatigue of a very hasty journey. He offered to mediate between them, and the King, who hated quarrels above everything, agreed. But Talleyrand would not listen to reason, and when he was told that the King was going on, exclaimed 'He wouldn't dare!'

The King did, in fact, have the horses put to at three in the morning to continue the journey. Talleyrand pitched on his clothes and reached the royal carriage just as it had started. Louis stopped it, and remarked with a smile 'So you are deserting us already, Prince? Your stay at the health resort will do you good. Let us hear from you now and then.' And with that he drove on. The prince, who till then had believed that nobody could excel him in cold-blooded arrogance, was beside himself. There he stood, at three in the morning in a street of Mons, with nobody to soothe his injured pride except Chateaubriand, whom he could not abide and had never taken seriously. Now he would actually be forced to let him act as mediator, lest the incident should lead to a rupture.

Even on the journey the King was exposed to intrigues, warnings and unsolicited advice; at every relay fresh messengers and counsellors approached him, and each time the King became weaker and more inclined to listen to them. Wellington and Blücher had allowed Fouché to convince them that he alone could keep the capital, and the whole country, quiet, and prevent a rising against the Occupation. It enraged Chateaubriand to think that a man like Fouché, who had earned a bloody reputation as a terrorist, and had voted for the death of Louis XVI, should be capable of becoming a Minister under Louis's brother. Talleyrand soon got the hang of the party relationships, and realizing that Fouché was completely master of the situation, he went over to his side. 'Oh, my unfortunate brother!' sighed the King, and signed the decree: Talleyrand was to be Minister for Foreign Affairs, Baron Louis got Finance, Pasquier the Ministry of Justice, and Fouché remained Minister of Police. Chateaubriand was eliminated, his brief span of office as Minister of Interior was at an end; Talleyrand had cheated him, and he now had both him and Fouché for his enemies.

The journey to Ghent and back was drawing to its close. The camp fires of the English and Prussian troops were burning on the

Plain of Saint-Denis when the King took up his quarters in the Abbey. Chateaubriand went to see him there in the evening, and sat patiently waiting in a corner of the antechamber because His Majesty had a visitor. 'Suddenly a door opened, and Vice entered silently, leaning on the arm of Crime: Fouché was leading Talleyrand by the arm. This infernal vision went slowly past me, entered the King's study and disappeared. Fouché had come to swear fealty and homage to his master. The faithful regicide, kneeling before him, laid his hand, which had caused the head of Louis XVI to fall, in the hand of the royal martyr's brother; the recreant Bishop stood surety for the oath.'

On the following day the King sent for Chateaubriand.

'Well, dear Vicomte?'

'Well, Sire? You are disbanding your regiments and taking Fouché?'

'Yes, dear Vicomte, it had to be. . . . What do you think of it?'

'Your Majesty, it is unfortunately an accomplished fact. Permit me to keep silence.'

'No, no, you know how much I have resisted ever since Ghent. Tell me what you think of it.'

'As you wish it, Sire, I can only tell the truth, and if you will put it to the credit of my loyalty, I believe it's all up with the Monarchy.'

The King was silent. Chateaubriand began to repent his audacious speech, lest he had gone too far. The King cleared his throat. 'Well, dear Vicomte', he said, 'I'm entirely of your opinion.'

PEER OF FRANCE

Was Chateaubriand's political ambition extinguished? To all that would listen he swore that it was, and he was sincere in so far as he would have found it impossible to sit at a conference table with Fouché. The King had hinted to him that he would be glad to see him as the Duc de Blacas's successor, but nothing more had been said about it. The King did, however, give him a token of his favour; he bestowed on him the title of Minister of State, which had no office attached to it, but a salary of 24,000 francs. The title did not mean much, the salary was small, but Chateaubriand could not afford to despise it, for his eternal money difficulties, of which he was actually rather proud, appeared to be greater than ever. Soon after this he was appointed President of the Electoral College of Orleans, and won the electors' loud applause by his opening speech, which overflowed with royalism. He would undoubtedly have been the first to be elected deputy, had not the King placed him on the list of those to be nominated peers of France. He hesitated for a time, because he thought the deputyship carried more political weight. The peerage was hereditary, but he had no children to inherit it. In the end, however, he accepted the title, and wrote home: 'Get the tailor, Le Bon, to come, and have him make me a Peer's suit. See to it that the fleur-de-lys embroidery doesn't look too scanty.'

Napoleon had been mistaken in numbering Chateaubriand among the ideologues. All he was after was actual political power, in the service of no matter what idea. His writing was often merely a means of cheating his hunger for power. He subscribed to no political system and had no political principles, since monarchism was with him merely a reflex of loyalism. Change, in his opinion, was the supreme law of the world; nations and individuals were in a perpetual state of change. He had read Vico, Herder and Hegel, and although he had often fought on Bonald's side, he was sundered from that great philosopher-statesman by his opportunism in higher politics. In the eyes of Chateaubriand, as a *grand seigneur* who had no need to run after favours and benefits, opportunism was not a defect of character but a political means, without which politics could never be carried on. Bonald, on the other hand, believed himself to possess an absolute political certitude that was eternal, and almost in the nature of a metaphysical truth. He was sundered, too, from de Maistre and Lamennais by the 'law of practice'. The latter wanted to make a god of the people, the former to deify the might of kings, whereas Chateaubriand declared 'I disapprove of the thesis that it is better that the people should perish rather than a principle. In the matter of government truths are relative, not absolute. Public freedoms are not always clothed in the same forms, they can exist in the most varied institutions.'

His temperament now, when his famous wavy locks were beginning to wear thin, was just as unequal as in the days of 'René'. Only a little while earlier he had exclaimed 'Why did I become a royalist against my instincts, at a time when a miserable race of courtiers were unable to understand me? How did I come to be mixed up with this herd of mediocrities, who take me for a madman when I preach courage, and for a revolutionary when I talk of liberty?' He was getting on better with these people now. The attraction of public life made him a trifle more patient with the courtiers and more confident in his future. He wrote to his wife 'Will you believe me at last? Will you leave me in peace? Will you cease to urge me to be this or that? Peer and Minister of State, the two first ranks in political and public life, what more do you want? We shall have money as well. I was certain I should be elected, certain of being made a peer. You haven't been very sensible. I'm steering my little bark in the right direction—after my own fashion, it's true—but everybody acts according to his nature. Work, our Valley, wealth, we shall be very happy. Come, then, be cheerful and content; no more foolish pretensions. Leave me a little independence if you really want my happiness.'

The electoral college in Orleans over which he had presided, and which he had stimulated by his Address, did more than its duty; it was more royal than the King, as was the case, moreover, throughout France. The elected Chamber displayed such strict royalism that the King called it, with a shake of the head, '*la chambre introuvable*'. Chateaubriand found himself being pushed right into the ranks of the Ultras, the unyielding reactionaries who wanted to re-establish the old régime, and believed it possible to return to absolutism. Their leaders were the Comte d'Artois, the Comte de La Bourdonnais, the advocate Corbière, Baron Vitrolles, Vicomte de Bonald, the great philosopher and party theoretician, and the Comte de Villèle. The King's authority was upheld by the nobility, the great landowners and the clergy, who were particularly active in preventing the rise of the liberal spirit among the people. An important part was also played by the so-called Congregation, which had been founded for benevolent purposes but had gradually assumed a political significance, and united in itself all the forces of militant catholicism. It surrounded its organization and activities with a certain secrecy, which contributed greatly to its prestige. Madame de Boigne called the Congregation 'a State within the State, a government within the Government, an army within the Army', but she may have been exaggerating.

Those months were no high-water mark in Chateaubriand's career. However happy his prospects might appear to him, he had entered upon a political path which was soon to prove a blind alley. He shut his eyes to the 'White Terror' that was raging all over the country. He took no part in 'hunting down the Marshals', but neither could he bring himself to disapprove of the countless acts of vengeance, the murders, maltreatment and plundering to which the men of the Revolution and the Empire were subjected. 'It is time to make an end of mercy.' This abominable slogan of the Ultras was certainly not of his coining, but his political ties did not allow him to oppose it. The King, who disliked all fanaticism, shook his head over the cruel zeal at work everywhere, and muttered 'They are irreconcilable. . . .' The fury of the purge wreaked on those that had not only remained in the country during the Hundred Days, but never emigrated at all, drew from His Majesty the ironical remark 'If these gentlemen could do as they liked, they would end by purging me too'.

Chateaubriand might have acted differently if he had been able to stomach the fact that Fouché was still playing such an important role. He was not alone in his aversion, even the sober Wellington characterized the employment of the great Policemen as an indecency. But the 'scandal' did not last long. Fouché was overthrown and dragged Prince Talleyrand down with him. Chateaubriand immediately came to his senses, and began finding fault himself with the policy of hate pursued by the Ultras, especially as the latter had not ventured to have purge lists drawn up by anybody but Fouché. The King, however, could not be persuaded to adopt the English system and entrust the leaders of the Opposition with the new government. He called instead

upon the Duc de Richelieu, who had, it is true, lived as an *emigré*
for over twenty-five years, but had sat in the Chamber among the
'Constitutionals', the adherents of the Charter, and could thus be
regarded almost as a Liberal.

The Duke saw clearly that it would be wise to find a place for
the Vicomte in the government; but Chateaubriand's ambition
was thwarted, as usual, by his personality. Richelieu had no liking
for this all-too self-confident, bumptious man, who was a writer
into the bargain, and was forever clamouring for recognition of
both his literary and his political accomplishments. He himself,
only lately, had almost fallen asleep in his chair while Chateaubriand was reading his very boring tragedy, *Moses,* in somebody's
drawing-room. Although in this case it would have been for the
author to complain, Richelieu felt offended by his general
sensitiveness. Besides all of which, it annoyed him that the
Vicomte should not be capable of keeping his money affairs in
order and was forever demanding royal favours in the shape of
hard cash. How he could bring himself to make such use of his
'ladies', especially Claire de Duras, as emissaries to obtain this or
that for him, passed his comprehension.

The atmosphere between the two men was therefore not a
friendly one, and did not improve when the Duke chose the young
Decazes, a former secretary to Napoleon's mother, Letitia, as his
assistant. Decazes, the son of a provincial attorney, was thirty-six;
he had served with distinction as a prefect of police and had every
prospect of cutting a figure in politics. His handsome appearance
and entertaining conversation soon made him a favourite with the
King, who took to addressing him as 'my son'. But this 'upstart',
who was thought to be a Liberal, was hated by the Ultras, and
even Chateaubriand disliked the choice. Richelieu, besieged by
the 'ladies', to whom his sister Madame de Montcalm now belonged, ended by offering Chateaubriand the Ministry of
Education in succession to Fontanes. As the post carried no
cabinet rank with it, he refused the offer as an insult, and took up
his pen again instead. Having discovered with horror 'the
ignorance of France concerning the principles of representative
government', he composed an essay on *The Monarchy according*
o

to the Charter, which he termed a 'Constitutional Catechism'. With this passionate advocacy of constitutional monarchy, to which he lent the brilliance and precision of his incomparable style, he was disavowing the Ultras without actually setting out to do so, and sounding an oppositional note. This led him into a position all the more paradoxical in that the government he was criticising was led by men like Richelieu and Decazes, who might themselves be considered as Liberals.

Chateaubriand still bore the title of Minister of State, and to this he appealed: 'As a Minister of State I owe the King the truth, and I shall speak it. If the Council of which I have the honour to be a member were ever to assemble, I might be told to speak in Council. But it does not assemble, so I must find a way of my own to make my submissive warnings heard, and fulfil my functions as a minister. What! When France appears to be threatened with fresh misfortunes, when I believe the cause of Legitimacy to be in danger, am I to keep silence because I am a peer and a Minister of State? My duty, on the contrary, is to signal breakers ahead, to fire the alarm gun, and to summon all hands on deck.' Why this excitement? He was defending parliamentary monarchy against absolutism, which was supported by the Permanent State as Bonald, de Maistre and Ballanche preached it. At the same time, however, he was complaining that the true Royalists were not being sufficiently considered, and that the old sinners were showing their faces again.

Just as he was about to send the essay to the printer, the Chamber was dissolved. This was the work of Decazes, who had convinced both the King and Richelieu that otherwise 'the intolerance of the Ultras would bring about a fresh Revolution'. Chateaubriand hastily wrote an addendum to his essay, in which he hinted that His Majesty had let himself be overruled by Decazes. The essay was published, the King read it, and a few days later the following Note appeared in the *Moniteur:* 'Since the Vicomte de Chateaubriand has cast doubt on our personal will, as expressed in our decree of September 5th (Dissolution of the Chamber), the Vicomte de Chateaubriand will no longer be numbered among our Ministers of State as from today.'

The rupture had come, the Vicomte was dismissed, the King was tired of him. He left the ranks of the Ultras, possibly with a sigh of relief. He was no doctrinaire, and without abjuring his fealty to the Legitimate Crown, he slipped into the camp of the Opposition.

The Duc de Richelieu still held the reins of power. A grandson of the famous Marshal, his features were still youthful in spite of his fifty years, in striking contrast with his grey hair. Madame de Boigne speaks of his 'fine, noble character', says he was 'liberal and patriotic at the same time', but finds fault with his disobliging manner, amounting to downright discourtesy. He had emigrated very early, almost in the first weeks of the Revolution, and had only lately returned, so that he did not know many people in Paris, and even spoke French with a slightly Slavonic accent. For his emigration had been of a quite unusual kind; he had not been content to sit about in England or Germany awaiting the miracle of a triumphal return, but had gone straight to Russia, fought against the Turks under Suvorov and been appointed Governor of Odessa by the Tsar. He had ruled over South Russia for several years, carrying out his task so brilliantly, and bringing the provinces entrusted to him to such a pitch of prosperity, that the Russian monarch had retained a grateful friendship for him. It was Alexander I that had urgently recommended the King to entrust the government to Richelieu, because he enjoyed the confidence of the Allies, and would be able to obtain much more favourable peace terms from them than anybody else could do. On leaving Paris, Alexander presented the Duke with an old map of France, on which all the territorial demands of the victors were drawn. France had been spared these sacrifices, so he added in his letter, solely on account of the confidence Richelieu inspired.

X

ENTIRELY WITHOUT CHATEAUBRIAND

THE PURGE

THE situation of France after Waterloo was one huge catastrophe. The French army, only yesterday the most glorious in the world, was now reduced to 'a horde of robbers'. The remnants of it were forced to retreat at once south of the Loire, and the entire country was soon occupied by the troops of the Allies. The victorious armies of Wellington and Blücher were joined by the Russian and Austrian forces and the contingent from the German States, making an army force of 1·2 million men in all, to which a Spanish corps had tacked itself on at the last moment, so as not to miss the share-out of the booty.

Vengeance! was the cry of the nations that had been plagued by the French conquerors for two decades. But France herself demanded vengeance on the authors of her misfortunes. All those that had served the fallen tyrant, or not resisted him, were to be brought to account. The purge was to be merciless and complete.

The long years of restless wandering from exile to exile had made of the King a psychologist and a philosopher without illusions. He mistrusted the over-ardent zeal of his adherents more than he did the French people, who for all their excesses had not yet lost their sound common sense. On June 25th he issued a conciliatory proclamation, promising forgiveness to his 'erring subjects', and abandoning to the severity of the law only 'a few guilty persons', who had taken part in the episode of the Hundred Days. Before the law in question could be made, however, a list had to be drawn up of the chief culprits, especially the high-ranking officers who had gone over to Napoleon, among whom were Ney and Labédoyère. This list was subsequently

increased by the royalist Chamber from 57 to 1,200 persons.
All superior officers and functionaries who had remained
at their post during the Hundred Days, in other words 'the
majority of those that had played a leading part in Paris or the
provinces during the last twenty-five years', were declared guilty.
A 'regular epidemic of vengeance' broke out. The administration
was ruthlessly purged, the denunciations assumed such proportions that the editor of the *Journal des Débats* complained of the
flood of notices. Royalist committees sprang up on all sides and
took the cleansing of public life into their own hands, on the
score of their members' sufferings in the past. Fouché, the
Minister of Police, was forced to intervene by a circular letter of
August 2nd: 'It is the will of the King that a veil be drawn
over mutual errors and lapses. We cannot obtain any favourable
terms from Europe until it has received a trustworthy pledge
of our peace and its own by the quelling of unrest in our country
and by the union of the People with the Throne.' To which he
added as a postscript 'Who dare think of personal vengeance
in the midst of public misfortune!'

But the vengeance went on; at daybreak on December 7th
Marshal Ney was condemened to death by the House of Peers
and shot according to martial law in the neighbourhood of the
Observatory. On the following day the Duc de Richelieu, who
had meanwhile become Chief Minister, laid a Law of Amnesty
before the House, and reminded them of the Peace Treaty that
had just been concluded: 'The treaty lately laid before you
requires for its execution the good will of each and the efforts of
all.' The debate, in the course of which Parliament considered
the cancellations already registered in the Conciliation Law, was
all the more violent because not a few among the deputies would
themselves be hit by the exactions proposed. A member of the
government, the Finance Minister Corvetto, was endangered
because he had been a Councillor of State under Napoleon. Con-
fiscations of capital were dropped after Royer-Collard had
remarked 'First we sequestrate because we have condemned, then
we condemn because we would like to sequestrate'.

In spite of this the law as accepted was no longer at all as conciliatory as Richelieu had wished. The courts-martial, which were entrusted with its execution, displayed such zeal that in many parts of the country a sort of civil-war atmosphere developed. Comical incidents were not wanting, and gave the purge a tinge of ridicule. A captain of the gendarmerie was condemned to three months' imprisonment because he was wearing 'seditious buttons', i.e., buttons showing the imperial eagle, on his coat. The same punishment was awarded an old soldier for having 'defaced a revered image' by painting a moustache on a bust of the Duchess of Angoulême. In the first three months of the year 1816, 70,000 arrests were made. The deputy de Serre said in the Chamber 'When we began, the demand for a purge was legitimate. But for the last six months everything has been turned topsy-turvy, and the entire administration has been remodelled. There is no sense in trumping up more accusations and demanding the purging of newly appointed persons. This frightful plague of talebearing is beginning to poison France. It is time to make an end of it. It must no longer be a crime to have a post'.

RICHELIEU FULFILS THE TREATY

The real trouble of the stricken country lay elsewhere. On November 20, 1815, the Peace Treaty between the Allies and France was concluded. It re-established the frontiers of 1792 and stipulated a war indemnity of 700 millions and the occupation of the country for five years. The Duke of Wellington was given supreme command of the Allied army of occupation, numbering 150,000 men. The cohesion of the victorious forces actually rested less on this treaty than on the Treaty of Chaumont concluded in March 1814—during the war—by which the Allies bound themselves to meet 'in a given time' to watch over 'the quiet of the nations and the peace of Europe'. France was excluded from this 'Concert', although she was admitted to the Holy Alliance 'in the name of the Trinity', founded by Tsar Alexander. But this religiously inspired league, which was simply a mutual insurance of crowned heads against the liberal tendencies of the nations; afforded the French government no possibility of regaining full equality of rights and ridding the country of the Occupation and of the financial burdens imposed on it.

The victors trusted the King, but not the French nation, which for twenty-five years had been active as an aggressor and an instigator of unrest, and had disseminated the 'poison of the Revolution' among the nations of Europe. The Treaty of November 1815 was intended above all 'to promote the progressive establishment of the new order in France' and to ensure the re-education of this turbulent people. The Allies were convinced that France had not yet returned definitely to the 'good principles', and that she must remain under tutelage until the last risk of a revival of the revolutionary danger was suppressed. The allied statesmen saw clearly that this danger might very easily be revived by the excesses of the purge and the reactionary fanaticism of the Royalists. Wellington wrote therefore to Louis XVIII, in his character of Supreme Commander of the army of occupation, 'Europe remains at peace on my word and on my responsibility. But it would only need a word to arouse it from this inactivity. This word will be spoken if you do not see to it that your government shows more wisdom and stability. The quiet of this country depends exclusively on the presence of the allied armed forces: their departure would be the signal for a fresh, veritable revolution. The extreme Royalists in the Chamber are nourishing discord and distrust'.

France must therefore give unequivocal evidence of her good behaviour, before she could be reinstated in the European community: such was the purpose of the Treaty and of the Occupation. With despair in his heart Richelieu, the *grand seigneur*, who was no place-seeker, and, as a Governor for twenty years in Russia, could hardly understand the moral embitterment of the French—agreed to the Peace Treaty 'more dead than alive'. He now saw only one way of lightening the burden laid on France, shortening the period of occupation and obtaining equality of rights for her, and that was by the strictest and most faithful policy of fulfilment. He made his Finance Minister Corvetto declare to the Chamber: 'We shall not dishonour our misfortune and exploit it to break our word; even in the midst of our ruin we shall show respect for the given word.'

In his struggle for revision, Richelieu recognized no other rule of conduct than keeping faith with the Treaty and laying all his cards on the table. In this policy he had, it is true, powerful helpers among the ranks of the Allies themselves, especially the Russian Ambassador Pozzo di Borgo, a Corsican whose merciless fight against Napoleon had its origin in an ancient family feud. Pozzo had emigrated from Corsica in 1796 and become one of the most influential of the Tsar's advisers. After the fall of Napoleon he had come to Paris as Alexander's ambassador and a true friend to France, cleverly supporting Richelieu's fulfilment policy without failing in his duty to the Tsar. At the regular ambassadorial conferences of the victorious Powers, over which Wellington presided, he expressed the conviction that 'any attempt to supervise the French, denuding and humiliating them, so that they can do no harm, would prove useless if it did not cease at the very earliest date provided for in the treaties. The internal order of the country must be the guarantee of peace, and not the foreign armies on the frontiers'.

Because of this support by a foreign statesman, and the confidence shown him by the victors in general, Richelieu was reproached with unpatriotic behaviour by the party of the Opposition. 'What can you do with a man,' cried Talleyrand hypocritically, 'who always needs a courier from St. Petersburg before he can come to a decision!' It was a fact that Richelieu found more support from men like Pozzo, whom Wellington accused of being 'more French than the French', than from his own parliament, or even from his Sovereign. 'What a fate,' he exclaimed, 'to have only foreigners to support one in one's own country!' Among his countrymen, for whose liberty and equality of rights he was fighting, he became daily more isolated. When, later on, he altered the Franchise Law, he was told that the idea had been forced upon him 'by the foreigners in Aix-la-Chapelle'; and it was without a word of thanks that this 'deliverer of the country', who had 'preserved the Rhine frontier for France'— as one may read on his monument in the chapel of the Sorbonne —would one day vanish from the political stage.

Meanwhile his struggle for the amicable revision of the Peace Treaty went on. In March 1816 he attempted the first official soundings as to the possibility of shortening the period of the Occupation. Castlereagh showed himself not adverse, and Wellington evinced some understanding of Richelieu's point of view. The latter wrote to the Tsar during the following month 'Our burdens are too heavy for France to bear them any longer, and I consider it essential that the Occupation should be reduced by the end of the year'. To his ambassador in London, the Marquis d'Osmond, he wrote confidently 'The force of circumstances must win the victory. They will evacuate our territory, and they will not dare to shut us out of the Grand Alliance much longer, however much they may want to ... The peaceful occupation must not last more than three years. If they want to prolong it we must go to war, for no country could ask the Chamber for the costs of the occupation after November'. The English now began making fresh objections, ostensibly because they wanted to wait for the result of the partial elections, and make sure that the internal situation of the occupied country offered sufficient guarantee of peaceful development. They had more reasons than one, however, to press for a delay; the demobilization of the English occupying troops would place London in a difficulty. Richelieu thereupon suggested the withdrawal of the Saxony and Würtemburg troops instead, 'which would rid us of our most troublesome and undisciplined guests'. The easing of relations was finally brought about by Metternich, who proposed to the 'Council of Four' that they should put the question on their Order of the Day.

'The 150,000 bailiffs keeping watch over us,' so Richelieu termed the army of occupation, for the foreign soldiers were not there merely to supervise the political opinions of the vanquished nation, they had also to assure the payment of the war indemnity. Seven hundred millions, spread over a period of five years, were to be paid in daily instalments. In addition there were 130 millions yearly in occupation expenses, and finally a still unfixed sum for so-called individual claims, to compensate the foreign governments, or their subjects, for war damage, supplies, loss of profits and so forth. Richelieu had tried in vain to get the amount of these claims fixed, since their unlimitedness made them highly dangerous. In order to raise the financial quota for 1817 the government approached the London banking house of Hope and Baring, to persuade it to give them support.

The unruliness of the Chamber, however, was not calculated to attract foreign capitalists, and it was only after the intervention of the mighty speculator Ouvrard, who for decades had always come forward in a crisis, that negotiations were set going again, and obtained the support of Wellington, so that a preliminary settlement could be arrived at. The English banking house first subscribed for 100 millions of government stock, and held out a prospect of a second, larger operation, which soon materialized, though still at an unfavourable rate. 'All the same,' as Pasquier said, 'the situation of the French government with regard to foreign countries was completely altered. Once all the English, Dutch, Hamburg, in short all European capitalists had become co-partners with France, they would necessarily become her allies'—who would advise their governments to reduce her burdens. In effect, the occupying troops were reduced by 30,000 men from April 1st. There still remained the question of the individual claims, which were being sent in from all over the world, and often under the most surprising pretexts. Claims were revived that went back to the Seven Years War. The Duke of Anhalt-Bernburg actually claimed the pay of 4,000 mercenaries placed at the service of Henri IV by one of his forebears.

On March 1, 1817, the list of claims was closed— it amounted to a total of 1·6 milliards! The banker Baring was so alarmed at this sum that he threatened to leave the country, for 'no sensible man could be prepared to place his fortune in a country threatened by a war debt equivalent to a complete liquidation of society'. Richelieu contradicted him, he intended to pay what France owed, but he must first ascertain to what extent these claims were justified. It proved impossible, however, for the allied governments to institute an examination of this kind, since it was mainly private claims that were involved, and France therefore tendered a proposal to agree on a lump sum of 200 millions.

Russia, who had made no claims, and England, who had settled hers a year earlier by a separate agreement, raised no objections. Austria and Prussia made all the greater difficulties. Richelieu reminded them of the higher interests of Europe, and pointed out that 'France was necessary to the peace of the European continent'. If the cord was stretched too tightly, the revolutionary spirit would reappear in France, 'and then, woe to Europe'. The argument was clear, and taken, moreover, from the victors' own stock: a durable order in Europe on the basis of 'good principles' was only possible, given a free France with equality of rights. 'I told them a score of times, when we were negotiating in November, 1815, that they would be doing too little or too much; either France must be so partitioned that nobody need fear her any more, or they must be reconciled to her by a generous treaty.' In the end Wellington, as arbitrator, fixed the total payment in satisfaction of the claims at 240 millions.

EQUALITY OF RIGHTS

A new stage had been reached. It was now possible for France to advance fresh arguments in her fight for an earlier evacuation of her territory. A few days later Richelieu presented a statute to the Chamber, which was to provide him with the means of satisfying the debt fixed by British arbitration. He had not been given such an attentive hearing since the dramatic session in which he had presented the House with the Peace Treaty and flung the text on the table in despair. The means were granted him at once, almost unanimously and without discussion. Of course it was no longer the old Chamber, the pressure from the Left was making itself felt, and was growing stronger with every partial election, so that by degrees the old heroes of the Revolution and the Hundred Days, such as Layfayette, Benjamin Constant, Manuel and finally even the Abbé Grégoire, were brought into Parliament, although the last-named had sat as a deputy in the Convention and introduced one of the first motions for the abolition of kingship, and for taking proceedings against the King,

This increase in liberal tendency was only interrupted for a short time by the murder of the Duc de Berry. In the meantime the Opposition, supported by the rising bourgeoisie, remained fairly tractable, and Police Minister Decazes exerted all his influence over the Prefects in order that the House to which Richelieu was now speaking should not number more than a dozen opponents. What the Duke had to say represented the *leitmotiv* of his entire policy, and could be summed up in three simple watchwords: Fulfilment, Liberation, Equality of rights. He quoted the decisive clauses of the Peace Treaty of November 20, 1815, according to which the military occupation of France could come to an end in three years if the country had fulfilled its duty and given proofs of its good conduct. 'The time has come for France to receive the reward of her courageous submission to her fate. With these treaties in our hands, the hardest conditions of which we have fulfilled, we shall not petition Europe in vain for the implementing on her part of the conditions favourable to ourselves.'

The deputy who reported to the House the bill that finally liquidated the financial bankruptcy of the Empire was no other than Napoleon's former Minister of Finance, Gaudin, Duke of Gaeta (notwithstanding Richelieu's declaration in his speech that France could attain to a better future if she hastened to sever herself irrevocably from the past). It was a great day for France, that spring day of the year 1818. The trees on the banks of the Seine showed swelling buds, even a hint of early green. There were a lot of people in the streets, for it was a fine day. 'All French hearts,' said Richelieu from the tribune, 'live in the hope of seeing none but French flags flying on the soil of their country.'

In the course of the summer it became known to the world that a Conference of the Allies was to take place at Aix-la-Chapelle for the purpose of clearing up French affairs. The three Rulers, so it was said, were to appear in person, and France would be represented by the Duc de Richelieu. The newspapers babbled their hardest about the difficulty of lodging such a distinguished company suitably in the little Prussian town, about the beauty of the room in the Town Hall in which the plenary sessions would be held, about the express communications that had been organized to supply the kitchen of the Conference with oysters, venison and confectionery, about the two ravishing lady parachutists, who had undertaken to afford the princes and statesmen an agreeable thrill with their *sauts perilleux*. In a word, excitement ran high, and it was rewarded—for when the Conference opened in September there were present, in addition, bankers like Rothschild and Baring, the English portrait painter Lawrence, a number of journalists (an innovation, this) and even the beautiful Madame Récamier.

The Duc de Richelieu had received from his Master a silver table service, several state coaches and a team of eight horses, to enable him to make a dignified appearance; but he had the wisdom to remain in the background and give the Allies an opportunity to settle their own quarrels among themselves to begin with. No doubt he also wished to wait and see what they would decide with regard to France. He had not long to wait, for on September 30th Metternich and Hardenberg told him in confidence that the curtailing of the Occupation was as good as settled. On October 9th the financial affairs of the Occupation were wound up, so that the evacuation of the country could be fixed for November 30th. The good news reached Paris sooner than the Duke had intended, and he begged the King to temper the jubilation in the capital 'so that it may not turn into demonstrations that might offend other countries'.

Actually everything was not yet won, for though the evacuation was the most urgent question, it was not the most important. France had still been left outside the European community, and did not in any sense dispose of equality of rights. The alliance of the victors, based on the Treaty of Chaumont and directed against France, was still in force. Richelieu proceeded by two stages: first the Alliance must be dissolved, and then France must obtain her place in the Council of the Great Powers. Things progressed very slowly and stickily. Richelieu became aware that mistrust of France as the focus of unrest was by no means extinguished. To begin with, Prussia, Austria and England were troubled lest the 're-integration' of France should finally upset the balance of power in Europe and transform the Holy Alliance into a European Directory under Russian leadership. Richelieu protested against this persistent suspicion of his country. If Europe were to maintain a system of mistrust of France, this could only discourage men of good will, isolate the King and even communicate the ferment of anarchy to other nations.

Richelieu, the resolute 'fulfilment' politician, was thus forced to threaten the victors time after time with the very danger on account of which they were hesitating to give France full liberty. He worked his way forward, step by step, and time was getting short. He could not prevent the Allies from organizing a military festival on the anniversary of the Battle of Leipzig, but he declined to take part in it, for although he had acclaimed the fall of Napoleon, the reminder of the defeat of French arms was none the less painful to him. At last an agreement was reached on all points, and the signing of the final protocol took place on November 1st, barely three years after the conclusion of the bitter Peace Treaty. France was declared to have fulfilled the Treaty 'with the most painful and honourable exactitude', the progressive stabilization of her internal situation was no longer to be doubted, and she was therefore invited to take her place in the Council of the Great Powers.

The conclusion for which the Duke had worked so hard and systematically had hardly been reached when the results of fresh partial elections in Paris were made known in Aix-la-Chapelle. Lafayette and Manuel, each a red rag to the Royalists, had entered the Chamber. 'It is a good thing,' wrote Richelieu to the King, 'that the negotiations are practically ended, for this news is bound to produce some effect.' Evacuation, full liberty and un- limited equality of rights had been obtained, but France had not yet seen the end of her miseries and confusions. The Royalists, who had supported the 'liberator of his country' so hesitatingly, and had more than once accused him of anti-national tendencies and 'submissiveness to foreigners', were already, without realizing it, sedulously digging the grave of the Monarchy. However, when Richelieu returned to Paris at the end of November, his travelling carriage met with the first Prussian and English troops marching homewards along the muddy high roads of northern France. The plumes on the cavalrymen's shakos hung dripping wet, the guns gleamed in the rain, the infantry stumped wearily through the mud and the rotting autumn leaves; but Richelieu's honest heart was at rest at last. 'I am beginning to believe,' he had written to the King shortly before, 'that it will be possible to bind Europe together with a federal tie.'

THE MAD QUEEN

Such is the history, in bare outlines, of the fulfilment policy pursued by Richelieu, which freed France from reparations and occupation sooner than could have been hoped. France's gratitude left something to be desired, and that of the Court still more so. The Chamber awarded him a gratuity of 50,000 francs, by way of honouring the 'Liberator of the Territory'. It did so, however, without enthusiasm and after a great many legal objections and captious quibbles. He presented the entire sum to the Bordeaux Hospital, and left the Ministry of Foreign Affairs as poor as he had entered it, 'taking his whole luggage with him in a portmanteau'. He became Chief Minister once again, after the assassination of the Duc de Berry (which the Ultras had laid at the door of Minister Decazes on account of the supposed tepidity of his opposition to the 'Liberals'). But he was forced to adopt so many reactionary measures, without succeeding in conciliating the Ultras, that he resigned the year after, weary and disgusted by the narrow-mindedness of his opponents.

One can hardly take leave of this generous, upright man without including an account of his death. This was connected, at once tragically and grotesquely, with the fate of the Desirée Clary who might have been married, in her youth, to General Bonaparte, if her parents had not considered they were more than sufficiently connected, through Joseph, with that adventurous family. Desirée thereupon married General Bernadotte, and thus became in course of time Queen of Sweden. She continued to reside in Paris, however, ostensibly because she suffered from a disfiguring facial eruption which she had brought back after a short stay in Sweden, and attributed to the climate of that country.

She lived 'an amphibious life', as Madame de Boigne expresses it, in her palace in the Rue d'Anjou. Her entourage, and her husband's ambassadors, addressed her as Your Majesty, and the remainder of society as Madame Bernadotte, an arrangement with which she was perfectly satisfied.

She wrote one day to Richelieu, while he was still Chief Minister, saying she wished to consult him on a matter of business. The Duke, a true cavalier of the old school, replied that it would be his duty to wait on her. He went to see her, fulfilled her request and was invited to dinner. The poor Duke, who was infinitely polite, but not in the least gallant, had no idea that he had kindled a flame in Madame Bernadotte's heart and 'laid the foundations of a madness that was to pursue him to the grave'. It began with flowers and other presents, so often repeated that he was obliged to beg his 'Mad Queen' not to place him in an embarrassing situation. But Desirée had quite lost her head, she maintained a set of spies to keep her currently informed of the Duke's movements. Her carriage was always ready, so that she could be forever on the heels of the object of her adoration. Everywhere he went, the Queen followed in his tracks; he concealed his intentions and his errands, he made detours, put up at the most modest inns on his travels, took his friends' carriages so as not to be recognized; but it was all no use, Desirée was at once on the spot.

He never spoke to her, never even looked at her, but in spite of this she never ceased to follow him. She took an apartment in Paris opposite his, and if ever he went up to the window without thinking, he was bound to see the Queen of Sweden at the window of the house opposite. She went into the shops he had just visited and bought the same object as he had, stationed herself in his path when he walked in the Tuileries gardens, so that, being nearsighted, he was often unable to make his escape in time, and ended by renting the hotel opposite the entrance to his château at Courteilles. The Duke was beside himself; he was no cynic, and did not attempt to be uncivil to the foolish woman, but he inquired in Stockholm, by diplomatic channels, whether it would not be pleasanter for the Queen to reside there. Bernadotte understood, and begged his wife to return home, but she answered evasively, and when he insisted, sent him medical certificates.

One morning in May of the year 1822 Richelieu left Courteilles to consult a doctor in Paris, for he felt seriously unwell and had decided that he must do something about it. Desirée was at her post; no sooner was the Duke's carriage on the road than she caught up with him and followed at his heels. When they were changing horses she succeeded in taking a peep into the other carriage, and saw the face of the adored one deathly pale, distorted by exhaustion, and then all at once violently flushed. She got hold of the adjutant and besought him to fetch a doctor because the Duke was seriously ill. If that were not so, she said, he would not have neglected to lower the blind, as he always did as soon as he saw her. Could a woman humiliate herself more deeply? She recognized the danger that threatened her beloved from the fact that he had forgotten to humiliate her. But she thought only of the danger, not the humiliation. By noon next day the Duke was dead.

XI

MADAME RÉCAMIER FOR ALWAYS

THE ETERNAL MONEY TROUBLES

CHATEAUBRIAND, meanwhile, had experienced some highly terrestrial embarrassments and an almost heavenly happiness. His greatest embarrassment was concerned with money, or rather the obstinate lack of it; his happiness was connected with Juliette Récamier. After the King had struck him off the list of Ministers of State, and ordered the essay on *Monarchy according to the Charter* to be confiscated by the police—though the author's rights in it were restored to him by legal decree—he had only the modest salary left that he was to receive in perpetuity as a Peer of France. The Restoration treated him worse than Napoleon had done, a paradox that his wife had foreseen. She had no illusions about the Court, she was aware of the secret antipathy the King nursed for the 'intellectual' Vicomte, and was convinced that her husband, with his royalist ambition, was chasing a will o' the wisp. Unfortunately she could not refrain from expressing a certain malicious pleasure at his discomfiture, which did not improve the domestic atmosphere.

It was easy for him to write twenty years later, looking back on this time, 'My nature made me quite insensitive to the loss of my salary. It simply meant going about on foot, and taking a cab to the House of Peers. In my public vehicle, under the protection of the *canaille* around me, I assumed the rights of the proletariat, to which I now belonged'. With a Peer's salary of a thousand francs a month one was hardly a proletarian in the year 1817, but at that moment he had pressing debts, some of them on bills of exchange, and his days were often full of care.

His faithful man of business, Le Moine, who had been trying

for some time to put the economic affairs of the couple in order, ran hither and thither to raise money and get the bills renewed, but he saw no way out except by selling the property in the Valley of the Wolves, of which Chateaubriand was so proud because he had laid out not only the house but the grounds with love and effort, according to his own taste. He began advertising the sale by auction of his library, and wrote to Claire Duras 'Herewith, dear Sister, the notice about my books. A writer selling his books is like a shopkeeper selling off his stock. All this is being done to the greater glory of His Most Christian Majesty'. The auction took place; it robbed him of essential books and fine editions, and this must have made his heart bleed, for he had always loved browsing among books, making extracts and rummaging through out-of-the-way tomes for equally out-of-the-way quotations. He was a mighty reader before the Lord, and loved not only the magic of the open page, but the spines of books, with the endless attraction of their half-revealed secrets.

'The library is sold,' he wrote to Claire, 'I also have permission to dispose of the Wolves' Valley by lottery. By this means I shall be completely denuded. Like Job I came naked into the world, and naked I shall depart from it.' The lottery, which it was hoped would bring in a large sum for his property, was a failure. Only four out of ninety lots were sold. Then by a miracle one of his nephews, Christian, appeared on the scene, with an ardent admiration for his illustrious uncle and prepared to do his utmost for him. Thanks to his assistance the money affairs were put in order; Chateaubriand no longer had a house or a library, but he was at least free of debt. Claire was pleased for his sake; she wrote to a friend 'His money affairs have been arranged, I'm so glad for his sake. Now he is independent, for thank God the arrangement has nothing to do with politics. It has done him good to go on writing his recollections. They are enchanting to read, but I hope he will not let himself be tempted to read them to anyone but myself. That would worry me for many reasons'.

So he had gone back to writing his *Memoirs from beyond the Grave,* which were to prove the finest and richest work of his life; but he was doing it for the moment at other people's tables in other people's rooms, for the couple were going from château to château, staying for a time with Colbert, then a few months with the Pizieux, leading, in short, the easy but uncertain life of guests, who are no doubt welcome, but have to conform to other people's ways. Chateaubriand did, however, go to Paris from time to time to see to his affairs, and to cast a secret glance at the politics of the day, which never left his mind. With his tendency to equate his own troubles with public misfortune, the situation of the country looked very black to him, and he sighed 'Poor France!' He even talked of leaving his 'ungrateful country' and going abroad again.

Possibly these plans had something to do with his visits to Madame de Staël, who had regained complete freedom of movement since the fall of her great opponent, and was now living in Paris again. Was he thinking of Coppet? A few years earlier, when she had complained of being restricted to Coppet, he had written to her 'If I had a good château on the shores of the Lake of Geneva, I should never leave it. The public would never have a line of mine. I should display the same zeal in making myself forgotten as I have foolishly spent in making myself known'. Germaine may have smiled ironically at the time, she may even have been annoyed. She can certainly not have believed a word of what her 'dear Francis' had written, and probably considered his lack of understanding of her position typical of the great egoist. Now he himself wanted to leave his country, not under duress, however, but from embitterment. But she was hardly capable now of giving him good advice, for she was ill. It was no longer Napoleon's police that were condemning her to immobility, it was her legs, which were failing her more and more. 'Good morning, my dear Francis,' she called out to him from her bed, 'I'm in pain, but that doesn't prevent me from loving you.' They talked of the changes in the times and the Powers. 'I have always been the same, lively and sad,' said Germaine, 'I love God, my father and freedom.' She asked him to have dinner with her on May the 28th.

He turned up punctually, and found Germaine in bed, more ill than before. She was too weak to sit at table, so the doors were set wide open to allow her to take part in the conversation, and Réne had to take his place at the table, alone with the second guest. This guest was Juliette Récamier. They had only met twice before in their lives, and had not then said much to each other. Now conversation was really difficult between them, hindered as they were by the thought of the dying Germaine, in her mental twilight next door. Their first conversation was a whispered one, and lent an involuntary intimacy to this strange encounter in the shadow of death.

The meal came to an end; they heard Germaine's breathing in the room alongside. 'I turned my head a little,' writes Réne, 'I raised my eyes, and I saw my guardian angel on my right. I am afraid lest in my old age my mouth should desecrate a feeling that has preserved all the freshness of youth in my memory, and whose charm only increases with the decline of life.' The great encounter of his life had come to pass. The connection was to last for thirty-one years, until death put an end to it. Of what nature was the tie that bound them so indissolubly together? Somewhere between earthly and heavenly love was born a feeling encompassing all human emotions. It was a mysterious relationship, which, whenever it appeared to approach the frontiers of a commonplace love story, retreated into the sphere of the purest spiritual exaltation. In a word, it was the perfect example of romantic love.

THE MOST BEAUTIFUL OF ALL

Who was Madame Récamier? Everybody knew her, but nobody knew of what elements her being was composed. She wrote hundreds of letters, notes and memoranda, but she never told the truth about herself. Must it suffice to call her the most beautiful, influential and beloved woman of her time? Of what time? Her social career began under the Consulate, she lived through the Empire and both Restorations, and did not leave this world till after the fall of the bourgeois King Louis Philippe. She made a conquest of Lucien Bonaparte, Bernadotte, both Montmorencys, Barante and Ballanche, in short everybody worth conquering.

The Duke of Wellington and Metternich were at her feet, Prince August of Prussia wanted to marry her, even women like Germaine de Staël cherished an exalted friendship for her. Benjamin Constant almost lost his wits on her account, he reduced his life to a heap of ruins for her sake. Only Chateaubriand, who was passionately devoted to her, was as ever in the happy situation of loving her a hair's breadth less than she loved him.

In the course of modern history no other woman is to be found exerting such a power of attraction over the best and most influential men of her time as Juliette. In spite of all the dramas she provoked, all the lives she lured to the brink of catastrophe, her image remains uniformly calm and untouched amid the confusions of her time. Nobody ever cursed her, hardly anybody spoke evil of her—despite the many separations, ruptures and frustrations. Her charm never failed, she never made even the most intelligent of her adorers regret that she was not on the same intellectual level as himself. No comparison ever arose between her and the men of powerful intellect who admired her and spent their time with her. Her abilities were of a feminine order, and so perfect that no man ever thought of demanding any intellectual accomplishment of her. Her smile, her conciliatory spirit, her sound common sense, her gentle irony formed a rampart round her that presented no hindrance to intelligent conversation. She made people talk, and listened to them: an incomparable gift, which amounted almost to genius in that she divined what the great people she associated with wanted to talk about. Literature, politics or social trifles, she always knew which of these was brimming the other person's heart, and she immediately made it overflow. Whoever talked to her believed that she understood him better than any other woman in the world. And this was true not only of men, for Germaine de Staël was a most intimate friend of hers for more than twenty years, and was never bored for a minute in her company, although she herself was intellectually far superior not only to her, but to most of the men of her day.

At the age of fifteen Juliette had married the forty-four-year-old banker Récamier, who until his financial ruin was famous for his extravagance and his grandiose style of living. What was the reason for this unequal marriage? The couple never had any children, and someone with an intimate knowledge of the situation swears that 'Monsieur Récamier never had any but paternal relations with his wife'. The same witness—Juliette's niece—declares that her aunt 'was never either mother or wife'. So it was inevitable that the rumour should get about that Madame Récamier was her husband's daughter, and that he had only married her to ensure her access to his great fortune. Two circumstances are in favour of this assertion: the banker was at one time a close friend of Juliette's mother, and the girl continued to live with her parents for two whole years after her marriage; besides which, at the time of the marriage, in 1793, Récamier was in a dangerous situation. It was the period of the Terror, and he was in danger of arrest and of having his fortune confiscated. Marriages of this kind often took place at that time of judicial uncertainty; those who felt themselves threatened often had no other means of insuring their possessions for the benefit, at least, of families closely allied to them.

However this may have been, Juliette, at an age when she might almost have been still playing with dolls, became the distinguished wife of a banker, though it was not till the fall of Robespierre and the drift of the Revolution into quieter waters that she was able to enjoy her husband's wealth and become known for her extraordinary charm. As soon as this was possible, she adopted the customs of a society that could not pretend to be the best, but was certainly the most amusing. She danced at balls in the post-revolutionary era in transparent garments that only imperfectly concealed her faultless body. Her husband encouraged her to display her famous feet, which presented no difficulty owing to the prevailing fashion of wearing light sandals. She exhibited her shoulders to the general admiration, and in fact did everything a woman can do, who wishes to please without overstepping the limits of decency. But Récamier never had cause to play the injured husband, for his wife never gave anybody more than her little finger.

Her social success was astonishing; from her twentieth year onwards she was the most admired woman in France. Every door was open to her, every house was proud of sheltering her as a guest. No dinner-party to great men, no ball with beautiful women was conceivable without her. But she was never entirely absorbed by social activities, she preferred houses in which not merely elegance but intelligence was the order of the day. She was chiefly attracted by serious converstaion, which she knew how to stimulate by her attentive listening and an occasional, more questioning than assertive word. Her elegance was of a special kind; she favoured an appearance a little reminiscent of the Vestals, the priestesses whose dignity and purity were the pride of Rome.

She never wore diamonds or jewellery of that kind; the only ornaments she tolerated were pearls, and those only sparingly. Madame Lenormant gives the following description of her 'A supple, elegant figure, shoulders and neck wonderfully proportioned, a small red mouth with pearly teeth, ravishing arms, if a little too slender, chestnut-brown hair in natural curls, a delicate, regular but very French nose, skin of a lustre that threw every-in the shade, a face full of innocence and sometimes of roguishness, which a gracious expression made irresistibly attractive. It could be said of her, as Saint-Simon said of the Duchess of Burgundy, that her gait was that of a goddess on the clouds'.

This description from the pen of a woman was one of many equally favourable, but there were others which admitted her overpowering charm with certain reservations. A certain Baron de Trémont, who had observed her closely, says: 'It would have been impossible to have a fairer face, but for all its attractiveness it was rather that of a grisette than a great lady.' Is it credible? He even gives her 'ordinary feet' and a 'flat breast', in flagrant contradiction of the general verdict. The numberless portraits by the painters of her day cannot of course be unconditionally trusted. One need only compare the famous picture by Gérard with the still more famous one by David, or the bust by Chinard, to realize how differently the academic but flamboyant brush of the first-named artist could present a human form from the more credible presentation by the great David or the honest sculptor. And as for the *décolleté* that Trémont disparages, a connoisseur such as

Brillat-Savarin was of quite another opinion. Moreover, Juliette, in later years, had the spring of the bosom in Chinard's bust covered up, which she would certainly not have done had the sculptor flattered her.

Madame de Boigne describes her fair friend with her usual mastery, in which a little acid is always mixed: 'Madame Récamier is the very type of the woman that has issued from the hand of the Creator for the happiness of man. She possesses every charm, every virtue, every inconsequence, every weakness. If she had been a wife and a mother, her life would have been more complete; the world would have had less to say about her and she would have been happier. Having failed of this natural vocation, she felt she must seek compensation in society. Madame Récamier is coquetry personified, she has carried it to the height of genius, and has thus become the admirable head of a detestable school.'

That she was the undisputed mistress of coquetry, that she wished to please without relinquishing her feminine reserve, was admitted by everybody, men and women alike. Barante wrote to Germaine 'Madame Récamier is busy, as usual, adopting every sentiment within her reach, relinquishing it and taking it up again. Last year Montlosier wrote me from Rome that he had met her just as she was thinking of becoming religious. But unfortunately that implies adoring God, whereas she demanded that God should adore her'. A malicious story, though there may have been a grain of truth in it, in so far as coquetry had become her element. It was far too brutal a description of her behaviour, for nobody could deny that she was a stranger to any form of obtrusiveness, that she possessed to perfection the art of appearing simple, not to say naïve, and that she was eminently kind and good-natured.

Of the many passions she had kindled, two had made a deep impact on her life: her romance with Prince August of Prussia and the passion she inspired in Benjamin Constant. The Prince, a nephew of Frederick the Great, had been taken prisoner by the French in Prenzlau. Napoleon took care that he should be splendidly treated, and even allowed him to go on a journey to Italy. He started off with his adjutant Clausewitz and went through Coppet, where he stayed longer than he had intended. He met Juliette there, and fell so passionately in love with her that he swore he would either marry her or perish. She was not indifferent to the Prince's homage, and agreed to a 'love pact' that was as good as an engagement. He promised to get rid of every hindrance to the marriage on his side, and she promised no less solemnly to make Récamier divorce her.

Meanwhile the conclusion of peace with Prussia had restored the young man to freedom; full of amorous hopes he repaired to Berlin, while Germaine did all she could to further the marriage project. Napoleon much regretted that the Prince should have absorbed the spirit of Coppet: 'The advice of his honourable father and his worthy mother would have been more useful to him than the lessons of the evil-minded woman he saw at Coppet, and the evil notions he heard there.' But the support that Germaine gave to the plan bore no fruit. Not only did Monsieur Récamier refuse to hear of a divorce, but Juliette herself was unable to live up to her vows of love, owing to her inborn coquetry. She gave up the Prince, and he wrote her a farewell letter, the furious anger in which hints at unknown complications: 'I could not have been happy with a woman who can simulate feelings she has perhaps never experienced. . . . I beg you not to write to me again, your letters give me too much pain. Adieu, for the last time.'

Madame de Boigne's statement that all the men who had been in love with Juliette remained friends with her, applies even to the Prussian prince, for only a few years later their relations were resumed on the most peaceable terms. And what of Benjamin Constant? This great thinker and writer, who was certainly one of the most fascinating intellects of his time, had been Madame de Staël's lover for many years, and made her very unhappy. Then he met Juliette, and with his heart still smarting from Germaine's lion's claws, and her amorous screams and curses, he flung himself into a fresh passion as if he were experiencing love for a woman for the first time in his tempestuous life. With a gift of introspection bordering on indiscretion he notes in his 'Intimate Diaries':

'Dinner at Madame X's. Madame Récamier. My God, I'm going mad.'

'The devil take love, which is plaguing me ridiculously.'

'I can think of nothing but Juliette. Gambled to distract my thoughts. Won.'

'The whole day given to Juliette. I'm not yet loved, but she likes me. There are few women that are not impressed by my habit of being absorbed and dominated by them. I feel a heat in my heart such as never before.'

'Neuralgia. This love for Juliette hurts me horribly. I haven't the strength to master the feeling, and yet what can come of it? A few enchanting moments, much suffering, and supposing Juliette is unexpectedly more emotional than I think, incalculable unhappiness.'

'I've seen Juliette again. I believe she is a great coquette, more so than she knows herself, but perhaps there is some feeling in her that I can develop. I must soon put her to the test. Beware of Madame de Staël if she discovers it.'

'Juliette promised to go for a walk with me. Didn't keep her word. Had dinner with her. I felt desperate at not being alone with her. At last a tête-à-tête. One mustn't pester her too much. She is capable of freeing herself from this beginning of a sentiment. I'm suffering idiotically.'

So it went on for more than a year. Benjamin was on a footing of a certain intimacy with the adored one, which, however, never crossed a sharply drawn line. He filled his diaries with candid observations on his condition (not intended for publication), and described his beloved with acute vision in spite of his intoxication.

This man of powerful intellect was at the same time a very self-conscious one, and greedy of sentimental excitement. Germaine had flung herself, sobbing, on the floor at his feet. But his suffering was genuine, none the less. Juliette saw to it that his longing for her should not fade, but refused to release him from his love-sickness. 'I'm out of my mind,' he wrote to her, 'I'm not joking, I'm suffering too much. I'm clinging desperately to the edge of an abyss. You can let a man suffer in this way with such indifference! Even angels can be cruel!' He had lost his head to such a degree that he decided to ask advice from Madame de Staël and her son. Germaine seems to have taken the confession quietly, although it was a good deal to demand of her, but Madame Récamier appears to have come off badly. He notes: 'Talked candidly about Juliette with Auguste and Madame de Staël. She is a regular libertine in woman's form. I must be mad! I must behave differently. This talk has relieved me a little.'

The relief can only have been of short duration, for the lover must very soon have discovered that this beautiful woman had absolutely nothing of the 'libertine' about her, but suffered, on the contrary, from too much virtue: 'Seen Madame Récamier again. Her presence always soothes me. She is so incapable of any feeling, shows such naïve indifference and coldness, not only towards me but to everybody, that one no longer loves her when one hears her. When she is absent one restores her to that which one desires, and the obstacles and outward difficulties in seeing her go to one's head. Moreover, she has good intentions and considers herself capable of friendship. I say this now, but at the least refusal I shall get worked up again, and capable of killing myself for pain. I simply must leave the place, and put an end to this madness.'

However, this great writer, thinker and statesman did not die of this love, nor did he go mad for its sake. His amorous frenzies had the same origin as his immoderate ambition, his cruelties, his changeableness in politics and friendship. The fact that such an uncertain character could have so much spiritual insight and political wisdom to dispense is one of the seductive and yet repulsive enigmas of the artist that he was, and always would be, in every phase of his activity. Compared with him, Chateaubriand, who was certainly not lacking in egoism, often unrestrained, appears a childish, generous creature, unsparing of his riches, never flirting with the abyss as he moves along the edge. Whatever may have been the nature of his connection with Juliette, what joys or disappointments she may have caused him, he never speaks of her with anything but the most loving respect and the most dignified emotion. Her image may have been surrounded by uncertainty and even ambiguity, but the light Chateaubriand sheds on her is never dimmed and remains pure to the end.

JULIETTE'S SECRET

She remains enigmatic, as a woman, all the same. Whom did she

ever love? By whom was she ever possessed? Was she perhaps
denied the fulfilment granted to the humblest of nature's children?
Even the most indiscreet of her admirers never boasted of having
enjoyed her favours. Among the meagre evidence of disappointed
or reconciled adorers, on the other hand, there are many references
to her purity and virginity. Her virtue, so Maxime du Camp said,
'was loudly acclaimed'. Merimée said in defence of her coldness
'Do not judge her unfavourably, I beg of you. She is to be pitied
rather than blamed; it is a case of *force majeure*'. A similar explana-
tion was given of the truly astonishing fact that she played the
part of one of the 'Three Graces' of the Directory, in the pleasure-
loving, immoral life of that period, without the slightest stain on
her reputation; which could certainly not be said of the other two
Graces, Thérèse Tallien and Joséphine Beauharnais. Was it
merely virtue that saved her from falling a victim to 'the sin of the
flesh'? Her virginal charm, her girlish attractiveness were too often
extolled for these epithets to be considered accidental.

   In Benjamin Constant's notes there are constant allusions to
the art with which she withdrew from attack, and thus fanned the
ardour of her impatient suitor. All that knew her refer to her
coquetry with indulgence or censure; but was this coquetry a
means, or was it an end in itself? Even in sexual love there is a
certain loyalty, which consists in not promising more than one
intends to fulfil. This woman, the most famous of her time, who
never had a successor in any country, was perhaps condemned by
extraneous circumstances to refuse the natural solution of a passion
between man and woman. In Sainte-Beuve's circle somebody said
'Nature has preserved her from ever yielding herself completely,
and none of her adorers has ever been able to overcome the
barrier that defends her virtue'. A physical hindrance, therefore?
But the Goncourts called her 'a virgin by inclination'; Madame de
Rémusat's son, in his Memoirs, which came to light only in 1959,
treats the 'case' with little ceremony, and ends his not very
chivalrous analysis in these words: 'A peculiar secrecy shrouds the
extent of the sacrifice she made to the pleasure of being loved.
There were successes that she contrived to renew with tireless,
insatiate greed, and even sought to advertise. She was endowed

with many good and lovable qualities, and yet was a coquette in the grand manner.'

The contradictions are resolved in the magic of her grace, and combine to form the harmonious image of a woman who could dominate even her enemies, so far as she had any. Chateaubriand had now become a permanent element of her life, whatever the nature of their connection may have been. She began at once to influence his work; they were hardly friends before he started writing—expressly for her sake—the most beautiful part of his Memoirs, the story of his youth: 'I was aroused from my thoughts by the fluting of a thrush perched on the topmost branch of a birch tree. This magical note conjured up a vision of our paternal estate; I was suddenly transported into the past, and into the surroundings in which I had so often heard the thrushes singing. This bird-song in the woods of Combourg spoke to me of a bliss that I felt I had now attained; the rich notes recalled the days I had wasted in pursuit of this elusive bliss. I intend to employ the little time that is left to me in describing my youth, so long as its essence remains palpable to me.'

Everything is combined in this passage: the innocent emotion transformed to poetry by the song of a thrush, the wish to tell the woman he loves about his youth—the simplest, most innocent period of his life—the mild melancholy of greying hair, which pleases rather than saddens him, the reawakening urge to work and the desire to speak of a happiness hitherto unattainable and now, perhaps, coming within his reach. These emotional stirrings were new to Juliette. She had known men who either spoke of nothing but themselves, or of nothing but her; now she was being carried off into a region that could be common to them both if only she chose—dream and remembrance. This sphere they now entered, never to forsake it again. Henceforth Juliette was to find repose in this half reminiscent, half expectant tenderness, although René would continue to play the Enchanter whom nothing and nobody could withstand. What he asked of her nobody knows, but there can be no doubt that she fulfilled every demand without hesitation, and accepted him as her lord and master. If she ever loved anybody it was him, and in full acceptance of her submissive role. René had no intention of suffering, so if suffering was unavoidable, it must be hers, not his.

He did not feel the intoxication of conquest, such as he had known hitherto. He had discovered all at once how enchanting a woman's face could be when it expressed joy and gratitude. He had no wish to triumph, he only wanted to love. In a word, he had become older. His one desire was to know that Juliette was happy, and happy through him—alone. This much-courted woman had never yet met a man who approached her with such open assurance, ruling her heart so tenderly and yet so decidedly, and speaking to her in such a wonderful, such a magical strain. The Enchanter had won his greatest victory, a gentle victory that swept over the surface of a woman's life like a soft breeze, and yet stirred it to its depths. She had at last found the man to rule her life; her heart unfolded to a passion she had never yet experienced, her 'coldness' and lack of emotion melted in the heat of a passion of which she had hitherto thought herself incapable: 'I cried all day long.'

Her friends were distressed, and no wonder, to see her losing her head for the first time in her life. She was now just forty, and though she had retained all the beauty of her face and figure, life was gradually assuming a sterner look and a hint of incalculableness. The faithful Ballanche expressed his anxiety: 'I felt quite sad and ashamed yesterday, for other people's sake as well as my own, to see the sudden alteration in your whole manner. Oh, Madame, what progress this malady has made in a few weeks, that you should avoid your nearest friends!' He adds, unwisely enough, a warning against this Chateaubriand, 'this spoilt man, intoxicated with himself, like all despotic rulers'.

Mathieu de Montmorency, too, evinced anxiety; he himself had once fallen a victim to Juliette's charm, but as a man of strict religious principles he had long since conquered his desire for her. He now watched over her safety and was not sparing of his warnings. Juliette, in return, urged him to purchase the house in the Wolves' Valley, which Chateaubriand had never been able to dispose of. He moved in at once, and persuaded her to spend part of the summer there with him. The Duchess de Broglie wrote to her 'I picture your little *ménage* in the Wolves' Valley as something quite enchanting. But when one of these days Mathieu's career is due to be included in the "Lives of the Saints", this tête-à-tête with the most beautiful and admired woman of his time will form a comical chapter. To the pure all things are pure, said Saint Paul, and he was right'. But Mathieu, like his cousin Adrien, was so famous for the strictness of his morals as to be above scandal, and nobody was offended by the idyll in the Wolves' Valley. He was less sure of her, it must be said, for when one day he was obliged to leave her alone at home while he went on a journey, he wrote to her 'I count on your perfect discretion not to receive the former owner of the estate too often'. She took care not to promise anything.

There were times, however, when she felt afraid of the power the Enchanter had acquired over her. She avoided him then, and went travelling, but she soon came back to him. They spent a few days together with friends at Chantilly, and during a secret walk at night in the park, which was surrounded by impassable woods, their intimacy reached its peak. Their tenderness knew no limits—except those drawn, perhaps, for Juliette by her nature and disposition—and for a long while afterwards the reminder kept appearing in his love-letters: 'Don't forget the woods at Chantilly!' They wrote to each other every day. Either a messenger carried the letters to and fro, or they made use of the post—in which case, however, it seems that the police opened the letters and often made extracts from them, with the result that many a page has come down to posterity. They poured out their hearts to each other. She wrote 'Love you less! Dear friend, you don't believe that yourself! After eight hours? Don't believe in these imaginary plans against you. It is no longer in my power, or in yours, or in that of anybody whomsoever, to hinder my love for you. My love, my life, my heart all belong to you'.

Old Récamier's affairs were taking a bad turn; a few miscalculations completed his ruin, and nearly everything Juliette still possessed was lost at the same time. The misfortune had this good side to it, that she could now, without offence, cease to share a residence with him, and make a home for herself. She found a modest lodging on the left bank of the Seine, in a nunnery where they accepted tenants and *pensionnaires* without any obligation to take part in the religious life of the house. This was the so-called Abbaye-aux-Bois, which in ancient times may have been surrounded by woods, but had now been overrun by the city of Paris, and lay in the Rue de Sèvres, not far from the life of the town. The apartment was small and inconvenient, but cheap, for Juliette was obliged to economize, since she now had to provide for her ruined husband's maintenance.

The apartment was on the third floor, and the stairs were steep. But the windows overlooked the gardens; a huge acacia reached almost into the bedroom; one had a view over roofs and towers and a glimpse of the wooded hills of Sèvres on the horizon. Chateaubriand was delighted with the modest refuge, for it afforded him 'silence and solitude above the tumult and noise of a great city'.

It is a testimony to Juliette's independence that she acquired greater influence from her 'cell' than she had ever had in wealthier circumstances. She never complained of the restrictions she was obliged to adopt; pampered though she had been, she accommodated herself to the narrowness of her present situation without a sign of discontent. Her friends came to see her as of old, and it seemed as though her radiance had been doubled by the narrowing of the frame of her life. According to Sainte-Beuve 'Madame Récamier never held a larger place in society than at the time when she lived in this simple refuge at the far end of Paris. She may be said to have perfected the art of friendship and helped it to develop further. The party spirit was then at its height. She disarmed anger, she smoothed out inequalities, removed acerbities and spread tolerance. In this way a woman can accomplish the work of civilization to the highest degree, without deserting her own sphere'.

Her role was less respectfully described in a contemporary but very superficial 'Dictionary of Conversation and Reading'; 'Evidence of the all-powerful influence of this politico—literary Areopagus is to be found in elections and academical examinations, in the distribution of ministerial portfolios and University

Q

Chairs, in a word, in all the high posts in the government. To be
protected by Madame Récamier was in fact, for thirty years, the
most unfailing of all recommendations; down to the illegitimate
son of her apothecary or her door-keeper, this kind-hearted,
complaisant woman found means to lodge them all in ministerial
offices'.

The connection with Chateaubriand soon assumed a semi-
public form; not only the circle of their friends but the whole of
Parisian society came to look upon the liaison as a sort of institution, demanding all the more respect in that the two lovers
behaved unusually correctly, almost ceremoniously towards each
other, and observed the forms of good society with the greatest
care. They were both conscious of their unusual situation and never
forgot that they were—each of them individually, and still more
so together—a favourite subject of Parisian conversation. Every
afternoon at three o'clock Chateaubriand appeared at the Abbaye-
aux-Bois to pay his respects, and never opened his mouth if he
found other visitors in Juliette's apartment. Mathieu, whose
friendship with Juliette was of longer date, if more resigned than
René's, wrote to her 'I cannot accustom myself to the fact that
when I present myself twice in one day to ask after your health,
you keep your door closed against me and make your maid tell
me tales, so as not to be disturbed in your tête-à-tête with
Monsieur de Chateaubriand'. To her friend Madame de Boigne,
who expressed astonishment at her subjugation, Juliette said 'It
may be the charm of novelty. The others were all preoccupied
with me, and he insists on my being preoccupied with him'.

However tender and affectionate their relations may have been,
there was never any question of another Chantilly. It is not to be
wondered at if throughout their time there was talk of the 'secret',
and even the 'case' of Madame Récamier. It was a day of conventional forms but violent passions. The 'longed-for storms'
conjured up by Chateaubriand filled the life of Byron, and later
found their greatest portrayer in Balzac. On the threshold of the
Romantic Era the surrender to passion was so violent as to disrupt
the order of existence. The fatal consecration the Revolution
had bestowed on embraces found a fresh form in the rebellion of

lovers against the order of society. In the case of such great and brilliant figures as Juliette and René this rebellion was not condemned, but it occasioned remark.

Chateaubriand, whose need to adore and conquer women, though accompanied by miraculous psychological tact, would appear to have included a healthy physical desire, was not the man to resign himself to a 'case'. Did Juliette reveal more to him than the world guessed at? Did she confide a secret wound to him, which formed a persistent offence to her womanly pride? However this may have been, his behaviour reveals a chivalrous side to his nature. He found fulfilment, of whatever kind it may have been; he was neither gross nor violent, neither cynical nor reproachful. His friendship with this woman was so tender and respectful that it remains one of the most beautiful love-stories among the memories of those times. Whatever nature may have denied Juliette, it never disturbed her mind, her temper remained harmonious throughout. There was nothing convulsive or distorted in her nature, which was strong enough to tame the brilliant egoist, now over fifty, and teach him a new form of adoration.

A VICTIM TO POLITICS

The influence of this woman on Chateaubriand's politics was at first hardly noticeable. She herself cannot be said to have had any definite political principles or designs, but only a general attitude that was definitely liberal and conciliatory. The Chamber was renewed annually as to one-fifth by partial elections, and the number of Liberals and Independents increased every time. Richelieu was succeeded by his nearest collaborator Decazes, a declared favourite of the King, who was trying, little by little, to do away with the vindictive exceptional laws passed at the beginning of the Restoration, and procure the Monarchy that breath of freedom, without which, in his opinion, Frenchmen could not prosper. He stood, therefore, between the two main party fronts; he wished 'to bring the one nearer to the King by means of the Charter, and the other nearer to the Charter through the King'. Decazes, at this period of the Restoration, was a bold, modern figure, and for that very reason pleased nobody but the King, who refused to be deprived of his charming Chief Minister, through whom he became a sincere, if unsuccessful, mediator between the two parties.

Decazes was too royalist for the Liberals, too Liberal for the Ultras—which shows that he was on the right track. Both parties were agreed in their hostility to him, and France thus beheld the paradoxical spectacle of two irreconcilable opposites cancelling each other out. Chateaubriand and his ultra-royalist friends founded the newspaper *Le Conservateur,* which did not live long. In the House of Peers he was now the unopposed leader of the extreme Right, which obliged him to co-operate more closely with Villèle, who was playing the same part in the Chamber of Deputies. The contact was purely political, however, for the two men were not made to understand each other personally. Villèle, an ex-naval officer, was a lesser nobleman of Gascony, shrewd and business-like, circumspect and taciturn, while the Breton Vicomte, to his great detriment, could never refrain from playing the wit, even in politics. Politics were for him merely a means of fulfilling his ambition and feeling his life doubled in intensity by the use of power. He was unwise enough to say to Villèle one day 'What does all this futile fuss matter to me? To me, that have never placed any trust in the times in which I live, that belong to the past, and doubt the mission of kings and the right to exist of nations, to me, that care for nothing but my dreams, and for them only if they last no longer than a night!'

This arrogant, grandiloquent confession was hardly likely to please the sober, dilligent Villèle, who had no use for dreams. But the two men were forced to hang together for the time being as leaders of the Opposition. The Vicomte put in appearance regularly at the joint deliberations, although they bored him: 'When I left these conferences I was a little more of a statesman, and a little more penetrated with the paltriness of the whole business. At night, when I'm half asleep, I see before me the various attitudes of the bald heads, the different expressions of the faces in that not very well-kept *salon.* Of course it was all very respectable, but I prefer the swallow that used to wake me in my youth, and

the Muses that filled my dreams.' Such phrases do not merely
express the self-assertion of a genius that feels itself superior,
and of another race, they show the conflict between fact and
fiction, politics and romanticism, which had caused so many
contradictions in Chateaubriand's life since Waterloo. If his
greatest and most faultless work—the *Memoirs from beyond the
Grave*—had not still been uncompleted, it might have been said
that his literary life was now over. *Atala* and *René*, *The Natchez*
and *The Martyrs*, the *Journey from Paris to Jerusalem* and
The Last of the Abencérages had been written, and with them a
period of life had come to an end. 'We seek consolation,' he said,
'for the lost illusions of our youth in the task of becoming a
famous citizen of the State. One need not fear old age if fame
rejuvenates it.'

But in the world of literature as in that of politics it would be
wrong not to take Chateaubriand seriously. His literary position
at the threshold of a great upsurge of Romanticism is undisputed,
and his political importance cannot be lightly treated. Even if his
hostility to the liberalism so discreetly displayed by Decazes was
genuine, this would not suffice to make him a reactionary. The
Ultra in him, which is certainly displeasing, was balanced by his
desperate attempts to introduce the elements of English parlia-
mentarianism into French politics and educate the leading class in
the country to this political form. What made him so obstinate,
even fanatical, was his ineradicable hostility to the Revolution.
The Revolution lay a whole generation back in time, it had had
new institutions imposed on it till it was past recognition, its
representatives and leading figures had been either exterminated
or transformed—again past recognition—but it had preserved its
political reality, and might at any moment be conjured up to walk
as a very lively ghost across the background of the political stage.
Upheavals of this kind, however guiltily stained, cannot be driven
out of the world, and become only the more malevolent the
deeper one tries to bury them. The Hundred Days had made this
suddenly manifest: Napoleon, in his predicament, invoked the
old Jacobin forces, and lo! they came to light from their holes
and hiding-places, and showed a liveliness that alarmed the

Emperor himself. Of all the spectres that haunted Chateaubriand during his political life, that of the Revolution was the most importunate.

At the last partial election the Abbé Grégoire had entered the Chamber. This apostate priest had sat in the Convention, and although he had attacked the 'planned vandalism' (his own expression) of those that wanted to burn the National Library and demolish the church steeples, he was nevertheless the first to move the abolition of monarchy and demand the indictment of the King. A historical figure, therefore, casting a bloody shadow. There was no need to be an Ultra to feel his presence in the Chamber offensive. Most of the politicians were agreed that the King ought not to have this deputy thrust upon him. Even Decazes could see this, and he set to work at once to draft an alteration in the electoral law which should prevent scandals of this kind. But he did not get far, for he 'slipped up in blood', as Chateaubriand horrifyingly expresses it. On February 13, 1820, the Duc de Berry was assassinated at the Opera. Berry, the son of the future Charles X, was not only the last hope of the Bourbons for the continuance of their dynasty, but also the hope of the Extreme Right, who were sure of his reactionary outlook and his hatred of liberalism.

The dagger-thrust that put an end to his life was delivered by a saddler named Louvel at ten o'clock at the Opera, and the murderer made no attempt to conceal his intention of bringing about the end of the dynasty. The victim could not be moved; he lay in the antechamber of his box, bleeding hopelessly but able to speak. His good feeling in personal matters manifested itself in his last hours. He begged that his wife, Princess Marie-Caroline of Naples, should be shown every consideration, because she was pregnant. He repeatedly implored those around him to show mercy to the murderer, whom he forgave. Finally he sent for his two illegitimate daughters, borne to him by an English lady long before his marriage, while he was an *emigré*. The two girls were brought to him, and Marie-Caroline clasped them in her arms. He had a kind word for everybody present until his death at five in the morning in the arms of his wife.

This behaviour of the murdered victim in his last hours increased the general indignation at the bloody deed. It was immediately given the widest significance and attributed to the spread of Liberalism. The Ultras cried aloud that 'the dagger that struck the Duc de Berry was a liberal idea'. One of them, Clausel de Coussergues, made Decazes responsible for the murder, and proposed to have the Minister indicted 'for complicity'. Marie-Caroline and the Comte d'Artois took the same view. When Decazes bowed before the corpse, the widow cried out 'Take that man away! I can't bear the sight of him, it is horrible to me!' Everybody that had been offended by Decazes's modernization of the legislation, and wanted to pick a hole in his coat for personal or political reasons, agreed with this verdict, and described the murder as a symptom of the evil spirit of the age, for which the Chief Minister was said, flippantly or maliciously, to be responsible.

Madame Récamier could not prevent Chateaubriand from assuming the same tone in his newspaper: 'The hand that struck the blow does not bear the greatest guilt; they that have murdered the Duc de Berry are those that have been introducing democratic laws into the Monarchy for the last four years; those that have rewarded treason and punished loyalty; those that have surrendered offices to the enemies of the Bourbons and the vassals of Napoleon. . . . Those are the real murderers of the Duc de Berry.' Every word of this diatribe is steeped in personal resentment, showing that the Vicomte could not forget his own personality even on the gravest occasions. But the way in which the King reacted to it was no less determined by personal feelings. He wrote to Decazes 'As a rule, my dear son, I read the works of Monsieur de Chateaubriand a bit superficially; but today I have laid the burden on myself of reading him right through. I am indignant. I should like to go to the author, who is doubtless a mean cur (all slanderers are), and force him to retract his infamous statements'.

But there could be no question of this. The Comte d'Artois threw himself on his knees before his royal brother and begged him to dismiss Decazes. The Duchess of Angoulême appeared, dressed from head to foot in black, and went through the same performance. The red-coated young men of the Bodyguard declared to all and sundry their intention to kill the Chief Minister. Chateaubriand continued to mingle his voice in the chorus of menace. The King resisted for a long while, saying 'His politics are mine'. Finally Decazes resigned of his own accord. Louis accepted the resignation much against his will, but he made his 'dear son' a peer, a duke, and an Ambassador to London. Before leaving for this new post, Decazes drove out to visit his estates. The feeling against him had been so well fomented that he was molested on the way, and to avoid recognition he travelled thenceforth under the name of Adrien de Montmorency, and made use of the relay horses that were being held in readiness for the latter's return to Madrid.

The English system of government, so Chateaubriand hoped, might be made use of now that a new government was to be formed, in which it was thought that the leaders of the victorious Opposition, including Chateaubriand, would be entrusted with power. But at the bare mention of the Vicomte's name the King shouted 'Never!' On the other hand, the Comte d'Artois begged him to write an account of the murdered man's life, and offered him a fee of 100,000 francs. Chateaubriand set to work at once, to the great joy of the widow, a little Neapolitan brunette who, seven months after her husband's tragic death, had given birth to a boy, baptized by the name of Henri, Duc de Bordeaux. For the christening, Chateaubriand presented the bottle of water of the Jordan that he had brought back from the Holy Land and carefully preserved.

The Duc de Richelieu was very loth to take office again as Chief Minister. He realized that he would not be able to do without the Ultras this time. But how was he to manage anyhow, since Villèle could not be included without Chateaubriand, who was now proscribed by the hostility of the King? Juliette Récamier solved the difficulty with her feminine diplomacy, guaranteeing her friend's reconciliation with the King, if he succeeded in persuading Villèle to take part in the government. Juliette knew her great friend; she knew that this commission would flatter his vanity; he would not be a minister, but he would be making ministers. . . . He did in fact render the King and Richelieu the desired service by inducing Villèle to enter the Cabinet. But Juliette had also seen clearly that the reward must not be wanting, and it was now necessary to rope in other friends to help. Claire de Duras and Mathieu de Montmorency busied themselves behind the scenes, but unfortunately the only vacant post was that of Envoy to Berlin. Fresh refusal, because Prussia was not a big country; fresh entreaties, until Juliette succeeded in procuring him the prospect of the honorary title of Minister of State, of which the King had earlier deprived him. At last he accepted. He wrote to Juliette 'Everything is ready. I have accepted according to your orders. I have been promised the Minister of State. Sleep now; at least the torment of uncertainty is at an end'.

The appointment was no diplomatic triumph. The post was of no first-rank political importance, but its occupant would be remote from Paris and unable to cause the King further annoyance, especially as he now stood in a certain disciplinary relation to the government. His removal was actually favourable to his reputation, since it shelved for a time the conundrum of a fundamentally liberal and freedom-loving man being at the same time a partizan of Reaction. In actual fact, the Restoration, strictly speaking, could not in any case reach full development in France, for its true, consistent champion was active, not in Paris but in Vienna. Metternich was the man that was seriously attempting to re-establish conditions supplanted and destroyed by the march of time. The fact that such fantasies could be born in such a distinguished brain was an after-effect, not so much of the Revolution as of the Napoleonic era. All the aggressions that Austria had had to defend herself against were, in Metternich's eyes, a result of the Revolution. He thought to serve the external security of his country by suppressing everything in the way of new currents in the world which had made themselves felt in the last thirty years. In France, on the other hand, this repression could not develop to the same extent, although it was more intelligently advocated there, because even the Unteachables were con-

tinually discovering that the surviving ideas and habits of the
Revolution had become a part of French daily life. In Paris,
therefore, any attempt to re-establish the past was an almost
hopeless undertaking. The sooner Chateaubriand could release
himself from this entanglement, the more unequivocal his intellectual attitude would become. Madame Récamier and the
Duchesse de Duras were following a sound instinct when they
persuaded the great man to go to Berlin.

Madame de Chateaubriand, the resigned but by no means defenceless wife, was glad to remain behind in Paris this time. She
had at last found the occupation for which she was suited. A year
earlier she had persuaded her husband to buy a property in the
Rue d'Enfer, and had fitted it up, under the name of the 'Marie-
Thérèse Home', as a refuge for 'aged clergy and distinguished
ladies'. She had gone begging to all and sundry in order to
furnish it and install the necessary staff. The Archbishop of Paris
and the difficult but pious Duchess of Angoulême had been
persuaded to become its patrons, and Madame de Chateaubriand
could now rule over a handful of old people, who for their part
were glad to be tended and controlled by such a dignified but
entertaining lady. Her pleasure in this new activity, in the
beautiful building and its garden, was not unmixed with sadness;
she sought fulfilment in this charitable occupation because she
was not allowed to rule over her husband, or even to be a real
help-meet to him.

ENVOY IN BERLIN

The Vicomte started for Berlin on New Year's Day of the year
1821. It was a cold winter, the Seine was frozen over, but the
diplomat travelled in a comfortable coach, wrapped up in rugs,
with his feet on a copper brazier filled with red-hot charcoal. He
enjoyed these comforts, and was glad not to have to concern
himself with extraneous details, since his secretary Hyacinthe
Pilorge was accompanying him and a courier was riding ahead
to order fresh horses at the relay stations, with refreshments,
and, if necessary, lodgings for the night. On reaching the Rhine

they stopped for a while, and he used the opportunity to write a long letter to Claire de Duras: 'This morning I went to look at the Rhine; there was the old Germany in all its beauty. When I get to the other side I shall really have crossed the river of oblivion. Do you know what I have been doing on the way? I've been re-reading Mirabeau's letters on Berlin.' He compares himself to the great statesman of the first years of the Revolution, whose advice and warnings the Monarchy heeded as little as his own. 'But Mirabeau, who was so shamefully ignored, took his revenge, whereas I shall not take mine. One can actually see the traces of his revenge here in Mayence: a city half shattered by gunfire, monuments and religious pictures mutilated by the sabres of Equality; death and life both profaned by that Revolution whose soldiers were first beaten in Mayence and then exterminated the people of the Vendée. Up, then! Let us remain incorrigible and begin all over again!'

The writer, as usual, was under the spell of his favourite images. If he crosses a river, and writes to his bosom friend about it, it can only be the river of Lethe, although in this case there is nothing to forget. On the contrary, he wrote letters to Paris incessantly, and was secretly determined to return there very soon. Far from drinking the waters of Lethe, he took more interest in the political events in his country with every step that led him further from Paris; he really felt he ought not to have left the country without his guardianship. All this was the opposite of forgetfulness, but the image had a power of its own, it forced itself upon his poetic fancy and had to be employed, whether it had any intrinsic connection or not. No opportunity for a figurative comparison, a poetical association, must be lost; this is what makes Chateaubriand's prose so fascinating, and the nature of the artist so ambiguous.

The Vicomte-Envoy pursued his journey through the wintry landscape. 'Frankfurt, the city of the Jews, delayed me only on account of one of its trades, namely, that of money-changing.' The streets were dismal-looking, he said, the covering of snow stretched from horizon to horizon, the branches of the fir trees were shrouded in hoar frost. Luther's grave in Wittenberg did not attract him, because Protestantism was 'as a religion, an illogical heresy, and politically an unsuccessful revolution'. The Envoy brought with him little knowledge of the affairs of the country in which he was to represent His Most Christian Majesty, but much goodwill. He had a high estimation of Prussia's share in the defeat of Napoleon. He said of the campaign of 1813 that it should be called 'the campaign of German youth, or of the Poets'. He speaks of the sympathy one must feel for 'these high-spirited youths that seized the sword in the name of independence', and adds, 'Each of these battles was a declaration of the rights of nations'. In his Memoirs he praises Theodor Körner, who was not one of those bards that express their enthusiasm in verse from a safe corner; he calls him an 'Apollo on horseback', and gives a prose translation of his 'Lyre and Sword'. He speaks of Arndt too, but his picture of him, although sympathetically drawn, is influenced by Madame de Staël and rather conventional. In any case he knows that the 'heroic generation' that fought against Napoleon 'has nothing left to say', and has been cheated by its Princes of the 'proud institutions' promised to it. 'In Germany there are now only worn-out Cabinets left, belatedly admiring the defeated Oppressor.' As though he, Chateaubriand, had not done the same!

In Berlin he lived in the little palace in the future Pariser Platz, which was the residence of the French Legation until it was destroyed. He found the house unhealthy and icy cold, and declared it gave him rheumatism. The winter was bitterly cold, and he often came home half frozen from his walks in the Tiergarten. But the climate of Berlin offers violent contrasts, and by May 'the heat is so intense even in Church, that I cannot take my walk at the usual hour'. He liked the beech trees in the Tiergarten, and strolled in their shade looking at the hearts and names young people had carved on their trunks; he found hearts pierced by a dagger and bearing the name of Karl Ludwig Sand, the youth who had stabbed Kotzebue. The evenings were long, for social life began early and was at an end by nine o'clock. The Envoy sat on for a long time afterwards at his writing-table, working at the fourth book of his Memoirs and hearing not a sound in the silent night except the shouts of the guard being relieved at the Brandenburger Gate.

His subordinates, who may well have awaited his arrival with a certain uneasiness on account of his reputation for arrogance, enjoyed working with him and were happy in his stimulating company. He called them his family. 'They do what they please ... I keep a carriage, more for them than myself, for I never make use of it. I see to it that the food is good, and I live among them. When they are short of money I always have something at their disposal.' The Envoy had no difficulty in seeing everybody he was interested in. He met Wilhelm von Humboldt, with whose brother Alexander he had long been acquainted; and he conceived a great liking for Chamisso, who lived in the Botanical Garden 'at some distance from Berlin'. The simplicity reigning at the Prussian Court made it easy for the French Envoy to get on a familiar footing with various royal personages. The King himself, Frederick William III, went out every day at the same hour in his little carriole, which he drove himself. He would get out in the Tiergarten to walk up and down smoking his cigar, and there he often met the Vicomte, with whom he exchanged a few friendly words. When he drove back through the Brandenburger Gate, the Guard stood to arms with an ear-splitting roar, and His Prussian Majesty touched the peak of his cap in return.

As was inevitable, Chateaubriand met Madame Récamier's former 'betrothed', Prince August of Prussia, who asked eagerly after their mutual friend. The 'Adieu for ever' had been wiped out long ago, when the Prince came to Paris with the Army of Occupation after Waterloo, and since then they had exchanged friendly letters. One could never be angry with Juliette for long. August possessed the famous picture that Gérard had once painted of her, the most magnificent, though not the truest, of her portraits. They both looked at it with emotion, August in melancholy remembrance, René with the nostalgia that led him to write her almost daily letters, to which she replied warmheartedly but irregularly.

He was far from his adored friend, but far, too, from all

annoyance. Madame de Chateaubriand was busy with her decayed protégés, and the 'ladies' were prevented from making any demands on him, especially as they imagined him to be overwhelmed by diplomatic work, which was far from being the case. But he could not live without the inspiring presence of some feminine creature, and he spent a good deal of time with the charming Duchess of Cumberland, *née* Friederike von Mecklenburg. He read passages from his works to this princess, who was familiar with everything he had written; he went for walks with her in the Tiergarten and met her at the theatre. His gift for treating women respectfully, not to say ceremoniously, while letting them feel his admiration, did not forsake him. The young mother of the last King of Hanover was flattered by his homage, his looks and words expanded the limits of her life at Court, and gave her hunger for romance a little nourishment. They wrote frequently to each other, and the sentimental correspondence was carried on even after he left Berlin.

In his despatches the Envoy paid little attention to Prussian affairs in their narrower sense, but he busied himself all the more zealously with the situation in Europe, which had reached a stage of pre-revolutionary excitement. In Troppau and Laibach the Powers were discussing the possibility of intervening in the 'revolutionary countries'—Spain, Naples and Piedmont, to reestablish the old order. Chateaubriand was dying to take part in these conferences as a representative of France; he was an ardent partizan of the right of intervention advocated by Metternich, provided it was for the sake of protecting the rights of the Sovereigns against the currents of rebellion. The Holy Alliance, originally intended as an instrument for ensuring the peace of Europe, was developing, under the leadership of the Austrian statesman, into a syndicate of monarchs for mutual protection against the demands of the People, so wantonly awakened during the wars of liberation. While these demands were flaring up on all sides, the 'Congresses' that had been provided for in the Treaty of 1815 were increasing in number and devoting themselves almost entirely to the elaboration of suppressive measures and interventions.

After the assassination of Kotzebue by the student Sand, the adherents of absolutism had had their eyes opened, at least as to the situation in Germany. 'Sand terrified Europe,' writes Chateaubriand, adding that the victim was not sufficiently important to deserve a dagger thrust. As usual, he advocates suppression, and issues a warning against it at the same time: 'A sort of political Inquisition Tribunal and the abolition of the freedom of the Press have halted intellectual agitation, but it must not be imagined that its mainspring has been broken. Germany wants political unity now, just as Italy does, and with this idea, which slumbers for a shorter or longer time according to events and persons, the German peoples can at any time be set in motion. Princes and Ministers may delay or precipitate revolution, but they cannot prevent mankind from developing.' He foresaw the course of events accurately, therefore, and his attitude was not as inconsistent as it appeared at first sight. Just as he desired more freedom for France combined with full preservation of royal authority, he wished the Princes would anticipate their peoples' demands and concede the rights that no country of Europe would be able to refuse much longer. He wrote to his political friends in Paris: 'Adopt the constitutional form of government openly, rescind special laws, but entrust official posts only to royalists.'

Pasquier, the Minister for Foreign Affairs, paid no attention to Chateaubriand's request to take part in the Congresses, although the Envoy had ended his letter somewhat imperiously: 'I beg you to give me a prompt answer.' Very well, he decided, if it couldn't be done by correspondence, he would go to Paris and plead his cause in person. He was in fact becoming something of a litigator, so insistent was his advice, so sharp his criticism of the government. He gave as his excuse that he must go and see his sick wife—'If I am not given leave I shall take it myself'—and complained that he had still not received his long overdue appointment as Minister of State. 'I wish to be spared vexations,' he wrote to the Minister of Foreign Affairs. 'If my services are no longer welcome, you can afford me no greater pleasure than by telling me so openly. I did not beg or wish for the mission with which I have been entrusted. My country desires me, my sick wife needs my care, my friends demand their leader. I deserve something either higher or lower than an ambassadorship or even a Ministry of State.'

Not a very tractable subordinate. The tone he adopts gives his Chief every reason for not wanting him in Paris. His suggestions became more and more persistent; according to him the French government did not know whether to co-operate in Metternich's policy of suppression or treat the increasing liberal currents in the country with respect. Chateaubriand was for intervening, especially by sending French troops into Savoy. The White Lily banner, he thought, needed glory to increase its authority: 'The Royalists will be delighted, and the Liberals can only applaud, if they see we are adopting an attitude in keeping with our power.' A quite new motive was thus creeping into his ideas on foreign politics. He was haunted by the ghosts of Napoleon and his time, compared with which the present appeared mean and dull. The era of the Bourbons needed more stirring successes than were to be obtained by government dexterity alone. The imagination and self-confidence of the French must be nourished if the country was not to be bored, and find life under the Lilies a mean affair.

The baptism of the Duke of Bordeaux, the posthumous son of the murdered Berry, was about to take place. The Vicomte was determined to be present, but Pasquier had still not replied to the request for leave. 'I will take my leave, for I am my own master!' he cried, behaving as no disciplined official should. At last Pasquier yielded. Chateaubriand rushed to Paris; he had scarcely time to pay the obligatory farewell visits. He said only a fleeting goodbye to the enchanting Duchess of Cumberland, since he dare not tell her of his secret intention not to return to Berlin. His last excursion took him to Charlottenburg: 'the villa, on the edge of a village, is surrounded by a not very extensive park, beyond which is fallow land.' The monument of Queen Louise gave him occasion to write some verses, which the Duchess of Cumberland had begged of him.

The trees were showing their first green shimmer when he entered Paris. All his friends were glad to see him again. Only old Fontanes was missing, he had died in the meantime, to the great grief of the returning traveller, who had remained loyal to him in spite of the difference in their political opinions. The King received him graciously and gave him back the dignity of Minister of State, of which he had deprived him some years earlier. He was also given the Legion of Honour, whose founder was now closing his eyes for ever on his rocky island in the ocean. This death at the other end of the world made little impression now; people had not forgotten the great Exile, but they had grown accustomed to thinking of him as something remote. Talleyrand, on hearing the announcement of his death, said 'That is a piece of news, but it is no longer an event'.

AMBASSADOR IN LONDON

The government was in the throes of dissolution. The Comte d'Artois had begun to disavow Richelieu, in spite of his solemn promise. On the occasion of a debate on the renewal of the censorship law, Villèle was left in the lurch by his party friends and quitted the Cabinet. Chateaubriand seized the opportunity to resign his post in Berlin. He wrote a ceremonious letter to Pasquier, in which he declared his solidarity with Villèle, and begged to be released from his Envoyship. This was immediately granted, and he now had time to devote himself to Madame Récamier, who was quietly keeping an eye on internal political events, so that her friend's cause should suffer no harm. Claire de Duras, too, had the pleasure of his company more often now, for he knew she still possessed a great deal of influence. He even saw the once so greatly loved Delphine de Custine; she had promised to remain 'a good friend', and had kept her word. The time of storms and scenes was over, and he spent a few carefree days with her and her son at Fervacques. Back in Paris, he wrote to her 'I have left peace and happiness behind me in Fervacques. Here I am surrounded by all the annoyances and vexations in the world, sickness, politics and persecution'.

The policy of the Restoration, which led to the final downfall of the dynasty, had not yet reached its peak, but it was already

R

stirring up heightened opposition. The liberal forces were being so hard-pressed that their spirit of aggression was increasing. Richelieu resigned; not only had the King let him down, and the Comte d'Artois broken his word, but the underground activity of the so-called Congregation was coming to light in threatening guise. The organization was becoming more and more neglectful of its role as promoter of works of Christian charity, and was being gradually transformed into a reactionary force meddling in internal politics. As 'Supporters of Throne and Altar', this Association, to which Jules de Polignac, Mathieu de Montmorency, the Marquis de Tonnerre, the Duc de Rivière and Baron de Damas belonged, was trying to isolate the King in order to do away with the remnants of the conciliatory laws of the Decazes era. Villèle, who had succeeded the Duc de Richelieu, was persuaded to promulgate two new laws against the Press, allowing the government, as Royer-Collard said, 'to seize upon as dangerous what they cannot prosecute as guilty'.

Whether Villèle had ever seriously thought of giving Chateaubriand the Ministry of Foreign Affairs is doubtful. René, who flattered himself that he was thoroughly familiar with every sort of machination, really moved among these intriguers like an unsuspecting child. When Mathieu de Montmorency was appointed to the Foreign Ministry instead of him, he exclaimed petulantly 'I'm too stupid and too decent!' He had in effect allowed himself to be completely cheated, for without his concurrence as party leader the new ministry could hardly have been formed. Madame Récamier succeeded in convincing Mathieu that people had really gone too far this time, and something must be done at once to conciliate the Vicomte. They must at least offer him an ambassadorial post. 'I won't accept anything but London,' declared René categorically, 'I must have the most important diplomatic post the government has to dispose of.' The government being only too anxious to get rid of him, as soon as possible, he was sent as Ambassador to London.

As usual, he took his time about it. In those days great men approached the posts they had accepted in a leisurely manner. The warning 'Above all, no zeal!', which Talleyrand had once

issued to his young men, was still in force. When one was
appointed Ambassador one began with long-drawn-out negotiations about one's salary, travel expenses and compensation
for other costs. If one owned estates—which had never been and
never would be the case with Chateaubriand—one first visited
these to put everything in order. Then followed the farewell
visits to official personages, the audience with the King, for which
one might easily be kept waiting for weeks, and the endless leave-
taking among one's friends and at parties. Domestic staffs and
secretaries were sent on in advance to arrange everything
according to the new Ambassador's wishes, and then one day
the journey might begin. The Vicomte pursued the same course.
It took him exactly three months from the date of his appointment
to arrive in London.

The parting from his Ladies took many forms. 'Do not grieve,
my beautiful angel,' he wrote to Madame Récamier, 'I love you,
and shall always love you. I shall never alter. I shall write to you.
I shall come back at once if you order me to do so. The whole
affair will not last long. And then I shall belong to you for ever.
Good night. The day after tomorrow I shall be writing from
Calais.' One or two servants were kept busy carrying little
letters and notes to and fro. As a newly appointed Ambassador he
may well have employed official servants of the Ministry of
Foreign Affairs to keep this tender correspondence going. The
letter to Juliette had hardly been despatched when another was
written to Claire de Duras. This 'dear sister', who was so helpful,
and so willingly allowed herself to be called on for a thousand
services, was less meek than her rival. She was impatient to see
him. 'What can I do?' he wrote to her, 'Your porter can testify
that the Minister of Foreign Affairs was with me. In these stirring
times one should not have an Ambassador for one's friend if one
cannot allow him to be taken up with business. I cannot come to
you till after dinner, at eight o'clock, and then only for an instant.
I am leaving tonight.' As for Madame de Chateaubriand, he had
been able to convince her that the climate of London was a lethal
one, and that for safety's sake the crossing of the Channel should
only be undertaken by the very robust. Whether she believed

these objections or not is another question. Probably the role of
Ambassadress to the godless English had little attraction for her
anyhow.

With great pomp, saluted by the guns of the Dover batteries,
the great man re-entered the country he had left twenty-three
years earlier, with his little bundle, as a poor *emigré* under a false
name. The comparison between the misery of that time and the
splendour of the present intoxicated him. However blasé he might
pretend to be, he was thoroughly alive to the colourful side of the
diplomatic service of those days, and it is probable that he contributed a good deal to the romance that surrounded the profession for a long while after. In his fine Embassy in Portland
Place he organized brilliant receptions, and conscientiously spent
the large sums at his disposal for the purpose. He employed the
best cook of his time, the famous Montmirel, who invented the
no less famous Pudding à la Chateaubriand (later known as
Diplomat's Pudding), and associated the Ambassador's name for
all time with the beefsteak known thereafter as Chateaubriand
tout court.

Reminders of the distresses of his emigrant days haunted him
at every step. On his way to present his credentials to the King,
he showed his Councillor of Embassy Marcellus the house where
he had lived with Hingant: 'My friend tried to kill himself there,
and I nearly died of hunger.' When one evening the chef sent a
specially successful dish to the table, he remarked 'A single one
of these gastronomical masterpieces, on which Montmirel spends
so much genius, calculated in gold thirty years ago, would have
sufficed to prevent me from starving, and Hingant from trying
to commit suicide'. The wine of Tokay, which flowed in streams
at the Rothschilds', reminded him that he had once, 'half dead
with hunger', greedily poured plain water down his throat. These
pictures from the past helped him not only to enjoy the present
but to compose wonderful meditations on the transience of all
earthly things. He wrote to Madame Récamier: 'I cannot move
a step here without recognizing something that reminds me of
my sufferings and my youth, of the friends I have lost, of the world
that has vanished, of the hopes I lulled myself with, my first

writings, my dreams of fame, everything in fact that belongs to
the future of a young man who feels that he is born to do something great. I have been able to grasp some of my dreams; others
have escaped me, and nothing of all this is worth the trouble it
has given me. . . .'

He employed what leisure remained to him to go on with his
Memoirs, describing in particular his experience as an *emigré* in
England. 'Those that read my Memoirs will scarcely notice that I
have interrupted them twice: once in order to give a grand festival
dinner for the Duke of York, the King's brother, and another time
to celebrate the anniversary of the day when the King of France
entered Paris. This fête cost me forty thousand francs. The
highest aristocracy of England, the Ambassadors and many distinguished foreigners were all gathered in my splendidly decorated
drawing-rooms. The tables glittered with the fiery sheen of the
London crystal, the golden shimmer of the Sèvres porcelain, and
threatened to break down under the superabundance of choice
dishes and flowers. London's finest carriages were drawn up in
Portland Place. Almack's music ravished the fashionable melancholy of the dandies, and the dreamy elegance of the demurely
dancing ladies. . . .'

A most lively ghost from his emigrant days emerged suddenly,
namely the Charlotte Ives of the Beccles parsonage, whom he had
loved and nearly seduced. She came to beg a favour of the Ambassador, or, more probably, to see the romantic hero of her
girlhood again. She was now Lady Sutton and according to
Marcellus, still beautiful if a little too stout. 'It was no longer
spring, summer was coming to an end and autumn was beginning
to appear.' Chateaubriand was moved by this meeting, but not
enough to lose sight of himself. 'How do you like me in my new
role? How do I strike you?' he asked her. Lady Sutton hit on the
brilliant idea of declaring that he had not altered in the least; upon
which he apostrophized her as 'a divine woman'.

Charlotte was not the only reminder in flesh and blood he met
with. Adolphe de Custine, son of the 'Queen of the Roses', paid
him a visit, and so did Léontine de Noailles, the daughter of the
unfortunate Natalie. He had seen both these children grow up at

a time when he was in love with their mothers. Charlotte, Delphine, Natalie—were they all embodiments of that Sylphide, that most perfect of all his loves, whose body and soul he had combined from his dreams? Had he really loved those enchanting apparitions, or had he been content to let himself be loved? 'And my soul, what was it? A little pain that faded and was lost in the wind.' 'Make haste to be happy,' he said to himself, 'one day more, and nobody will love you!'

In London, however, it was difficult to make haste, if one happened to be an Ambassador and exposed to public attention. He had the reputation of being irresistible. Had not Madame de Beaumont died in his arms, had not Natalie, the beautiful Duchesse de Mouchy, lost her wits on his account? Feminine interest was greatly aroused by these romantic half-truths. Lady Fitzroy was said to have a *penchant* for the Ambassador that was more than literary. But a simple Madame Lafont, wife of a violinist, seems to have pleased the Vicomte more than all these ladies. Madame Récamier, who was always kept fully informed, even evinced a certain jealousy, which was most unlike her. Claire de Duras, too, made mortified allusions in a letter, to which he replied 'You say you will not say anything to me, because you might otherwise say disagreeable things. I know what those things are: that I love nobody, that I am a complete egoist, that one must talk to me of nobody but myself, that I am false, unfaithful, etc. . . . . Use up the whole dictionary of insults; you will not prevent me from loving you'.

The most famous woman in London at that time was Frau von Lieven, the wife of the Russian Ambassador. She and the Vicomte took a thorough-going dislike to each other, which found written expression on both sides. According to Chateaubriand 'Frau von Lieven had a sharp, repulsively ugly face; she was a mediocre creature, mediocre and wearying. Her only subject of conversation was the politics of the day'. For which reason, of course, the Ambassador should have cultivated her acquaintance. She was intimate not only with George IV but with Metternich; her influence was far-reaching and she knew more about the state of international affairs than many a Minister. Her verdict on Chateaubriand was equally severe. He looked, she said, 'like a hunchback without the hump'. She thought his blasé attitude very affected, although he had brought it into fashion himself. 'He puts on a dreamy air in drawing-rooms, and carries his old heart, that nobody wants to buy nowadays, in a sling.' When he confessed his boredom to her, she offered to introduce him to some intelligent women.

'Oh, Madame,' he said wearily, 'I don't care for intelligent women.'

'So you prefer stupid women?'

'By far, Madame, by far.'

Frau von Lieven, who was herself accounted far and wide the cleverest of women, was not slow to take the hint.

With other important personages he knew better how to behave. The King was well-disposed towards him; Wellington also showed him his better side. Londonderry was very hospitable and enjoyed the famous Frenchman's company, but he was a stiff kind of man and never talked of State affairs, so that he was quite unproductive as a political source. Far more frank were his relations with Canning, who like himself had come to politics by way of literature, and agreed with him in complaining that kings would have nothing to do with intellectual men. 'If people take our ideas,' said Chateaubriand, 'they must take our persons with them.' As for London society, he did not care for it because it did not care for him. Each side thought the other stiff and proud, and his social life was restricted as a result. He found time for his literary work and was very considerate towards his younger assistants, who in return grew very fond of him. But he devoted himself to the business of his Office far more than he had done in Berlin. He sent an enormous number of reports to Paris, and composed them with great care. He kept a strict watch on the work of his assistants too: 'Be careful of your adjectives,' he said to Marcellus, who profited by the advice, and learnt to write so well under his Chief as to produce some excellent volumes of memoirs in later years, among them one of Chateaubriand himself.

In one of his reports the Ambassador wrote 'The French Embassy, which had fallen into neglect for so long in this country must take the lead in social life again, as well as in political affairs. The influence of society extends to politics, and in the sphere of diplomacy balls can be of use in the service of the King, though this part of my duty is not the one I like best'. In effect he was more concerned with international politics, on which unfortunately his outlook differed widely from that of the English. The London government opposed the Tsar's inclination to intervene in foreign countries that failed in obedience to their sovereigns, whereas Chateaubriand had an ardent desire to see France taking part in the Spanish Civil War and reinstating the King in his rights. He was convinced that it was still possible to control the movement for reform in those countries still under absolutist rule. He saw clearly that the hour of Liberalism must strike sooner or later, but he would have liked the change to come from above and not by means of insurrection. England was all the less disposed to meddle in the Spanish situation, because she felt certain that Spain was about to lose her commercial monopoly in South America. Even Metternich, the inventor of intervention, was cautious in this case, because France, on whom the police work for the Holy Alliance must naturally fall, would be unnecessarily strengthened by a military success in Spain.

The Powers were to assemble in Verona for a Congress, to solve the Spanish question and examine the Italian situation. Chateaubriand felt that his great hour had struck; he was determined to be a member of the French delegation, and he wrote letters to his 'ladies', in which tenderness and ambition were ruthlessly mixed. To Madame Récamier: 'The Congress would have the immeasurable advantage of bringing me to Paris, and this whole manoeuvre signifies only one thing, that I'm dying to see you . . . to be loved by you, to live peacefully in some little refuge with you and a few books, that is the whole content of my wishes and my heart. . . . Think of the Congress!' To Claire de Duras he merely wrote 'Dear sister, arrange everything with Villèle!' But both Villèle and Mathieu de Montmorency hesitated to give him a place in the delegation. He declared angrily, in the tone his superiors were accustomed to, 'If people mean to reward me in this way for my loyalty, I shall have more to say.

I'm not going to allow people to laugh at my expense'. Nobody wanted to laugh at him; he did not realize that they were beginning to be afraid of him. His moods, his sensitiveness, and the obstinacy with which he clung to his recipes for foreign politics, were gradually making him a terror to his political friends. He now went over entirely to Villèle's side, and was commissioned by him to go to Verona.

Chateaubriand described the Congress later in two volumes, written in a very attractive and politically instructive manner. The meeting of so many crowned heads, Ministers and other dignitaries formed a brilliant spectacle. The Austrian Imperial couple, with Metternich, Gentz and four Ambassadors, the Tsar with Nesselrode, Lieven, Pozzo di Borgo and a swarm of adjutants and councillors, the Duke of Wellington, the King of Prussia with Prince William, Bernstorff and Humboldt, the Kings of the Two Sicilies and Sardinia, the rulers of Tuscany and Modena, all these were crowded together in the city of Romeo and Juliet. Even Marie-Louise, the 'widow' of Napoleon, now Duchess of Parma, came accompanied by her Count Neipperg. She invited Chateaubriand to dinner, and he found her most cheerful: 'Now that the universe had taken upon itself to remember Naploeon, she no longer had the trouble of thinking of him. Besides which she was pregnant.' Chateaubriand was deeply offended by her forgetfulness, and as so often, he had melancholy remarks to make on the decay of earthly greatness. This gave him a gloomy look that put everybody off. Pozzo di Borgo called him 'an old child of fifty'. The Queen of Sardinia asked him affably if he was related to the Chateaubriand who wrote books. Metternich, instead of talking high politics, irritated him by describing circumstantially how to prepare the best macaroni. The Vicomte was not attentive, which annoyed the Austrian statesman and gave him occasion to joke about the Ambassador to the Tsar. Chateaubriand wrote of Metternich to Claire de Duras 'He has a mediocre brain without principles or point of view; he has power only over the weakness of Mathieu de Montmorency'.

But the gloomy looks of the 'old child' cleared up when he was given the leadership of the French delegation. Mathieu had gone

to Paris to win the King and Villèle over to French intervention
in Spain, which he had promised Metternich to do. Villèle believed
erroneously that Chateaubriand would support the English policy
of abstention; but he at once vehemently advocated intervention:
'If the—actually little dangerous—hostilities with Spain lead to
the recovery of our military standing in Europe and make us
forget the tricolour, we shall have nothing to complain of.'
Through the mediation of Countess Tolstoy, herself incited by
Claire de Duras, he was able to approach the Tsar, and had some
far-fetched, not to say fantastical, conversations with him. He gave
free rein to his dislike of England, and discussed with the ruler of
all the Russias the possibility of forming France and Russia into
a bloc to hold England in check. If France could obtain the left
bank of the Rhine and a complete revision of the Treaty of 1815,
which would be possible only with the help of the Tsar, she would
undertake to ensure that Russia had access to the Bosphorus.
These conversations pleased both the writer and the Tsar; their
fancy roamed free through wide expanses, which were unfortunately still in the hands of their owners. The Tsar complimented
the Vicomte: 'I'm glad you came here; it's a good thing for people
to see each other.'

Chateaubriand was inwardly resolved to make war on Spain,
and France was to wage it alone, without sharing the 'glory' of it
with other Powers. He was playing a bold game, for Villèle, the
head of the government, was convinced that the delegation in
Verona was acting in accordance with his instructions and refusing the war with Spain. His Foreign Minister, Montmorency,
who had arrived in Paris meanwhile, contradicted him, and
pointed to the fact that in Verona he had already practically
pledged himself to the Powers to restore full rights to the King
with the help of French arms. Villèle decided to disavow his
Foreign Minister, and this being so, Montmorency preferred to
resign. Thus the office so ardently coveted by Chateaubriand fell
vacant, and it was hardly possible now that it should not be
offered to him. But he controlled his feelings, and suggested to
Villèle that he himself should discharge the duties of the Foreign
Ministry for the time being. Upon this the King intervened, saying

'Accept. I command you to do so'. He could not but obey, and
hastened to accept, writing at the same time to the Duchesse de
Duras 'The King has commanded me to accept. I have obeyed,
but like one that is being led to the gallows'. Claire knew what to
think of such statements.

XII

SHOULD WRITERS BE MADE
FOREIGN MINISTERS?

CADIZ AND CORDÉLIA

At long last Chateaubriand was Minister of Foreign Affairs. He wrote at once to Madame Récamier, assuring her that no one but himself was capable of conducting foreign policy. 'I shall be sleeping tonight in the ministerial bed that was not made for me, in which one scarcely sleeps, and remains only for a short time.' He did actually move that very day into the building on the Boulevard des Capucines, on the Right Bank. 'I feel as if by crossing the bridge I was going away from you on a long journey. It breaks my heart, but I shall get the better of this impression. I shall come and see you in our little cell every day at our usual hour.' He meant it seriously: although he had now attained the peak of his political ambition, he had no intention of letting himself be engulfed by official business; he looked forward to recovering from the bustle of affairs in the soothing intimacy of these regular meetings. But he had not reckoned with his ambition, or with his eternal craving for fresh excitement.

The Foreign Minister from the realm of literature proved a hard worker: 'I write all my personal letters myself, I never entrust them to anyone else.' He wrote till late at night not only to his Ambassadors but to the Tsar and to Canning. However garrulous, this correspondence had always the same refrain: France must move into Spain with an army, to strengthen the principle of Legitimacy, to dam up the revolutionary spirit in Europe, and to weld together the French forces, in which the great spectre of Napoleon was still alive. Villèle was aghast at the determined attitude of his Foreign Minister, who had thus circumvented him in the Spanish Affair, but he was forced to indulge him for the moment, because he needed the votes of his friends in the Chamber. Had he many friends left? Mathieu and the Congregations were hostile to him, in spite of Juliette's zealous preaching of conciliation. To the Liberals such as Lafayette, Broglie, Lafitte, Manuel and Foy, he was now a stumbling-block, a statesman demanding war on his own account, preparing to spill French blood in order to give the Crown fresh splendour and satisfy his personal vanity.

The greatest hostility of all came from England, which was turning to direct encouragement of the revolutionary party in Spain. Chateaubriand wrote to Canning 'You say the war might overthrow our not yet quite established institutions. Maybe, but there are two ways in which a government can be defeated, by reverses and by disgrace. If revolutionary Spain can boast of having made monarchical France tremble, if the white cockade retreats before the Descamisados, people will look back to the might of the Empire and the triumphs of the tricolour cockade. Think what an effect this reminder will have on the Bourbons! The French people is essentially militarist; success would bind the army to the King for ever; the whole of France would rush to arms. You cannot imagine what can be achieved in this country by the word Honour'.

The Chamber was asked to grant a hundred millions for the campaign. The Opposition resisted the demand for nearly a week. There were unheard-of tumults. Manuel, who fought hardest against the proposal, declared that this intervention might release a dangerous wave of patriotism in Spain, and reminded his hearers of the effect that the invasion of France by foreign troops in 1792 had had upon the country. This reference to the Revolution roused the Royalists to the utmost fury; they called for the expulsion of Manuel. Refusing to go of his own accord, he was dragged out of the Chamber by gendarmes; sixty deputies followed him of their own free will, and remained absent till the end of the session. This incident could not, however, affect the success of Chateaubriand's great speech.

On April 7, 1923, an army of a hundred thousand men

crossed the frontier river, the Bidassoa, under the supreme command of the Duke of Angoulême. The campaign proved a very
easy undertaking, although it lasted six months. The revolutionary
spirit was almost entirely confined to the educated classes, that is
to say those that could read and write. The mass of the people
greeted the French troops with cries of 'Down with the Constitution! Long live the absolute King!', which greatly facilitated
operations. Whereas fifteen years earlier France had come up
against the most bigoted resistance by the Spaniards, who shrank
from neither sacrifice nor cruelty, this time everything went like
clockwork. It became obvious that the Spaniard was open to
anything extreme and bordering on absurdity, but that moderate
plans of reform left him cold. By May 24th Angoulême's
troops were entering Madrid, but the Cortes had withdrawn to
Seville and Cadiz, taking the King with them as a prisoner.
Chateaubriand had some difficulty in keeping the aggressive spirit
of the Supreme Commander from flagging, for he was trying to
lead the rebellious Spaniards back to the true path by conciliatory
means, and had ordered his army to see to it that vengeance for
the Spanish monarchy remained within humane limits. He hoped
in this way to obtain the liberation of the King without further
bloodshed.

The Foreign Minister noted these efforts with discomfort, he
knew better than Angoulême that the rebels had got their teeth
into things and would not voluntarily set the King free. He
exhorted the Supreme Commander to proceed with more vigour,
and encouraged the Chief of Staff to open artillery fire on Cadiz,
where the King was, without regard to Ferdinand in person. 'I
hope nothing will happen to him, but we are really concerned
with the Monarchy as such; he must bear the brunt of the fight.
You may be sure that you will accomplish nothing without a
coup de force, and complete success can only be attained by speed
and audacity.' And later 'I have told you, and I repeat it, that
Cadiz will not be abandoned so long as I have a seat in the Council.
I would rather die than see France retreat. I repeat once more,
Cadiz must fall, and then the Spanish Affair will succeed'.

Chateaubriand the writer urged the generals to act realistically,

as a thinker he warned them not to lose themselves in philan-
thropic speculations, but to fire bombshells and carry operations
through. The result proved him right; the key to Cadiz, the out-
works of Trocadero, were taken by assault in the only major
engagement of the campaign. Ferdinand was liberated on October
1st; he immediately revoked all the decrees and laws of the constitutional government and signed the first measures of retaliation.
The French Supreme Commander, who had occupied the country
in the manner he wished to, was now obliged to be the helpless
spectator of the excesses and barbaric reprisals of the Spanish
Royalists. The leader of the rebellion, Colonel Riego, was taken
prisoner. They demanded not only the death penalty, but that his
body should be torn in four pieces, one of which was to be given
to each of the four great cities of the country for public exhibition.
Villèle directed the Duke of Angoulême to 'protect the vanquished, without any appearance of partisanship'. The Duke
made every effort, and though he failed with regard to Riego, he
did contrive to protect the refugees and help many of them to flee.

Once again Chateaubriand found himself in the unhappy
situation of having brought about a result that offended his
deepest instincts. An eloquent advocate of constitutional
monarchy, he saw the adherents of this form of government in
Spain being persecuted and punished in the cruellest fashion.
His fight for the principle of Legitimacy had not only restored
a brutal, mediocre autocrat to the throne, but at the same time
strengthened the influence of the English in Spain. For retribu-
tion came speedily; the bloodthirsty fury of the 'Avengers' was
beginning to disgust the population and provoke them against
the French, a trend of which the English cleverly took advantage.
Chateaubriand's misgivings arose too late: 'France wished Spain
to be peaceful and happy; she is opposed to all dangerous reactions and all spirit of revenge. We do not wish to appear as
accomplices of stupidity and fanaticism. We would rather give up
Spain than lend our arms to those that prefer to see blood flow
on the scaffold rather than on the field of battle.'

In the opinion of the government offices of Europe, however,
the Foreign Minister was conducting his affairs most brilliantly;

he was acclaimed as an outstanding worker, a man not to be trifled with. Those that had thought of him as a poet gone astray in politics, a dilettante who could be easily dealt with thanks to his vanity and his deficient understanding of current affairs, were disappointed. His success incited him to more extensive projects. He wanted to make an end of the fluctuations of French foreign policy between England and Russia. He fancied himself sure of the Tsar's assent if he attempted to bring about more decisive co-operation with Russia. He wrote to his Ambassador in St. Petersburg—'for his instruction'—'We are again becoming the natural bulwark of Europe against England'. A few months later he expressed himself more definitely in a memorandum: 'Our true policy is the Russian policy, by which we can create a counter-weight against two decided enemies, Austria and England.' 'The Tsar,' wrote his Ambassador, 'is convinced that you are the man of the hour, and that you are destined to carry out, in agreement with him, all social and political changes in Europe. He has often given us to understand that France and Russia could ensure the peace of Europe and force the other Powers to do what we wish.'

No wonder Chateaubriand now thought it possible to wipe out the last traces of the Peace Treaty of 1815. To his late Councillor of Embassy, Marcellus, he said in confidence 'This war must be the signal, the first act, of our resurgence; we shall then need the whole of the left bank of the Rhine'. This became the leitmotiv of his diplomacy; what he called 'the lawful expansion of our frontiers' had taken such a hold on him that even the prospect of a war with England did not dismay him. He dreamed that he was destined to 'make the laurels of Waterloo fade'. Dangerous dreams, which show only too clearly that he was in a state of intoxication which intensified his sense of living. He thought every sort of revolution in the world would be possible if he lent his powerful hand to it. 'The Spanish War is to my policy what René was to my literary output'—a masterpiece, that is. He boasted of his intimacy with the grandees of the day; he was enraptured with his world-wide reputation; he felt he was the Great Man of his time, and was incapable of keeping this feeling to himself.

10 Cordelia, Madame de Castellane

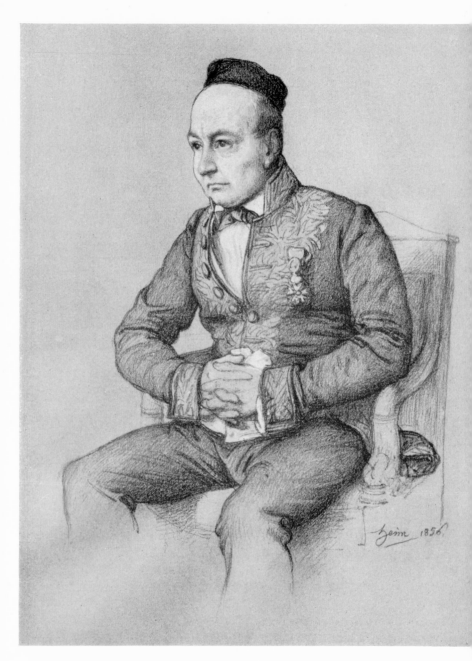

11 Sainte-Beuve

This exalted frame of mind was due not only to the success of his foreign policy, but to a woman. The twenty-seven-year-old Cordélia de Castellane had come into his life, and with such violence that she seemed to have turned everything upside-down. This was not the first interruption his connection with Madame Récamier had suffered; her serene purity had driven him here and there to women 'for whom the soul is not everything'. But this young woman meant more to him, she deprived him for a time of sense and understanding; the sensual madness of the fifty-five-year-old statesman assumed such a form that scandal appeared almost inevitable. Cordélia was the daughter of the banker, Greffuhle, a very wealthy man, and was married to an insignificant officer, of the famous family of the Castellanes. She had the figure of an angel, and was possessed by a devil. Her golden hair, milk-white skin and sparkling blue eyes gave her an appearance of innocence, which, however, did not last long. She was no coquette, she made no promises she did not at once fulfil. She was too much the great lady to pay attention to people's gossip; with her there were no scenes or complications, she was so completely in love with love that the sudden flaring up of desire in this grey-haired man, who was both a writer and a great statesman, aroused her own desire. He had begun the siege at the time he ordered the troops to surround Cadiz; she had yielded before Trocadero had fallen.

On the morning after their first rendezvous she proposed that he should escape from the crowds and the turmoil of the capital and spend a few days with her by the sea near Dieppe. He agreed at once: 'My angel, my life, and I know not what else! I love you with the whole madness of my first years. For you I shall become Amélie's brother; I forget everything since you permitted me to fall at your feet. Yes, I'll come to the seaside, anywhere you like. At last I have seized the dream of happiness that I have pursued for so long. It is you I have adored all this time without knowing you. You shall know my whole life, you shall know what one can only know with me . . .' He wrote this to her at his immense ministerial desk, at which Vergennes had written to all the Powers of the world in the name of Louis XVI. He broke off a letter to Canning;

s

he wrote a few lines in a hurry to Claire de Duras, saying he could not come that evening: he left everything in disorder and fled to the sea with his *inamorata*.

Was it a passion? If so, it was of a very simple kind, and for that reason René yielded to it entirely without reserve. Cordélia cared nothing for politics and attached no importance to connections in that sphere. She was not romantic by nature, had hardly more than an average interest in literature, and was neither a connoisseur nor a blue-stocking. She simplified his existence during these politically agitated weeks; the tie that bound them was purely erotic, in so far as such a many-sided nature as Chateaubriand's was capable of yielding to a single, simple emotion. For in his wooing and his seduction he was always conscious of his success, and the fascinations induced by his great position—by all that he called his fame. She must have been greatly moved when he kept declaring to her 'I would sell my future for your kisses'. What woman would not be thrilled by such words from such a man! But he was also expressing his own emotion: it seemed incredible that such a young and beautiful woman could love him for the sake of erotic bliss.

He began writing verse again, amorous verse with cryptic expressions almost disagreeably suggestive of intimacy. He missed ministerial councils, sent excuses to the King, refused to see ambassadors, all for the sake of meeting Cordélia. But he did not neglect his political correspondence; on the contrary, his imagination had been stimulated, he seemed to be carried off his feet, and began filling page after page with political projects that were often on the border-line of fantasy. He waited patiently in his office for the postman to bring him further news of the taking of Trocadero. He did not stir from his work-table, but while he was waiting for details of his greatest triumph he wrote to Cordélia 'Now I can write to you without reserve, and tell you that I would give the world for one of your caresses. If only I could press you to my throbbing heart and unite myself to you with long kisses that give me the breath of your life and you mine! You might have given me a son, you might have been the mother of my only child. Instead of which I am sitting here waiting for an event that gives me not the slightest happiness. What do I care for the world without you! You have even robbed me of my pleasure in the success of this war, which I alone had determined upon, and for the glory of which I was so eager. Today everything has vanished from my sight except You. I see you everywhere. All this fame, which would turn any other head, cannot distract me for an instant from my love. Come again soon, compensate me for all that has slipped through my hands. Come and forgive me for the liberation of the miserable Spanish King. I'm afraid you will hardly be able to read my letter, for I am writing to you after writing to all the Kings and Ministers of Europe. My hand is tired, but my heart is awake'.

While he was balancing the account of this intervention in Spain with great political discernment, his other self was revelling in the intoxication of personal satisfaction. The whole war, it would appear, was being carried on only that he might look deeper into the mirror of his ego. Never did Narcissus express himself with greater unrestraint than in the letters he sent to Cordélia at this time. The guns in front of the Dôme des Invalides were firing a salute, a Te Deum was being sung in the cathedral of Notre-Dame, Ambassadors were having to give receptions, Ministers having to be notified, the King having to be informed. But the Minister of Foreign Affairs, the hero of the day, was counting the hours till he could see Cordélia again.

Gossip was beginning to seize on the love affair; his closest friends were shaking their heads and uttering discreet reproaches. The most noticeable disapproval was expressed by Madame Récamier in her gentle, tactful way. The recklessness and extravagance of her friend's behaviour wounded her deepest feelings. Montmorency and other political enemies tried to involve her in intrigues against him, and to escape from all these complications she suddenly started on a journey to Italy that was to keep her away from Paris for five months.

TIME TO CATCH MICE

Chateaubriand was seriously alarmed at the sudden departure of

his most recent friend, of whose love he had—quite rightly—
felt assured. Had he gone too far? Had he demanded too much
of those two upright, sensitive women, Juliette and Claire? But
at the same time, with the naïvety of men spoilt by success, he
began complaining that women were always plaguing him—the
busy, famous statesman—with their 'fusses'. He wrote to Madame
Récamier 'This journey of yours is quite unnecessary; I shall
never be tired of you, and even if I have many years yet to live,
my last days will still be filled and beautified by your image. Will
you find me again on your return? Obviously you don't care
much whether you do or not. When one is determined, as you are,
to break everything in pieces, what does the future matter? I've
written to you twice to Lyons and once to Turin, and you have
not answered me. . . .' Thus he concealed his bad conscience under
a feeble attempt to be offended. Nevertheless all that he wrote
here of his 'last days' was to prove true.

Juliette knew too many people, and had too close connections
with the sphere of political power, not to be thoroughly informed of the growing criticism of her volatile friend. The
arrogance with which he aired his mental superiority to the rest
of the world, together with his insatiable thirst for honours, made
him fresh enemies every day. He wanted to be perpetually distinguished, celebrated and decorated, without foregoing the
pleasure of looking down on those that had such things to award.
He was given the Golden Fleece, the Grand Cross of the Re-
deemer, the Order of the Annunciation, the Order of the Black
Eagle, the Ribbon of St. Andrew's Cross, to say nothing of
decorations by the lesser Powers. But he now demanded of the
King the blue ribbon of the highest French distinction, and
obtained it only after plaguing friends and foes to death with the
affair. Juliette sent him discreet warnings. He replied with a little
masterpiece of false modesty and irritated self-conceit: 'People
have been telling you that success has gone to my head. Come
and see for yourself—its effect on me is quite other. My greatest
fault is that I can never feel enthusiasm; I should be much happier
if I could set my heart on something. Naturally I'm not quite
indifferent to the fact that France is enjoying so much respect

abroad and is flourishing and prospering at home, and that the glory and welfare of my country have coincided with my entrance into the Ministry. But if you deprive me of this satisfaction of an honest man, nothing will remain to me but an abysmal boredom with my office, great weariness, and a longing for death far from all noise, in peace and forgetfulness, somewhere in some remote corner of the earth.'

The burden of power, which appeared to cause him so much disgust, was to be taken from him sooner than he expected. His relations with Villèle grew daily worse; he allowed it to be seen too plainly that he considered himself qualified to succeed him. His foreign policy plans were not progressing, least of all in South America, where English influence was increasing with the movement for independence. 'I don't mix poetry with affairs of state,' said Villèle to all who would listen, 'all those fine countries down under will soon be nothing but markets for England, if Chateaubriand spends another year writing confidentially to Canning.' The head of the government was particularly irritated by the resistance his Foreign Minister offered to the conversion of government stocks. Villèle expected a great result from this operation, which was to lower the rate of interest from five to three per cent. . . . But the House of Peers did not follow the Chamber in this respect, chiefly, so Villèle was persuaded, because his Foreign Minister was setting the Peers against it. It came to a discussion in the Chief Minister's office, in which Villèle sharply attacked the Vicomte. Those in the antechamber heard loud voices and the sound of chairs being violently pushed back. The conversion was refused by the Peers. Villèle wanted to resign, but the King pleaded with him: 'Villèle, don't abandon me to these bandits!' Several members of the government suggested simply depriving Chateaubriand of the office of Foreign Minister and thus removing him from the government. The Vicomte was warned by Claire de Duras. 'Dismiss me?' he said. 'At once, if they like,' and went to bed.

Next morning—it was Whit Sunday—the Vicomte went to the Tuileries to listen to the sacred music in the Court Chapel. It was a fine morning; lost in thought he was listening to a festival

motet when a servant whispered to him that he was wanted outside. Softly, so as not to disturb the rest of the congregation, he
went out and found his secretary, Pilorge, in the passage, who
handed him a letter, adding 'Monsieur le Vicomte is no longer a
Minister'. The letter, which was signed by the director of the
political department, read as follows: 'Monsieur le Vicomte, by
command of the King I herewith communicate to you a decree
which His Majesty has just issued.' The decree read: 'Comte
Villèle, President of Our Ministerial Council, is provisionally
entrusted with the portfolio of Foreign Affairs and replaces the
Vicomte de Chateaubriand.' Chateaubriand immediately signed
the acknowledgement of receipt, ordered six cabs to be fetched,
with the help of which he removed his possessions from the
Ministry, and wrote to Villèle, an hour after receiving his dismissal, that the King's command had been carried out. He was
deeply wounded by the brusque fashion in which he had been
dismissed; his self-conceit had suffered a blow—salutary or in-
jurious—that entirely altered his relation to the outer world,
and above all to external power. 'They have turned me out,' he
exclaimed, 'as though I had stolen the King's clock off the mantelpiece.' Not only was his sense of honour wounded, he had
suddenly realized that his ambition had driven him to take a
road incompatible with high art. A writer, he now saw, was
intended to remain an outsider, to live alone and work alone.
Political activity is team work; he had persistently acted in
opposition to this fact, and he was now made aware that he had
foundered, not so much with regard to political circumstances
as to the best part of himself, his artistic power. He had ad-
ministered his office brilliantly, had proved a brilliant Foreign
Minister and Chief Minister, but he had been a different man all
the time from those usually occupying these posts. It was not
incompatibility of opinions that had brought about his downfall, but incompatibility of types.

At home he told his two cats, which he had brought with him
from the Foreign Ministry, that their life of luxury on sofas
adored with fleur-de-lys was at an end: 'The day of playing the
great ladies is over; now you must set to work catching mice.'

Weeks earlier he had arranged a diplomatic dinner for forty persons for that evening. All these guests had to be put off, Montmirel the chef had to get rid of his countless frying-pans, saucepans and casseroles, and content himself with preparing a modest family meal, to which the dismissed Minister invited his wife and his man of business Le Moine. Everything passed off peaceably and amicably, but he was boiling internally. He 'turned the crowd of sympathisers away', that is to say he received few visitors, and was sorely distressed because his two best advisers were out of reach. Claire de Duras was seriously ill, Madame Récamier was still in Italy; there would be no getting any sensible encouragement from Cordélia, who had no head for politics and was absent from Paris anyhow. Madame de Chateaubriand was no help, for she shared her husband's indignation—was even more indignant than he—and could do nothing but rage against Villèle, Mathieu and the King.

The fallen Minister had no gift for forgiveness or even forbearance. He roared like a wounded lion, and set to work at once to attack Villèle's government. Later on he declared that it was the idea of a parliamentary régime he had adopted in England which had led him into the path of opposition. There was some truth in this, though it served to conceal the strength of his resentment, for in spite of all his political violence and exaggeration he had always been an advocate of constitutional monarchy, supported by a parliament. It was, moreover, beneficial to his state of mind at the moment to be able to seek revenge on the grounds of his political convictions. He started a controversy which the *Journal dés Debats* published. Villèle answered very quietly at first. 'I'm not jealous,' he said once at a party, 'he has far more intelligence than I have, but I have more judgement.' An excellent formula, expressing the eternal hostility between politicians and intellectuals. Villèle knew very well that one can make a politician out of a writer in case of need, but a politician can never be transformed into an intellectual. He claimed on his own behalf, however, that the pure politician can judge the situation better at a critical moment and is thus better able to act. At this stage of the quarrel Chateaubriand could not refrain from showing spite: 'It is always wrong to make business men into statesmen; their policy is inspired by the Bourse. As for literature, anybody that can write is suspect. To be a statesman one must first be unable to speak French.'

He was trying hard to bring the forces of the Opposition together, to unite the Extreme Right with the Liberal Left, and he succeeded in leading men like Hyde de Neuville and Clausel de Coussergues on the one hand, and Royer-Collard, Benjamin Constant and Casimir Perrier on the other, to oppose the government. Even so it would have been difficult to move from a common basis if Villèle had not made the mistake of reintroducing the censorship. According to him he was doing this in order that the population should not be distressed by the news of the King's progressive illness, but in reality the criticisms of his policy were proving too much for the Chief Minister. Now the freedom of the Press was an ideal that Chateaubriand, otherwise so frequently vacillating, had never failed to defend. Every action by the Censor, and above all every attempt to revive painfully abolished forms of censorship, had always brought him into the arena. This time he wrote a pamphlet in which he flung out the question 'What has really happened? That the Ministry has made mistakes, that it has parted from the Royalists, in a word that it is hardly capable and has been told so—these are the serious reasons that force it to rob us of the basic freedom of institutions that we owe to the wisdom of the King'.

The death of the King interrupted all political disputes for a time. Louis XVIII, who was suffering from gangrene, and whose right leg was beginning, so to speak, to decay on his living body, bore his last weeks of suffering courageously. The distinguished, cultured old gentleman knew it was not pleasant to nurse him. The diseased parts of his body gave off a terrible stench, and as he always complained of the cold, his sick room was kept suffocatingly hot. He never complained, and he tried to keep visitors away. At the moment of death he felt no pain; he followed the prayers for the dying, and the extreme unction, with great attention, and expired quietly behind the curtains of his bed. It was four in the morning; a gentleman of the bedchamber went to the Comte d'Artois, who was resting in the next room, and said to him 'The King is dead. Long live the King!'

The new sovereign took the name of Charles X. He was a handsome man of seventy-six, and had more charm but less majesty than his late brother. He knew how to please by an amiable manner, but he was, and always had been, an inconsiderate creature, giving no thought to the results of his decisions. His arrogance was almost world famous; and he only got on well with the lower ranks because in his eyes they were hardly real people—one need not take care what one said in their presence. But his arrogance had nothing to do with his present situation, he had displayed it when wandering homeless in a foreign country, obliged to depend on other people for his subsistence. Unfortunately for France and for his dynasty, he lacked his brother's intelligence and self-possession. His political gifts were small, and he was firmly convinced that everything which the storms of history had swept away could be re-established, as an outward sign of which belief he had himself anointed in Rheims Cathedral with the oil of the sacred ampulla, and went through the ceremony of the laying on of hands, with which, in ancient usage, the sick were cured.

The new King commissioned the Vicomte to write a eulogy for his accession, and paid for it in princely fashion. Moreover, he issued a decree restoring the title of Minister of State to the dismissed Foreign Minister. As the appointment had to be countersigned by Villèle, Chateaubriand declined it; he did not wish to accept any favour from the hands of that government. He was obliged to attend the anointing ceremony in Rheims in his character of Knight of the Order of the Holy Ghost. He thought the decoration of the cathedral miserable; in Berlin, he said, a performance of the *Maid of Orleans* made a far better show. As bad luck would have it, at the reception of the Knights of the Order he found himself standing beside Villèle. He was feeling very uncomfortable in his black velvet mantle lined with red silk, while Villèle, quite at his ease, as though he were in the habit of wearing such mantles and plumed hats, looked right through him 'with the profound indifference and contempt of a man who has a portfolio for a man who has only his genius'. He felt angry too because Marshal Moncey had some sort of sacred sword to carry in front of him at the ceremony, the Moncey who, in the army of the Republic, had always distributed double rations on the anniversary of the execution of Louis XVI, and was afterwards promoted under Napoleon, and refused to take part in the prosecution of Marshal Ney.

Juliette Récamier had returned from Italy. Their meeting was peaceable and free from reproaches; their old familiarity was at once re-established, as though they had seen each other the evening before. René was again completely under the spell of this incomparable woman, who was sparing of reproaches but never backward with encouragement, and always able to conciliate opposites. She was as beautiful as ever, but her hair had turned white, and this first sign of age moved her friend almost to tears. He could not look his fill at this contrast between the unaltered face and the white hair; a peace and tenderness were diffused by this whiteness which awakened in him a feeling of reverence for the unalterability of the soul. The tie between them was strengthened, they were both penetrated with the certainty that nothing earthly could part them any more; the indulgence she nursed for his weakness and naïve egoism had assumed an almost maternal character.

Her little drawing-room became once more the centre of social life, in which politics, literature and good manners mingled in equal parts. As before, people who avoided one another elsewhere met amicably in this *salon*, whose chief ornaments were a harp and a portrait of Germaine de Staël. The Rochefoucaulds, senior and junior, Mathieu de Montmorency and Chateaubriand were forced to exchange conversation, in spite of their differences on home politics, and contrived to do this creditably under the gentle but firm glance of Juliette. Cuvier and Ampère put in appearance from time to time; Benjamin Constant, too, came back again, his free and easy manner quite restored. He read the company passages from his manuscripts, and found attentive if often critical listeners. The great actor Talma, now more than ever king of the French theatre, often entertained the assembled guests by reading some brilliant passage from one of Chateaubriand's works. The Duchess of Abrantès—'Laura' to her friends—once brought a stout young man with her who was a stranger to them all. His name was Honoré de Balzac, and he listened with great attention to the conversation around him.

One evening Madame Récamier produced a voluminous manuscript—the first three books of Chateaubriand's *Memoirs from beyond the Grave*, which she and her niece had copied out between them. She begged the author to read some of it aloud, and the circle of friends heard for the first time the story of his young days in the old castle of Combourg, deep in the Breton heathland; of his sister Lucile and their long walks together, their shared sorrows and solitude. The audience listened with deep emotion to this great fragment of French literature; they were spellbound by the reader and by the romantic passion of his prose, and their attention never slackened although the reading lasted two hours. Chateaubriand melted, as Goethe would have said, at his own fire. When he laid down the last sheet he could no longer restrain his tears. But Juliette's delicate skill converted the general emotion to a subdued conversation, in which they all recovered their composure.

Juliette wielded her sceptre with charm but insistence. She saw to it that Mathieu should be elected to the Academy, and procured René's vote for the purpose. But he had hardly been adopted as an 'immortal' when he died of a stroke. Death overtook him on a Good Friday, while at prayer in the church of Saint Thomas Aquinas—a fine death for so pious a man, but a great loss to Juliette, who had never had a more devoted, unselfish friend. Her tact and delicacy, however, were at their greatest in her relations with Chateaubriand's wife. Céleste had long since become reconciled to Juliette's domination, and had dubbed her 'the Arch-lady' by way of distinguishing her from the others. She was in constant need of money for her Old People's Home, and importuned not only her friends, but ministers, diplomats and the Court for assistance. Madame Récamier took the greatest interest in the Home, and canvassed the whole of Paris for it, which so softened the heart of the shrewd Céleste that she paid Juliette several visits, and was soon convinced that she was a good soul, well qualified to soothe her husband and give him a measure of stability. Céleste had gained a friend, but she had lost one of the targets for her spiteful remarks.

It became known that a speculator was planning to establish a sort of Fun Fair on the land adjoining the Home, with a scenic railway and other attractions, and Chateaubriand decided on the spur of the moment to buy the plot of ground and the house upon it, although, as usual, his coffers were empty. The couple now had a handsome property in the Rue d'Enfer, spacious enough for them both. But where had René found the money? He had succeeded, as few writers do, in making his publisher his banker. The publisher Ladvocat had contracted with him for a complete edition of his works, and placed the enormous sum of 550,000 francs at his disposal. After the purchase of the property he still retained a prodigious balance, the counter-value of which consisted of thirty-two volumes, including thirteen volumes of unpublished writings. He went to Lausanne for a few months with Céleste, whose health was not all that could be desired, and began revising his earlier work. The death of his old friend Delphine de Custine, with whom he had had so many quarrels and delightful reconciliations, had affected his spirits; there were times when he felt old. The coquettish *weltschmerz* of his earlier years was beginning to give way to genuine melancholy; his hair still stood up in a 'wind-swept' shock, but it had turned grey.

At home, in the Rue d'Enfer, the newly acquired villa was still occupied by workmen carrying out their trade, whistling and singing amid the smell of paint. But he had never been particular about his study, and soon found a corner in which to revise the work of his American period, *The Natchez*. The old priests, Céleste's pensioners, wandered round the fountain in the garden reading their breviaries, the tired old ladies sat quietly on the garden seat, the little bell sounded the Angelus; a more peaceful world could not be imagined. Here René could work and collect his thoughts, here he could live as a writer whose recollections were beginning to outweigh his present existence.

THE WORLD UNDERGOES A CHANGE

But politics proved stronger once again. Was it a 'wished-for storm' working up? Was the writer plagued by his old desire for action in the midst of this calm, although he would not have confessed it? The cause was an imperative one: Freedom of the Press. Villèle's ministry had made itself disliked during the last two years by several reactionary laws it had passed, especially the so-called law of sacrilege and the law concerning the right of primogeniture. Now it was attempting to increase the severity of the censorship and prevent the circulation of newspapers, the majority of which were in the hands of the Opposition. Ever since the return of the Bourbons the question of the freedom of the Press had continually brought Chateaubriand into the arena; it was still the point of contact between his political friends and the Left. All his liberalism, which he had contracted in England, and had so often been forced to conceal in the ranks of the Ultras, flamed up on the subject, which actually concerned him in his most personal activity, for the Censor had forbidden newspapers to advertise fresh publications from his pen; he had even struck out the word 'wonderful' from a notice of his forthcoming *Natchez*. But it was not his personal vanity that was injured— he was on no point so little conceited as this—his political foresight told him that the Bourbon monarchy would founder on the reef of the freedom of the Press if it did not listen to reason.

Charles the Tenth's government attempted to stick to its guns. The Academy presented the King with a violent protest against the Press regulations planned by Villèle. Chateaubriand published an article against the 'Vandalic law' in the *Journal des Débats*, of which 300,000 copies were circulated. In the Chamber he led the Opposition, together with the Duc de Broglie, and supported by Molé and Pasquier. Resistance was so violent, and went so deep into principles, that Villèle suddenly lost courage and withdrew the law. The importance of the whole proceeding did not dawn on him, however, till the citizens lighted up their houses that evening to celebrate the 'victory over the enemies of free opinion'.

Once again Chateaubriand had become the leader of political feeling in France. He was more powerful than ever at that moment, for though he had no direct share in the course of events, he had an inner vision of their development, which made people believe him. He saw the fall of the old Monarchy approaching, and the perpetual admonitions he expressed in newspaper articles and letters all harped on the reminder: 'The world is changing.' The introduction of the machine into industry was producing its effect; what blind reactionaries mistook for a noxious aftermath of the Revolution was in reality the first sign of the painful but ceaseless transformation of society under the influence of the progress of industry. Chateaubriand foresaw the effect of railways; he foresaw the Panama Canal. 'The universe is changing all round us; new nations are appearing on the stage of the world; astonishing discoveries herald a speedy transformation of the arts of war and peace. Religion, politics, morals, are all assuming a fresh character. Are we aware of this movement? Are we keeping pace with society? Are we following the march of time? Are we preparing to keep our rank in this transformed or growing society?' Warnings of this kind proved the writer's superiority to the politicians of his day; Chateaubriand was at that time almost the only party leader and politician who could see beyond his nose and warn his contemporaries that storms were brewing, whose violence would rule the century and drag daily politics in their train. He tried to widen the mental horizon of the French and prove to them that Paris was not the hub of the world. 'The Atlantic is now a mere stream that one can cross in a few days. The political influence of the States now in formation in America will make itself felt in Europe.' And again: 'Republics are in possession of an immense portion of the earth on the shores of both the oceans. The perfected civilization of ancient Europe can render assistance to these nations, still in the full vigour of their youth, to these still virgin lands with their powerful, energetic nature. The machines of England will exploit the mines of America. Steamships will ascend the rivers, railways will run through reputedly impenetrable forests . . . the barrier of the isthmus that connects one America with the other will be broken down. The new Marine, owing its propulsion to fire, defies the seas; there are no more currents, monsoons or contrary winds. Missiles of unknown shape and force will be invented . . . What are we doing in the midst of this world movement?'

All this—in the year 1825—was not said for the sake of prophesying, but to point out that the French government was not in tune with these revolutions, nor even capable of realizing them. His conclusion was a moderate one, and practically useful, but it did not suit the outlook of Villèle's government: 'If a statesman must be mad to attack the torrent of the century, it is still more senseless to yield to it blindly. We are adherents of monarchical order on rational grounds, we consider Constitutional monarchy to be the best possible form of government in this era of our society.' He defends the Charter for the same reasons: 'Not because it is a charter, a constitution, a code, a principle, but because it is the expression of the needs of the age.' He does not lose sight of the fact that the Charter offers the government a pretext to misuse it, and he detects the very point at which the July Revolution was to catch fire, namely Article 14, which allowed the King 'to proclaim decrees and ordinances necessary for the execution of the laws and the safety of the State'. He thought it 'quite possible that one fine morning the whole Charter would be suppressed for the sake of Article 13'. Which was exactly what happened.

The special laws promulgated by Villèle betrayed a barely concealed clerical influence, and stirred up the people not only against the clergy but against the Congregations. The influence of the latter, first brought into being for charitable purposes, had spread throughout all circles and institutions, and its secret-society behaviour had inflamed public imagination. Even Chateaubriand issued a warning against it in a letter to Mont-losier: 'I want religion as much as you do; I hate the Congregation as much as you do, and all these confederacies of hypocrites that turn my domestic staff into spies, and go to the altar merely in search of power. But I think the clergy, once they are delivered from these parasites, will adapt themselves very well to a constitutional régime.' These and similar criticisms struck at the foundations of Charles the Tenth's government. Chateaubriand was becoming a 'Monarchist against the Monarchy', with the result that the Liberals, and even the Republicans, drew nearer to him. General Lafayette, the old idol of the Left, sent him a laurel leaf as a token of his admiration.

Thus fate willed it that the Vicomte de Chateaubriand, convinced Royalist and former leader of those that were more royalist than the King, became the man to bring about the fall of the Bourbons. He had not had the least desire to do so, but he drove the King and his government to such extremities that they had either to listen to reason or abdicate. The concurrence with his ideas expressed by Benjamin Constant is very significant: 'I am glad to join my weak activities to your powerful influence. The frenzy of a Ministry that afflicts France and seeks to degrade her affords me the consolatory assurance that this state of things cannot last. You are contributing powerfully towards bringing it to an end.'

The Opposition had come into the open some months earlier. A parade of the National Guard had given rise to demonstrations. The Duchesses of Angoulême and Berry were hissed. The King himself was mostly greeted with politeness, but several companies of the 6th Legion shouted 'Down with the Ministers! Down with the Jesuits!' At the end of the parade a number of Legions marched past the Ministry shouting 'Down with Villèle!' The Chief Minister, in a fury, made the mistake of ordering the disbandment of the National Guard, which had been the idol of the Paris populace ever since the Revolution. This measure was only partly sanctioned by his government, and the break-up of the Cabinet began. He ended by dissolving the Chamber and ordering fresh elections. The Royalists, led by Chateaubriand, under Royer-Collard and Guizot, formed an electoral league with one another and procured an overwhelming defeat for Villèle. The government resigned. Contrary to the general expectation, the King did not appoint Chateaubriand to succeed Villèle, but

Martignac, a distinguished deputy who was generally believed capable of easing the situation. The King, it seems, could not make up his mind to overrule the resistance to Chateaubriand of the extreme royalists and the clergy. The fallen Villèle, who had the ear of Charles X, urgently advised him against entrusting power to the 'traitor', who was hardly more than a revolutionary in disguise. This dishevelled Vicomte and poet, with his solemn Cassandra warnings, his perpetually wounded conceit, and the stability of a rope-dancer—such was the picture of Chateaubriand painted by his enemies—could not possibly be selected to strengthen the position of the Throne and the Church and oppose the increasing clamour of free thought. Chateaubriand was indignant at the King's perfidy and this gross trespass against the political rules of the game. He had an attack of fury which nearly suffocated him, and leeches had to be employed to lessen his blood pressure. During the night the gall entered the blood-stream and he became, so says Madame de Boigne, as green as a lizard.

The King, Martignac, and the rest of the Ministers were afraid of him and of his political power, which would permit him to perpetrate any act of vengeance he chose. No price appeared too high that might bind him, however loosely, to the Cabinet, and at the same time remove him to a distance. They would have made him Envoy to China if that had been possible. Where should they send him? The King ordered the post of Ambassador to Rome to be offered him. 'The word Rome had a magical effect on me,' wrote Chateaubriand later, 'I experienced the temptation that anchorets in the desert are exposed to.' This was more than a fine turn of speech; the thought of going to Rome stirred his latent readiness to retire from the political strife of the day and give himself up to the melancholy scene, stamped with the decay of earthly glories, in which guise Rome had appeared to him twenty-five years ago. Rome, to him, was not only the city in which he had buried Pauline de Beaumont, but the city of all graves. Greatness and transience, ruins and monuments had not yet lost their witchery for him. The idea of re-experiencing the gentle melancholy of the Eternal City in all the splendour of high

T

office and at the same time as a solitary poet, tempted him so sorely that he accepted the offer forthwith.

The Curia made a few difficulties, of which he was not informed; his criticism of the French clergy and especially the 'hypocrites' of the Congregations, were not forgotten. But the Nuncio advised that no objections be raised. 'If the Holy See were to reject him now, Monsieur de Chateaubriand, whose conceit is great and his *amour-propre* sensitive, would wage bitter war against us.' The Nuncio believed the new Ambassador would not remain long in Rome, but would soon wish to enter the government. Besides which he was bringing his wife with him this time, on whom he depended almost as much as a child on its mother, and who was as pious as she was benevolent. There now remained only the problem of inducing Adrien de Montmorency, brother to the deceased Mathieu, to vacate his ambassadorship, in Rome in favour of Chateaubriand. This ticklish task was performed by Madame Récamier with the greatest *savoir-faire*. Adrien agreed to go as Ambassador to Vienna.

Chateaubriand started on his journey with melancholy feelings. He had made many enemies in recent years, and lost some of the few good friends he possessed, Joubert, who had contributed so much to his literary education and had shown himself such a good friend, had been dead for some time. Claire de Duras, too, had died in Nice the preceding January. His 'Dear Sister' had loved the Enchanter with a selfless and untiring passion, and he had taken much advantage of her helpfulness. Ten years before, she had confessed her love for the magnificent egoist: 'I am sad to death; what are outward things without him? He is the light that illumines them; everything becomes dim and lifeless when he leaves me. . . .' Poor Claire, he had often told her clearly, even harshly, that he could not love her, that she must be content with the friendship he could offer her. But she never wavered in her feelings, and found her happiness in working for his. Now she was dead; he could entrust her with no more missions, great or little, and must rely solely on Madame Récamier, for without the services of women he could not exist.

The parting from Juliette cost him much pain. As he journeyed southward beside his wife, in a comfortable travelling coach with postilions, lackeys, and a courier riding ahead, he thought of her incessantly and wrote letters to her when and where he could: 'Believe me when I say that nothing in the world can distract me now, or separate me from you. Always think of this, that we must end our lives together.' At the frontier he wrote 'I am writing to you in a miserable hut, that in France or out of France, this side or the other side of the Alps, I live only for you and wait only upon you'. The Ambassador travelled towards his destination at a leisurely pace, beside his pious, devoted Ambassadress—whose little spitefulnesses were losing some of their sharpness with time—and arrived at the end of three weeks.

During the ten months of his tenure of office he had to deal with a Conclave, with Eastern affairs, and with certain great religious questions, on which he made careful and lengthy reports. But he performed, as he says himself, 'all this diplomatic work like any other ambassador, without giving it a thought, as a peasant girl in Normandy knits stockings while she tends her sheep'. He lived in great style; the government had given him a heap of money, which he spent faithfully on their behalf. His banquets, fireworks and garden parties exceeded all the patriotic efforts of other diplomats: 'I have given balls and soirées in London and Paris, but I had no idea what parties in Rome could be like. They have something of the poesy of the ancients, which places death beside pleasure.' His reception for the Grand-Duchess Hélène was far-famed, notwithstanding the weather drove the guests out of the garden into the house. At times he wondered if it was not a pity to be devoting his brain and his time to these worldly efforts, and then his thoughts would revert to the beautiful young women 'floating in music and flowers like swans heading for luminous southern lands'. 'What pleasure is it that allures them?' he asks. 'Some seek what they once loved, others what they do not love as yet. And at the end of their journey they sink into the ever open graves, into the old sarcophagi from which sparkling fountains spring, to add to the fine, light dust of earthly transience.'

But there were evenings when the spacious Palazzo Simonetti, which served as the Embassy, remained empty and dark. The couple then stayed quietly at home. Céleste busied herself with embroidery; René played chess against himself or stood with his elbows on the mantelpiece, staring into the mirror above it. Was he studying his face, looking for traces of age, or was he seeking that strange thrill that seizes one like the beginning of a dream, when one's own face becomes that of a stranger? The house was quiet, the woman silent in her armchair. René smoothed back his hair with both hands and contemplated his powerful forehead; but the longer he stared, the more confused his thoughts became, his sense of identity faded, the longed-for storms were silent; for a moment his vitality was paralysed by the realization that what a man creates is always greater than himself.

He drove out of the gates of the Holy City and roamed about the Campagna, armed with a sporting gun. The light of the Campagna, its colours, and the marvellous haphazardness of its contours, always delighted him. A quarter of a century earlier, in a famous letter, he had given the classic description of this scenery. But day by day it seemed new and inexhaustible: 'I can't stop wandering about the Campagna; there is no path between two hedges that I don't know better than the paths at Combourg. I collect flowers from the grave of Caecilia Metella; mignonette and Apennine anemones have a soft effect on the white of the ruins and the soil. . . . I often go on foot round the city walls of Rome, my excavations are merely another form of the same pastime. Perhaps I shall give my dust to the earth in exchange for the statue it will erect to me.' The old melancholy of graves and ruins seized him again: 'This city of Rome is a beautiful means of forgetting everything, despising everything and dying.'

Gloomy thoughts, which he confided to Madame Récamier: 'I assure you I often wish for death. What am I doing on the earth? Yesterday, Ash Wednesday, I knelt all alone in the church of Santa Croce, which leans against the walls of Rome not far from the Naples Gate. I listened to the monotonous dirge of the monks in the midst of that great solitude, and wished I were a monk too, to be able to sing among all these ruins. What a place in which to bury worldly ambition and strip oneself of earthly vanities!'

How these words, written on the morrow of Ash Wednesday,

must have troubled Juliette's heart! They made her anxious about him, he ought not to be left entirely to his gloomy dreams. She was not to know that the very next day a young lady had called on the Ambassador with a letter of introduction, and dispersed all his ideas about human dust and the renouncement of earthly pleasures. This was the twenty-seven-year-old Hortense Allart, who succeeded in a single hour in restoring all his enterprise to the ageing writer.

If Madame de Chateaubriand had hoped there would be no 'ladies' in Rome, she was soon undeceived. The fact that a long letter was despatched to Juliette that Friday no longer troubled her. But there were other correspondences she viewed with less confidence. A Marquise de Vichet, mother of a handsome lieutenant, wrote as an enthusiastic reader, but retreated when the author, on the spur of the moment, invited her to visit him in Rome. Léontine de Villeneuve, twenty-five and unmarried, wrote to him 'I really don't know why I am writing to you. Thousands of others before me have wearied famous men with their correspondence'. Which resulted in a lively exchange of letters that rapidly assumed a most intimate character. He did not forget, however, to mingle a few grains of bitterness in the heady potion of his erotic eloquence: 'I can give nobody happiness, because I do not possess it myself. Happiness is not a part of my nature, it does not suit my age.' And again: 'Good morning, my beautiful Léontine, my Sylphide, my charming Unknown, love me and write to me.' Next time: 'Léontine, I must see you; I love you too much, I'm an old fool!' Perhaps he was right, for he suddenly warned her against him: 'Every creature that has attached itself to me has repented it. They all suffered: all of them, before they died, had more or less gone out of their mind. For this reason I shudder when people wish to attach themselves to me.' In the end he turned really wise, and wrote to her 'The rendezvous you promised me on earth I shall only beg for in heaven'.

These were letters and dreams that could be destroyed when they threatened to assume palpable form; but Hortense Allart was actual, an attractive and—it must be added—a highly palpable reality. The first time she visited the Embassy to deliver her letter of introduction the Ambassador was not at home. 'What is she like?' he asked the secretary who had received her. As a result of the flattering description given him, he at once paid her a return visit, with a flower in his buttonhole and more alive than ever. In spite of her youth, Hortense was a shrewd, experienced woman. She was convinced that 'you only know a great man when he is your lover', but she took her time. She gave him the manuscript of her new novel to read—'splendid', he thought it—they chatted, quarrelled over politics, laughed together, and saw each other more and more often. She had little virtue, but no great illusions either. 'Monsieur de Chateaubriand,' she wrote later, 'was acting a part, as I soon realized; but there was something really exciting about him, he was so fond of women.' In this seductive company he forgot for a time both his boredom and his political ambition, which was forever driving him towards Paris. He remarked one day to one of his assistants 'If Madame de Chateaubriand wishes to go to Paris herself, I can very well spend my summer here; I should feel lost away from Rome'.

THE POPE'S CAT

Pope Leo XII had received him in an unusually friendly manner. The Lord of Christendom was a modest old man, whose colourless face was marked by ill-health. His study, in which he received the Ambassador, was as bare as a monk's cell, and had only one easy chair, which was intended for the visitor. In the ample folds of his plain white cassock lay hidden the great cat Micetto, with which the Pope shared his tiny meal when he was alone. The Ambassador often saw him again, and had long discussions with him, which he reported to the Minister of Foreign Affairs at length and in exemplary form. His Holiness asked him for his opinion of the Greek question, which was not really within his sphere of office, but with which he had for some time been much engaged. Otherwise he was not exactly overwhelmed with business. Not until Leo XII succumbed to his disease and the Conclave assembled to elect his successor was he confronted again by any serious task.

The dead man left the French Ambassador his cat, which had

taken his fancy so much on his visits. She was brought to him at the Palazzo Simonetti—'all grey and very gentle, like her dead master'. She was to keep him company for many years, and be treated with great respect, as 'the Pope's cat', by the pious inhabitants of the Home in the Rue d'Enfer. He had always known how to get on with cats, and he succeeded in making up to her for the Raphael saloons in which she was born and the sunshine on Michaelangelo's cupola, on which she had once gone walking high above the earth.

The representative of France had his candidate, the same as Austria, but the chances of influencing the election were small, however much Chateaubriand may boast that Pius VIII, who issued as victor from the Conclave, had actually been his candidate. This was true only in so far as Cardinal Castiglione, who now wore the tiara, had been on the list of the Princes of the Church whose success would be welcomed by France. Cardinal Albani, on the other hand, who took over the office of Secretary of State, was decried as a zealot, and enjoyed the full favour of Austria. The Paris government was highly displeased at this appointment, and reproached the Ambassador in a rather unkindly worded despatch for not doing all in his power to eliminate Albani. Chateaubriand, knowing very well that the Minister for Foreign Affairs had written this despatch himself, replied at once with calculated severity 'This clumsy despatch, composed by some ill-bred scribe of the Ministry of Foreign Affairs, is not of the kind I had the right to expect after the services I rendered the King during the Conclave: some little regard should have been paid to the person to whom it was addressed'.

He decided precipitately to leave Rome. Not only did he refuse to tolerate the reprimand he had suffered, he had also heard that the Foreign Minister had fallen ill and the King was about to appoint someone else. Would it be himself? Hasty letters went to Paris, to Madame Récamier and other friends: 'I shall arrive a few hours after this letter.' But all his hurry was wasted, for the King had already entrusted the office to the Foreign Minister's deputy, Portalis. Chateaubriand had once more suffered disappointment, but this time he tried to take it quietly: 'The decision I have now to make must be calm and dignified. I shall not send in my resignation, I shall make no fuss; I still have a period of leave to the good, and I shall make use of it to go quite peaceably to Paris when all is over. There I will lay my resignation at the feet of the King. I can no longer be of use to the government. At the moment when I have succeeded in getting the Pope elected whom the King wished for, the King thinks it necessary to look for a Minister outside all political probability. Perhaps I needed this outrageous lesson to subdue the last flights of my pride. I accept it submissively and shall put it to good use.' But was it wise to give up the ambassadorship just now? Juliette Récamier, with her wonderful flair, sensed the storm rising over France during these weeks of the year 1829. She had been so indescribably happy to have her old friend back again. 'His arrival,' she had said to her neice, 'reawakens my life, which was threatened with extinction.' But she foresaw that the government could not hold out much longer, and as soon as it had resigned, the King would root out the last traces of Liberalism. She felt that Chateaubriand ought not to be on the spot in Paris when this change of government occurred. If the King took him into the Cabinet, he would side with a cause that was bound to be wrecked. If the King rejected him he would lose his head and do things he would regret. She did all she could to make the idea of returning to Rome attractive to him, she promised to visit him, she appealed to his political wisdom, to his affection and his friendship for her, till at last he promised to do as she wished.

He would resume his life in Rome. The sky of France was so grey and depressing! If he could no longer be ambassador he would write a History of France; he would lodge in a little room in the Monastery of Sant' Onofrio, alongside the cell where Tasso died. Juliette would be there, he would form an intellectual centre in the Eternal City, young writers like Lamartine, Sainte-Beuve and de Vigny would come on pilgrimage to him. Then the cell became a palace, in which he would give brilliant parties for the most beautiful women in the world. Enough of these politics, which had so often injured his pride! Perhaps after this King was dead? No, the Dauphin didn't like him either. 'I alarm their mediocrity.' Thus he played with reality as though he were twenty years old.

Juliette was a true friend. She did well to urge him to leave Paris, for he had all sorts of follies in his head that did not beseem either his age or his office. Hortense Allart, who had shown so little resistance to him in Rome, was in Paris for the purpose of pursuing her adventure with the great man. She shared his taste for endless rambles through the streets and outskirts of Paris; she listened to him when he talked of his depression and his thoughts of death. 'His conversation,' she said later, 'was often melancholy but always kindly. I quite forgot his age, but he did not. He often spoke to me of his death, and was pleased if my eyes filled with tears.' They frequently visited a little inn, in an upstairs room of which they dined tête-à-tête. The mood was then less despondent. 'He had a good appetite, and everything amused him.' Hortense sang some of Béranger's songs to him, 'and then', she says without the least prudery, 'he did what he pleased'.

Was she merely a plaything, whose role need not cause the loving Juliette any anxiety? There was a carelessness about her that enchanted him, she did not belong to the society in which he usually mixed, she knew none of the politicians, diplomats and statesmen that held such a large place in his life and were beginning to weary him in all seriousness. With her he could behave as he liked, in her company he felt free of all restraint and every affected attitude. At the same time he recognized that she was clever, and had a genuine understanding of literature. He often dictated to her passages from the *Historical Studies* on which he was working at the time, and in this way she came to know him better than in ordinary conversation. She discovered that the *weltschmerz* of his youth had turned into a fruitful pessimism, which had been further strengthened by an immense acquaintance with history. His historic sense enabled him to find reflections of himself in every phase of the past, but it also inspired him with a feeling of resignation, contrasting with his pleasure in political activity, which exasperated his enemies and enchanted his friends. 'His boredom, his indifference,' says Hortense, 'have a kind of grandeur; his genius is everywhere apparent in his boredom. He reminds me of the eagles that I sometimes see of a morning in the Botanical Gardens, fixing their gaze on the sun and flapping the great wings that their cage is too narrow to encompass.'

He was still Ambassador to the Holy See. Juliette took care that he should not start any quarrel with the government, and urged him to return to his beloved Rome, where she would soon follow him and help him with his work. To help him to while away the time in Paris, and no doubt to lure him away from his gay, frivolous Hortense, she made him more and more the point of attraction of her *salon*. She had now taken a larger apartment in the same house, the 'Abbaye-aux-Bois', and assembled a select company there one evening to listen to a reading by Chateaubriand. Unfortunately he chose his drama *Moses*, of which he was specially fond, but which is certainly one of his weakest works. Lamartine, who was beginning to be much spoken of among the younger writers, was present at this socially brilliant party, and describes it somewhat unkindly: 'Below the portrait of Madame de Staël, like an Oswald grown old, sat Monsieur de Chateaubriand. Thanks to the fans and chairs of the ladies he contrived to conceal the ugliness of his unequal shoulders, of his thick-set body and skinny legs. One only saw the manly bust and the Olympic head with its sparkling eyes, a mouth at one moment pursed up in a solemn expression, at the next expanding in a smile more polite than cordial; the cheeks furrowed like Dante's, thanks to Time, which has driven as many years as ambitious passions through them; an expression of false modesty, assumed as the cosmetic of fame—such was the figure-head in the background of the drawing-room, between the fireplace and the portrait. He greeted all arrivals with an awkward politeness that visibly begged indulgence.' The actor selected to read the piece did not do it well, and the author took it from him to deliver the conclusion himself. He was a good reader, but even so the work did not succeed in capturing the audience. Madame Récamier, in her usual charming fashion, bridged over the embarrassment that spread between silence and forced compliments.

Now, however, he must think seriously of leaving, for even a Chateaubriand could not stay away from his post for ever. But first of all he wished to spend a few days at the healing springs of Cauterets, not because he felt ill but because his correspondent Léontine, whose written declarations had so flattered him in Rome, had suggested a rendezvous with him there. Poor René, surrounded by all the glory of the world, loved by the most famous woman of the day, feared as a statesman who had reinstated kings and whose present sovereign kept anxiously out of his way! His heart was still restless, his senses curious, his life still not anchored, still as of old abandoned to every gust of wind! He roamed with Léontine along the mountain streams of the Pyrenees and surrendered his life to her, passionately and blindly, although he was well aware that it was drawing nearer and nearer to the final shadows. Léontine was decidedly not the equal of his dreams, she had not the measure of the eternally desired Sylphide, and nothing much came of the adventure but the sketch for a novel to be called *Love and Age*.

It consists only of a few pages, confessions of a Réne grown old. 'I am,' he says, 'an old wanderer without a home, of an evening I see everyone going home and closing the door behind him; I see the young lovers gliding through the darkness, I sit on the milestone, counting the stars and relying on none of them, and await the dawn that has nothing new to tell me.' In another passage of the work he says 'When you tell me that you love me like a father, you make me shudder; when you declare you love me like a lover, I don't believe you. . . . When you were sitting with me yesterday on those rocks, when the wind in the tops of the pines brought us the murmur of the sea, I nearly died of love and melancholy: I said to myself "Is my hand light enough to caress that golden hair? What can she love in me? A dream that reality will dispel" '.

This sentimental rambling in the Pyrenees had hardly lasted three weeks when disturbing rumours reached him from Paris. The King had at last found an opportunity to dismiss Martignac, whom he had come to dislike as an enlightened, progressive Chief Minister, and had entrusted Prince Jules de Polignac with the government. The news soon proved true, and this meant that a confict between constitution and government would sooner or later become unavoidable. Chateaubriand feared the worst, and started for Paris there and then; he was determined to leave the King's service, although his dream of an evening of life in Rome was more alluring than ever. On reaching Paris he begged to be received at once by the King, but the latter had himself denied to his vistor, for he had no wish to hear the warnings and threats of this 'solemn Cassandra'. Jules de Polignac begged the Ambassador not to resign but to return as speedily as possible to Rome: 'Am I not your friend? Your resignation might occasion fresh rifts. I beseech you, dear Vicomte, do not commit this folly.' But the Vicomte stood firm, although Polignac swore that he was as devoted to the Constitution as himself, and would never do it any injury.

Chateaubriand was not to be deceived, he declared that the new government was most unpopular, and that the people foresaw a curtailment of the freedoms guaranteed by the Charter, and would never accept this. As a believer in these freedoms, he would not join a government which the King had only set up for the sake of returning to absolutism. Madame de Boigne asserts that the King made every effort to persuade him to remain; that he offered him the title of Duke, the settlement of his debts and a highly paid post at Court for his wife. If this is true, Chateaubriand's steadfastness is doubly admirable, for he was again deeply in debt, and his publisher Ladvocat, from whom he still stood to receive a good deal of money, had gone into liquidation. But he had only too clear an idea of the intentions of Charles X and his 'dear Jules'—as he had called his new Chief Minister ever since the days of their common exile. The end of the old Monarchy was near, it had no use for monitors and prophets, he himself had exhausted every means of persuading it that the world had altered.

The name of Polignac stirred painful memories in the French people. The revolutionary hatred of Court and courtiers, which had exploded with such terrifying force forty years earlier, still clung to this family, closely connected with Marie-Antoinette as it was, and still ranking as a symbol of reactionary corruption. Jules de Polignac, who had grown up as an *emigré*, had early made friends with the present King and had taken part in Cadoudal's conspiracy. Even during the first Restoration he had proved a merciless persecutor, and had fought every attempt to form a constitutional régime. 'Dear Jules' was exactly the kind of Chief Minister the King had longed for all these ten years. With him he would be able to do away with the Charter and obtain a compliant Chamber. Polignac was no coward, but there was not much else to be said of him. He had a high opinion of himself, was immensely pious, and declared that the Holy Virgin had appeared to him and appointed him to be the saviour of France. His appointment of General Bourmont to be Minister of War, who had gone over to the enemy on the eve of Waterloo, brought popular opposition to him to its peak.

The resignation of an ambassador is no great political event, but in the case of a Chateaubriand, exerting such an important influence not only on a number of deputies but on public opinion in general, there was bound to be a noticeable repercussion. The liberal Press was triumphant: 'One of the greatest geniuses of Europe has remained true not only to his reputation but to himself.' No wonder the Liberals sought union with him; but he knew that he was 'more a banner than a leader', and he was anxious, moreover, to avoid contact with a movement aiming at 'changing the dynasty'—replacing, that is, the 'incorrigible Bourbons' by the House of Orleans. The aged Talleyrand and Baron Louis cherished notions of this kind, and had them disseminated by such powerful publicists as Mignet and Thiers. They called their paper the *National*. Chateaubriand would have nothing to do with endeavours of this kind; even if he could no longer save the dynasty that was rushing blindly to destruction, he would remain loyal to it, for his loyalty was not of the mind, it was a vital instinct.

Charles X opened the session of 1830 with a severe Speech from the Throne, which sounded like a declaration of war against all those who were not prepared to support his policy. A no less significant 'Address' from 221 deputies was the result. It had been composed by Royer-Collard and Guizot, and was to the effect that the government's policy was entirely at variance with the wishes of the nation, and that 'an orderly conduct of affairs' was no longer possible. The King dissolved the Chamber, and although a few days before the fresh elections, the town of Algiers had been occupied by a French army, which caused rejoicings in all quarters, and Polignac expected this military success to turn greatly to the advantage of the government, the elections resulted instead in an enormous success for the Opposition.

This time the air was not 'full of daggers', but it smelt of powder. Everybody was prepared for a *coup d'état*, and Paris, as restless and ready to revolt as ever, the starting point of so many uprisings that had spread throughout the country, made its preparations. A populace that had always had a weakness for street fighting began fishing its toys out of the cupboard again. Arms came to light from nowhere, and were distributed at night; the purchase of gunpowder, *couteaux de chasse* and duelling swords assumed striking proportions, and secret gatherings of students, workmen, artisans and members of a resolute middle class increased in number. The Court and the government alone remained unmoved, or too proud to take the general unrest seriously. Villèle urgently advised his former colleagues not to throw a spark into the powder barrel, because one never knew 'what might not blow up with it'. The Tsar, at that time the most absolutist ruler in the world, sent a courier to the King, suggesting that he should immediately take suitable measures of conciliation, rather than conjure up troubles that might spread to other countries as well. Charles X replied defiantly 'Concessions destroyed Louis XVI; I have no alternative but to mount a horse or else the executioner's tumbril'.

Early on the morning of July 26th Chateaubriand left for Dieppe, where Madame Récamier was staying, as she had done the year before, to enjoy the freshness of the sea air far from the all-too summery capital, and watch the children and young people devoting themselves to the pleasures of sea bathing, which had just come into fashion. She had taken a handsome apartment in the Hotel Albion, with windows overlooking the sea. The two old friends sat there together, talking in lowered tones, as usual, of the threatening political situation, and of the happiness of being together, never to lose each other again. Juliette was aware of all the follies committed from time to time by her white-haired friend; she had no high opinion of his feminine acquaintance, especially Hortense Allart but she was far from reproaching or even teasing him about them. Her invincibility, against which no woman, however young, clever or aggressive, could prevail, was due to the delicate calm she respired. Her prestige as a woman outweighed her white hair; her worldly wisdom and her constancy, which never became oppressive, formed the peaceful zone to which René always fled as though he were going home.

So they chatted, often falling silent too, to listen to the regular plash of the waves upon the shore or to watch the sails disappearing into the summer haze. Then a visitor arrived from Paris, a mutual friend, who could hardly wait to be announced. He brought them the infamous ordinances the King had just issued. These were four decrees, brought into force by the King on the grounds of the authority given him by Article 14 of the Charter. The first suppressed the freedom of the Press, the second dissolved the Chamber, the third altered the electoral franchise and the fourth fixed a day for a fresh election. Chateaubriand could not believe his eyes; the paper fell from his hand: 'Yet another government hurling itself intentionally and of its own free will from the towers of Notre-Dame!' His decision was as impulsive as when in his youth, sitting with settlers in a lonely mill at the edge of an American forest, he had read in a newspaper lying on the ground 'Flight of the King'. He immediately ordered post horses for his return to Paris. He could no longer be absent from the centre of the drama that might begin at any moment. He was painfully aware of the conflict in his breast. He must save the King; but he must also save the freedom built up by the Constitution. 'I must not give up for lost either the King or the Charter, Legitimate Power or Freedom.' But at the same time he felt it was beyond the power of man to solve the contradiction.

THE FALL OF THE LILIES

At Gisors, on the way, he heard that Paris was in revolt. The great upheaval, known later as the July Revolution, that convulsed heads and hearts in Europe and America, had begun. He questioned the inhabitants, who were all greatly excited. It was obvious that they had fully realized the importance of the Constitution to their daily lives, and to the future of the country, and that they felt personally threatened by the King's breach of it. He was shown a copy of *Le Temps*, in which somebody had underlined the sentence 'The reign of law has been interrupted, that of force has begun. Obedience has ceased to be a duty'. In Pontoise there was fresh news, showing that street fighting had started in earnest. The King appeared to be cut off in the castle of Saint-Cloud. The postilion of the carriage discarded his jacket because it was embroidered with the royal lilies; he advised Chateaubriand not to try and enter the city by the Porte de l'Etoile because barricades had already been erected there, but to go through the turnpike at the Trocadero. Chateaubriand told him to pull up on the hill of Chaillot, at the spot where Napoleon had intended to build a palace for his son, the King of Rome. From this lonely eminence he could overlook the city; isolated shells were falling, there was a rattle of musketry at intervals, and ever and anon the alarm-bell rang. White smoke was rising between detached groups of houses. His eye was caught by the tricolour flags, already visible on a number of building. The white lily banner of the Bourbons was nowhere to be seen. 'I knew now that it was no longer a question of revolt but of revolution. I foresaw that my role was about to be changed; I had hastened here to defend public liberties, and now I should be obliged to defend the Monarchy.'

The Vicomte drove by wide détours through a strangely empty city—for the positilion avoided all the centres of disturbance—to his house in the Rue d'Enfer. Madame de Chateaubriand received him with tears of trepidation and relief. She had seen too much rioting and fighting in the streets of Paris in her youth not to tremble now with fear. He did what he could to reassure her and then wrote a letter to Madame Récamier in Dieppe. He described the situation in the capital and his own internal conflict, which condemned him to inactivity: 'There is nothing I can say or do; I am waiting, and weeping for my country.' Later on he wrote her a second letter: 'It is possible that this letter will not leave here, for martial law has been proclaimed. Marshal Marmont is in command for the King; people say he has been killed, but I don't believe it. Try not to worry too much. God protect you. We shall see each other again.' Next day he wrote again: 'It is all over. The people's victory is complete. The King has yielded on every point, but I fear things will now go far beyond the concessions made by the Crown. I wrote to His Majesty this morning.'

The letter did in fact reach the King, but he could think of no instructions to give the writer, and sent it on to the Duke of Mortemar, whom he had appointed Chief Minister. The Duke was not to be found, he had been attacked on the way from Saint-Cloud to Paris, had been shot in the heel, and did not arrive till late in the night at his house, where he at once settled himself in a bath-tub and sent for the doctor. Hearing nothing from the King, Chateaubriand went to the House of Peers. He was still hoping to find a means of persuading the King to abdicate in favour of the little Duke of Bordeaux, and thus preventing the Duke of Orleans's appointment as Lieutenant-General of the Kingdom from leading to a change of dynasty, for he knew there was a movement spreading throughout the capital to make Philip of Orleans King. He made the journey to the House on foot, to see things for himself. He took no heed of the gunfire, which was becoming restricted to certain quarters of the city with the gradual withdrawal of Marmont's troops. Compared with the great days of the Revolution, the city seemed 'a model of order and silence'.

On the Pont-Neuf somebody had given the statue of Henri IV a tricolour flag to hold. Going through the Colonnades of the Louvre, Chateaubriand, who liked going bareheaded, was recognized by a party of students by his wild shock of hair. 'Long live the defender of the freedom of the Press.' they cried. They were delighted to have the great man among them on this great day, and they carried him over the Pont des Arts, up the Rue de la Seine to the Luxembourg Palace, where the Peers were sitting. People looked out of the windows and waved to them. 'Long live the Constitution!' shouted the students. 'Yes,' agreed Chateaubriand, hanging on to the mane of the young man carrying him pick-a-back. 'Yes! Long live the Charter! But long live the King

v

too!' Upon which the students roared in chorus 'Long live Chateaubriand!' Which saved any further argument.

It was a scene entirely after his own heart. The People, Youth, fine enthusiasm, a triumphal progress—glorious! The Peers looked on in amazement as their colleague was deposited on the cobble pavement of the courtyard by a laughing horde of young undergraduates. He bade his admirers farewell, and according to Molé, said a few words to reassure them as to the fate of the Bourbons (As if there had been a single student in Paris that wasn't longing for the fall of the dynasty!): 'Don't worry! So long as we can preserve the freedom of the Press, you have only to give me pen, ink and paper, and if the dynasty is really overthrown, I shall have set it up again in three months time!' Whether he really said this may be doubted, for Molé was no longer the friend of old days, and had taken to telling spiteful tales of the pompous Vicomte, who always referred everything in the world to himself.

The Peers did not share his optimism—if he really harboured it —they knew that everything was not yet over. The dead, the dying, the smoking ruins and barricades, the streets laid waste by artillery fire; all this could not be washed out so soon. Each of the political parties—Legitimist, Orleanist, Republican—was still opposed to the others. The Duke of Orleans had been persuaded to go to the Hôtel de Ville, to wave the tricolour and allow himself to be embraced by Lafayette, the old rhetorician, who must always be on the spot 'when the People spoke'. It did not look at all as though the street-fighters were prepared to go home peaceably, now that their bloody work was done and many of their number had lost their lives. Louis Philippe, who had already tried to make himself popular—one of his worst miscalculations—invited 'the People' to the Palais-Royal. Courtyards and passages were immediately filled with a noisy, cheeky, jocular crowd, opening all the doors, lounging on the seats, unpacking their provender all over the place. 'The shouting, and the singing of "The Marseillaise", could be heard so loudly in the drawing-rooms that it was difficult to make oneself understood. Nobody dared close the windows for fear of annoying the people. It was not a popular triumph, it was merely the joyous orgy of a crowd with no malevolent intention. . . .'

Louis Philippe was not yet 'King of the French'; there was still a plan afoot to get Charles X and the Duke of Angoulême, the successor to the Throne, to abdicate in favour of the little Duke of Bordeaux. This would ensure the continance of the dynasty and at the same time the destruction of its political influence. Louis Philippe, the 'lieutenant-General of the Kingdom', would then be appointed Regent. The nine-year-old boy, who was to take the name of Henri V, was the posthumous son of the Duke of Berry who had been murdered at the Opera in 1820. His mother, Marie-Caroline, the fantastic Neapolitan, who was staying at Saint-Cloud with Charles X, had now become a perpetual source of unrest and disorder. At one moment she had the absurd idea of taking her son, the last of the Bourbons, to the Hôtel de Ville and putting him under the protection of the People; at the next she was urging the old King, who seemed half paralysed by perplexity, to leave Saint-Cloud at once because it was too near to Paris. She presented herself to the King in male attire, with a sword at her side and two pistols in her belt—she was waving a third in her hand. The King sat motionless in his chair, in the company of his First Chamberlain, the Duc de Maille. Marie-Caroline besought him to leave, fired her pistols at the ceiling, and rushed out again. 'What do you think of that, Maille?' asked the King, shaking his head. To which the Chamberlain answered with a nasal drawl 'Hair-raising!'

At last the King started off—towards the coast. He signed his abdication in Rambouillet, and then the journey went slowly on. He was surrounded by an enormous retinue, which, however, grew smaller at every stage. These people trailed a ceremonial along with them, the fussy observance of which greatly delayed the journey. There was a great deal of brain-racking, for instance, because according to ancient usage the King must not dine at a round table. In Laigle, where he spent the night, a table had to be sawn up to make it rectangular. Louis Philippe determined to make this pompous company find their legs, and collected a band of insurgents to catch up with the King and 'take over his protection'. Although Charles still had 12,000 crack troops with him, he speeded up his journey under this pressure, and on August 16th went on board an American ship in Cherbourg, which was to take him to England. Once aboard, all danger was over, but the Duchess of Berry broke into His fallen Majesty's cabin, crying treason. She had heard on deck that the Captain intended to carry off the whole company to 'Saint-Helena'. The poor Captain, however, was only referring to the English coastal village of St. Helen's.

So ended the exodus of the Bourbons, who had ruled over France for centuries and brought her so much of both glory and misery. However great the force of history, however defenceless the individual against its dynamic, the burden of guilt still lies on mortal shoulders. Charles X had a will, and he got his way. He left his country in a state of ferment and unrest; the anointing oil of Rheims had not succeeded in calming the waters of the age.

Louis Philippe begged the Vicomte de Chateaubriand to call on him, so that he might obtain the advice of the great man who had so clearly seen the revolution coming. In the Palais-Royal he was greeted with cries of 'Oh, Monsieur de Chateaubriand, we are so unhappy! What are we to do now?' The Vicomte had only one answer: 'We must recognize the little Duke of Bordeaux as King Henri V, and Louis Philippe must act as Regent until his majority.' 'Of course, of course, that would be the ideal solution, dear Vicomte, but events are more powerful than we are, and I fear . . .' The visitor could see that the speaker was burning with eagerness to wear the crown. When his friends asked him afterwards what they had talked about, he said 'What would you, he wants to be King, and Madame the Duchess of Orleans wants to be Queen. . . . They both gave me to understand that I could be useful to them, and neither of them dared look me in the face.' A few days later the Duke of Orleans was 'King of the French'.

The Peers assembled to swear fealty to the new Sovereign, but Chateaubriand refused to take the oath. At nine in the evening he mounted the tribune to give the reasons for his attitude. In the dismal light of the lamps that only sparsely illuminated the vast Hall of the Luxembourg, the apparitions facing him bore all the marks of uncertainty and cowardice. They held their heads down, they turned their eyes away, they were nearly all resolved to follow the new régime and seal the fate of the old dynasty. The House listened to him in profound silence. He declared that the parliamentarian republic was to be the future form of States all the world over, though its hour had not yet struck in France. Meanwhile only the Legitimate Monarchy had authority enough to ensure respect for public freedoms, but it had condemned itself to destruction 'by the conspiracy of hypocrisy and stupidity'. 'It is not out of sentimental devotion that I plead for a cause which would turn against me in every way if it triumphed. I am not seeking after romanticism, or chivalry, or martydom. I do not believe in the divine right of kings, I believe in the forces of revolution and reality. I am proposing the Duke of Bordeaux quite simply as a necessity that is weightier than the one under discussion here. I have wearied Throne and Country enough with my unwelcome warnings as a useless Cassandra. All that is left to me is to seat myself on the ruins of a collapse that I have so often foretold. I credit misfortune with the power to do everything except to release me from my oath of loyalty. My life must remain consistent. After all I have done, said and written for the sake of the Bourbons, I should be the lowest scoundrel if I were to deny them—now, when they are going into exile for the third and last time. All I ask is to preserve my freedom of conscience, and the right to die where I can enjoy independence and peace.'

He spoke the last words with difficulty, he could hardly restrain his tears. He was rent by a storm of emotion, weeping over the grandeur of the moment, for say what he would, nobody had reached after romanticism and chivalry more than he. He wept over the helplessness of men in face of a changing world, but also over the sinking dynasty whose last representatives were so little equal to the greatness of their name. They were the tears of a man who knew his day was over, but that no day could affect the immortal core of his being. He had been the moulder of his life, of which he had intended to make a work of art, and lo! he had succeeded. He went calmly down the steps of the tribune, calmly

through the silent, oppressed Assembly to the door. Once
outside he divested himself of his splendidly embroidered Peer's
coat, his sword and his plumed hat, removed the white cockade,
put on his black coat and slipped the badge in his pocket. Then
he wrote a declaration to the effect that he was renouncing the
title of Peer and of Minister of State, and the emoluments
connected therewith, and strolled home under a misty moon,
through the great gardens, past the spot where Marshal Ney
had been shot fifteen years before.

XIII

HAPPINESS AND SORROW
WITH WHITE HAIR

THE LAST OF THE SYLPHIDE

CHATEAUBRIAND'S political life was at an end. Just as he had withdrawn from the service of the First Consul after the execution of the Duc d'Enghien, and retired into solitude to pursue his literary work, so he now drew a final stroke under his public ambition. But whereas at that time he was awaiting his hour and carefully cherishing his dreams of power, today he was determined to re-establish the unity of his personality and oscillate no more between romanticism and politics. Of course he would defend with all his literary energy the dynasty now living in exile, to whose undermining he had himself contributed so much. But the perpetual tension between fiction and fact, in which he had lived for so many years, was broken; the day of hesitation was over. He no longer needed to oppose Napoleon while admiring him, to despise the policy of the Bourbons and pay homage to them; he need no longer be a monarchist against the Monarchy, or a Liberal against Democracy. He could now, without internal conflict, agree with the younger Republicans like Armand Carrel, Arago and Béranger in their hatred of the 'Bourgeois Monarchy' and contempt of the régime of the *juste milieu*, which leaned for support on bankers and business men, and which he called 'this soup-tureen of a housekeeping monarchy'.

His great idea, adopted during his lengthy sojourn among the English, of endowing the French with a political system in which a hereditary monarchy should be mated to English institutions, had suffered shipwreck. But had he really done everything he could to establish the idea in France? Had not the radical

royalism to which he had yielded after the fall of Napoleon contributed substantially to the breach between the rule of royalty
and the will of the people? Whenever he had behaved fanatically
instead of practising the decent opportunism whose usefulness he
had so early recognized, he had found himself in a blind alley,
and not himself alone. Now the time had come to turn to principles and see that they were maintained unalloyed, outside the
sphere of practical usefulness. No road was now to lead him back
into the chiaroscuro of daily politics, in which he had tried in
vain to find a way into himself. In everything he had done he had
been concerned with his own personality, he had loved politics
only for the sake of the frame it had afforded his ego. In his quest
of himself he had threaded the mazes of politics, and had paid for
this romantic ambiguity by an uneasy conscience. Now it was all
over; the writer could return to his hermitage, he was in harmony
with himself.

'As a Republican by nature, a Monarchist for wisdom's sake,
a Bourbonist for honour's sake, if it was not possible to retain
the Legitimate Monarchy, I could have found my place in a
democracy far better than in this mongrel monarchy, which has
been foisted on us by I know not whom.' His complete abstention was genuine; the government would have been only too glad
if he had accepted some high office, and thereby pledged his
authority for the bourgeois kingship. But the dividing line had
been crossed; his dress sword, plumes, gold embroideries,
buckles and sashes, all the glittering finery of his former offices,
had been sold to a Jewish dealer in old clothes, who had given
him seven hundred francs for the costly lumber. He could make
good use of the sum, for as he had stripped himself of all his
income the night before, there was no money in the house. He and
his wife had suddenly become poorer than they had ever been
before. He had now only his pen with which to provide for their
daily needs. So now the time for work had come, as he had once
told his cats that the time had come to catch mice. He immersed
himself in the *Historical Studies* which he had begun in the
Valley of the Wolves. A new publisher had applied for the rights
of the *Complete Works*, and offered him an advance of 25,000

francs on the historical work. He riveted himself to his writing-
table for months on end, working ten to twelve hours a day.
When a law was introduced in March forbidding the Bourbons
to enter France, he composed a polemic *Of the Restoration and
the Electoral Monarchy*, which had an enormous success, and
brought him enough money to go to Switzerland with his wife,
whose poor health necessitated a change of air. But he could
only endure it for a few months, and in September he returned
to Paris, under the pretext of negotiating the sale of the house
in the Rue d'Enfer, but in reality for the sake of being near
Juliette again. It had been rumoured in Paris that he intended
settling abroad for good—being an *emigré* again, in fact. He was
dining one evening at the Café de Paris with a party of distinguished Republicans, including Carrel and Béranger, the
popular national song-writer, when the latter stood up, glass in
hand, and sang some new verses he had composed specially for
the occasion, beginning:

'Chateaubriand, why desert your country?'

The song soon became popular, and Chateaubriand was not
unwilling to let it be thought that it had played a part in bringing
him back to France for good. His country was unhappy, he said,
and he would not desert it. He told Madame Récamier that he
could not live abroad because he could not do without her
company, which was only too true, for he could not endure his
wife and her perpetual sarcasms unless he could go to Juliette
every day in search of the peace he so badly needed. Victor Hugo,
the rising star of French literature, made critical comments in
his diary on the Master's comings and goings: 'Monsieur de
Chateaubriand goes to Geneva, comes back to Paris, goes off to
Geneva again, gets on our nerves, gives himself airs, leaves us a
pamphlet and flies off again. . . .' The pamphlet was a protest
against the strengthening of the law forbidding the country to
the Bourbons. It had been sought, by an amendment, to introduce capital punishment for any infringement of this law, but
Chateaubriand's protest made such a stir that the amendment
was in fact withdrawn. Napoleon's nephew, who was living with

his mother Hortense in Arenburg, on the Swiss shore of Lake
Constance, wrote to the author in enthusiasic agreement: 'How
fortunate are the Bourbons to be able to lean for support on such
a genius as you.' René answered him at length: 'You know,
Prince, that my young King is in Scotland, and that so long as he
is alive there can be no other King of France than he. But if
God in his inscrutable wisdom had rejected the race of Saint-
Louis, and if the customs of our country prevented the establishment of a republic, no name could better represent the glory
of France than yours.'

The race of Saint Louis was eating the bitter bread of exile in
the royal Scottish Castle of Holyrood, in which Mary Stuart had
once resided. The old King and the Angoulême couple had
resigned themselves to their fate, and no longer cherished any
hope of treading the soil of France again; but the Duchess of
Berry, mother of the boy Chateaubriand called his king, had lost
none of her enterprise in the sharp northern air. Vivacious, and
greedy of sensation, she combined her struggle for her son's
pretensions to the Throne with a taste for travelling about the
world and setting conspiracies on foot. The little Neapolitan
brunette had a head full of adventures, not all of a political
nature; her later destiny revealed the limits set to a woman's
participation in the affairs of this world.

Although she was forbidden to enter France, this enterprising
woman was making definite plans to do so. She was trying to
form a 'secret Regency Council' in Paris, and wrote to Chateaubriand inviting him to join it. But in spite of the admiration she
had always expressed for him—the only member of the Royal
Family to do so—he declined politely. Cholera broke out in
Paris about that time, carrying off thousands of people and
striking terror into the great city by its insidious ravages. Marie-
Caroline wrote again to Chateaubriand, assigning him 12,000
francs with a commission to distribute it to the victims' familes.
He felt unable to refuse this request, but he found it difficult to
reach the intended recipients, for most of the mayors would
have nothing to do with the affair.

He was hoping to hear no more of the Duchess of Berry,

when the restless lady landed on the south coast not far from Marseilles with a small retinue, for the purpose, as she said, of repeating 'the return from Elba'. She was set down on the coast at midnight in a heavy storm. Loving nothing so much as masculine dress, she was disguised for the occasion as a cabin boy. Thirty-four years old and not exactly beautiful, but always in the best of spirits, she was starting now with cheerful laughter on a dangerous undertaking. But her hopes that the population would at once rally to her side and begin the fight against the bourgeois monarchy were sadly disappointed. The gendarmes were on her track, and she had perforce to clear out of their way without delay. But instead of going aboard ship again she decided to travel across France to the Vendée, where she hoped to find support among the remainder of the Loyalists.

This journey across a country she had been forbidden to enter she found vastly entertaining. The little company amused themselves romantically by impersonating characters in historical novels. Walter Scott was the great fashion just then, so the plotters gave themselves names out of his novels and adopted their sentiments. The Duchess was not only courageous but lucky. She found hospitality everywhere, and was never betrayed by those that recognized her. She was sometimes obliged to spend the night in a stable, and once even in a ditch; but she arrived safely in Nantes, disguised as a peasant woman this time, though she would rather have played the peasant boy, and found refuge in the house of two sisters, passionate Royalists, who had belonged to every loyal conspiracy during the Revolution and had built a hiding-place into their house at that time, which was supposed to be undiscoverable. It was on account of this hiding-place that the house had been selected for Marie-Caroline

Although the undertaking was far from delighting the adherents of the 'young King Henri V', they did not wish to leave her in the lurch. The famous attorney Berryer was sent to bring her to her senses and facilitate her departure. On his way back he was arrested. The papers seized at his house contained the names of persons associated with the Duchess, among them that of Chateaubriand. On June 16, 1832, the police fetched him out

of bed and took him into custody 'for taking part in a conspiracy against the security of the State'. Chateaubriand took it
calmly, but his wife, still haunted by her memories of the prisons
of the Terror, was in despair, and could only be soothed in the
course of the day by Madame Récamier's efforts at consolation.
Her husband spent a few hours in a cell, which he at once
attempted to compare with Tasso's; but he soon realized that
there was little by way of tragedy or sinister comparison to be
extracted from the whole incident, and decided therefore to look
on it from the comical side. Gisquet, the Prefect of Police,
appeared a few hours later and offered him accommodation in
his official apartment. Mademoiselle Gisquet was turned out, and
the great man moved into her chaste bedroom, where he was
thoroughly comfortable and beguiled the time by composing
little poems, listening to the young ladies playing the piano to
him, and enjoying the sympathy of numerous visitors. The first
to appear was Madame de Chateaubriand, laden with parcels,
and still horrified at the idea of his imprisonment, although the
sight of the dressing-table trimmed with frills and ribbons
gradually pacified her. Then came Madame Récamier, her
beautiful eyes full of tears of sympathy. But she found her friend
very cheerful, and set to work thinking out the practical measures
to be taken for his speedy liberation. Béranger, with whom the
Vicomte had lately made friends, came too, so there was no lack
of variety in the fair Mademoiselle Gisquet's room.

Madame de Chateaubriand, however, had not been able to
see anything funny in the incident, and when at the end of a
fortnight her husband was freed again, she insisted that they
should return to Switzerland, her health having suffered from the
agitations of the last weeks. But travelling costs money, and they
had not yet found a purchaser for the house in the Rue d'Enfer,
or rather, they had given up seriously looking for one. For once
Chateaubriand was pleasantly surprised by his Bourbons; the old
King sent him from his grey castle in Edinburgh the handsome
sum of 20,000 francs, begging him to regard it as the settlement
of a debt on the part of the Crown. Céleste begged him to go on
ahead of her and look for a suitable place to stay in. He was

delighted to travel alone; he had arrived at a stage in life in which
he was glad to meditate on the past and strike the balance of his
years. Before leaving, he had tried unsuccessfully to renew his
old relations with Hortense Allart, but she had now turned her
attention to a handsome young Englishman, Lord Bulwer-
Lytton, and had not replied. His sad thoughts were no longer a
pose, he realized that he must concede its dignity to age, that age
need not mean renunciation so long as one changed the objects
of one's desires and wished for nothing that might lead one
astray. 'When I was young,' he sighed, 'I was lonely; now, in
my old age, I am merely isolated.'

He started off without really knowing where his first halt was
to be. On the St. Gothard Pass he spent a night of thunder-
storms in a modest inn. It was a time for delving into the deepest
recesses of his melancholy, which was, however, in no way
induced by any lowering of vitality. He was more than ever
aware of his strength, but just as passionately aware that the
dreams which had accompanied him throughout his life could
never be fulfilled. The artistic power that formed the core of his
existence demanded of him that he should renounce the uttermost gifts of life. That night the written word appered to him as
the highest fulfilment. 'These mountains, this thunderstorm, this
night are lost treasures to me. And yet how much life I feel in
the depths of my soul! Never, when the most fiery blood flowed
from my heart into my veins, did I speak the language of passion
with such energy as I could at this moment. I feel as though my
Sylphide of the woods of Combourg were issuing from the
flanks of the St. Gothard. Have you found me again, enchanting
phantom of my youth? Do you pity me? As you see, only my
face has changed; I am still chasing fantasies and devoured by a
fire without cause or nourishment. Come, sit on my kneee, don't
be afraid of my grey hair, stroke it with your fingers—fairy or
spirit, whichever you may be—; perhaps under your kisses
it may turn dark again. This head, which the fading of the hair
has not made any wiser, is as full of folly as when it gave you
existence, you, eldest daughter of my imagination, innocent
fruit of my mysterious love affair with my early solitude. Come,

let us mount the clouds once more; with the lightning we will furrow, illumine, set fire to the abysses I shall drive past to-morrow. Come, as you used to, but do not bring me back . . . Someone is knocking at the door, but it is not you: it is the driver, the horses have arrived, we must depart. There is nothing left of this dream but the rain, the wind and myself—dream without end, eternal thunderstorm.'

Madame Récamier, meanwhile, was on her way to Constance, having hesitated a long time before undertaking the journey. She found it difficult to break with her habits and leave her apart-ment in the 'Abbey', which, as Ballanche says, was 'the hub of the world for her friends, as the temple of Delphi was once for the Greeks'. Her friend Madame de Boigne, who had little liking for Chateaubriand anyhow, warned her that 'life at our age is so difficult to make bearable, that one should not upset it once it has become more or less settled, especially when there is so little equality between what one gives and what one receives'. But Juliette could no longer resist the desire to see her beloved friend again. One day in late August they met in Constance. They sat for a long while hand in hand, silently contemplating the smoothly shimmering surface of the lake.

Juliette was now fifty-five, Chateaubriand sixty-four. They had loved each other for fifteen years with a feeling that had long since assumed the highest form of friendship. His many in-constancies and deceptions had scarcely touched the core of their love. He was still the man whose eyes best reflected her being, and told her best and in the deepest sense how beautiful she was and what a hold she had on his life. It was too late for either of them to question the origin of their mutual bond; they could no longer live without each other.

Amid the glitter of lake and sky he read her, in a low voice, the lines he had lately written in the mountains. The passion of his prose scorched her like fire, and disturbed the peace she was offering him. She spoke to him of the life still in store for them, and of death, with which she knew he was equally in love. He listened, soothed as always, and wrote in her note-book 'I could wish to see the sun for a long while yet, if I might end my life beside you. May my days expire at your feet like these waves, whose murmur you love. August 28, 1832'.

They travelled together to Geneva, where Madame de Chateaubriand soon joined them. Although Céleste had submitted to her husband's friendship with Juliette as an unalterable institution, he still had to suffer from her ironical allusions and eternal discontent, only a little tempered by her native wit. For the sake of peace he buried himself in his *Memoirs from beyond the Grave*. This work, which was to make his name immortal, and outlive all his other writings, was progressing. He was slowly beginning to organize the pile of sheets, passages and chapters into books and give them the right sequence, completing them and writing fresh ones. To Hortense Allart, who had turned up again, he wrote that even she could no longer keep him from his work: 'You talk of power and love. It is all over. I am reserving the remainder of my life for myself alone; nobody would want it, and I will not give it to anybody.'

Hortense was the last person to whom he would have confessed that this 'remainder' of his life was reserved for Madame Récamier. He saw Juliette daily in Geneva. They went for excursions together; in Coppet they sought out the grave of their mutual friend Germaine de Staël, who had brought them together. While he rested on a seat she walked about the garden; he followed her with his eyes, embracing in thought the pale, lovely figure, which seemed endowed with the immortality of a divine shade. That evening he wrote 'Now, as I write this page, at midnight, while everything is at rest around me and I can see through my window a few stars twinkling above the Alps, I have the feeling that all I have ever loved I have loved in Juliette; she was the hidden source of my affections. True love or folly, I have always only loved her. She orders and rules my feelings, as Madame de Chateaubriand has brought order and peace into my duties'.

THE DUCHESS GETS STUCK IN THE CHIMNEY

In October, when the first leaves were falling, and the Lake of

Geneva had begun to have melancholy moods, Juliette returned to Paris and left Chateaubriand to his work, which soon began to pall on him because he could think of nothing but excuses for following his friend. Then he received the news that the Duchess of Berry had been arrested in Nantes, where she had been in hiding for months, and had been taken to Blaye. He immediately wrote her a long letter, saying he was hastening to her assistance in order to defend her. He sent copies of the letter to all the Paris papers, and started packing his trunks. 'Nobody,' writes the spiteful Madame de Boigne, 'got more satisfaction out of the arrest of the Duchess de Berry than Chateaubriand. He was dying of boredom and couldn't think up an excuse to return to Paris.' Now he had the excuse. He left Geneva on November 12th, to rush to the assistance of 'the virtuous mother of his King'.

This enterprising lady had actually succeeded in fooling the police for months, corresponding with all and sundry from her hide-out. Possibly the authorities might have made even greater efforts, had the government known what to do with the royal conspirator once they had arrested her. But they could not prevent the police from carrying out their duty. The town of Nantes was swarming with policemen and spies; the government had sent their best detective officer there, a certain Joly, who had caught the murderer of the Duke of Berry and was now set on the track of his widow; but even this expert was unable to discover the Duchess's refuge.

Then Thiers, who had succeeded Monsieur de Montalivet as Minister of Interior, received a letter in which some anonymous person begged him to come to the Champs Elysées late at night to receive an important communication. Although the Prefect of Police urgently advised him against following up this strange rendezvous, Thiers betook himself to the appointed spot—with two loaded pistols in his pockets—and was approached by a frightened-looking man, who offered to deliver up the Duchess of Berry against payment. The man, whose name was Deutz, was in fact in the confidence of the lady, for whom he had carried out many secret errands. The bargain was concluded; the traitor being promised half a million in cash. He was accompanied to Nantes, where he at once pointed out the Duchess's place of concealment, and then dashed headlong back to Paris while the police broke into the house.

But Marie-Caroline was nowhere to be found. They searched the building for five hours while two battalions cordoned off the street. They threatened the owners that they would pull the house down stone by stone, since the person they were looking for could not have left it. But threats were of no avail; the hideout, which had remained concealed at the time of the Revolution, could not be discovered. Gendarmes remained in all the rooms overnight, even in the attic, where two of them lay down on the floor, shoved the old newspapers lying about under their heads, and attempted to sleep. As it was cold, they lighted a fire in the grate, which went out after an hour. In the morning they rekindled it, throwing bundles of the old newspapers on it to warm up the little room. Suddenly they heard a sound of knocking, which was soon repeated. From the smoking chimney came a voice: 'Clear away the fire, we're coming out!'

And out came the Duchess and three of her followers. They had spent over twelve hours in the narrow refuge contrived behind the fire-back, from which the smoke, and the heat of the iron fire-back, had finally driven them out. They were half suffocated, covered with burns, and looked ridiculous into the bargain. The Duchess's face was black with soot, and she had torn off half her dress because it had caught fire. They were all taken to the citadel of Nantes and sent on next day to Blaye, under safe custody. Deutz the traitor had earned his half million. He was an abomination to all Europe, and Victor Hugo castigated him in a furious poem. The Secretary-General of the Ministry of Interior, who was entrusted with the payment of the reward, sent for his ten-year-old son, led him behind a screen and said to him 'Watch carefully what is about to happen, and never forget it!' Then he placed himself behind his desk, on which the money was stacked in two packets. Deutz came in; Didin signed to him with his hand to stay where he was, then he took the tongs from the fireplace and held out the bundles with them to the traitor.

w

Not a word was exchanged. Deutz stuffed the money inside his coat and left the office.

While the conspiring lady, whose fate was still undecided, remained in custody at Blaye, Chateaubriand wrote a magnificent pamphlet in her favour, ending with the sentence 'Madame, your son is my King!' The pamphlet was sold out in a few hours, the final sentence was in everybody's mouth, bands of young men marched past Chateaubriand's house shouting it in chorus, and it went the round at certain banquets in honour of the Duchess. Thousands of appreciative letters were sent to him or published in the newspapers. In the end the government bestirred itself and took legal proceedings against him and against the publishers of some of the papers. Berryer took up the defence of the men of the Press; Chateaubriand declined his assistance. The jury acquitted all the accused, and the author was carried shoulder-high by the crowd and brought home in triumph.

Yet another glorious moment—but unfortunately the pleasure did not last long, for it had become known that the heroine of Blaye, the 'Mother of the King', who had been a widow for twelve years, was in an advanced state of pregnancy. A gale of laughter spread throughout Europe, while the well-disposed hung their heads in sorrow. The government allowed the Duchess to be quietly delivered in her prison; they were only too glad she should lose her reputation at a single blow, and no longer have to be taken seriously as a political figure. Who the father was, nobody knew—if she knew herself, as her enemies said. A marriage was hastily arranged with a Sicilian Count, but the great adventure was at an end, the French authorities shoved her over the border into Italy.

To Chateaubriand this tragi-comic dénouement of the drama must have been somewhat shattering, but he was tied, so to speak, to his famous refrain, and Don Quixote that he was, he now felt bound to champion the 'Mother of his King' in all seriousness. Charles X and his family would have nothing to do with the Amazon, and had broken off all relations with her. She begged Chateaubriand to act as mediator, and he at once declared himself ready to travel to Prague, where the Bourbons were now lodging as guests of the Emperor of Austria in the Hradschin. An old barouche, which had belonged to Talleyrand, was furbished up, and one day in May he started on his journey across Europe, accompanied by his secretary Pilorge.

How lovely is the world when one is not in a hurry, and has no half-finished manuscript demanding one's return! The journey, so he emphatically declared, was to serve 'the greatest of his missions', although, as Madame Récamier asserted, he was of all Frenchmen the last to believe in the return of the Bourbons. The route led through Germany, and had this additional charm that he knew himself to be under police observation the whole way. He had never enjoyed strange scenery and people as he did now; nothing escaped his heightened senses, no cornfield, no woodland border, no girlish smile, least of all the moon, the ancient partner of his meditations, wending its solitary way and shining down upon the nocturnal fields between which ran the road.

The old castle in Prague rang like an empty suit of armour; winding, bare and majestic it received the traveller, who imagined himself, for a moment, in the awe-inspiring Escorial. The little Court of the ex-King, which had been installed as best it might on the second story, like some embalmed object, lived in the bonds of etiquette as if it were still in the Tuileries; the reactionary prattle of Blacas and Damas, the unctuous absent-mindedness of Cardinal Latil, all this may have been pathetic rather than ridiculous, but it was not in any way imposing. 'Good morning, good morning, Monsieur de Chateaubriand!' cried the King from the depths of an armchair, 'I'm delighted to see you! I was expecting you. Please don't stand, let us sit down. How is your wife?' The visitor was deeply moved at the sight of His grey-haired Majesty. All the representations he had intended to make vanished into thin air; he had great difficulty in approaching the real object of his journey, and his intercession for the adventurous Marie-Caroline did not perhaps turn out quite as ardent as he had planned. The King did actually turn the ear in which he was not deaf towards him, but he was too listless to take the matter up himself. In his high-pitched old man's voice he murmured evasive politenesses: 'But my dear man, I'm not reproaching anybody.

Everybody must behave as they think right.' Then he invited him to luncheon on the morrow, when they would be able to discuss the matter further.

Next day the Vicomte realized that his mission had fallen through. The ex-King repudiated all the Duchess's requests and insisted that her son should remain separated from her. The Courtiers may well have had a hand in this decision, especially the Duc de Blacas, Chateaubriand's old enemy, 'who had a high opinion of himself—a French malady'. The conversation with the King then revolved, comically enough, round money matters: the two old gentlemen described their financial situation to each other. Charles, by his own account, was devouring his capital, which was, however, very considerable.

'How much,' asked the old monarch, 'do you need to be rich?'

'Sire, do not waste your time. If you were to give me four millions this morning, I shouldn't have a red sou left this evening.'

'I like that! But what the devil do you need your money for?'

'To be honest, Sire, I haven't a notion, for I have no fancies, and never spend anything. It's a mystery.'

Conversations of this kind did not further the cause of the Amazon, whose advocate Chateaubriand had set out to be, so he took his leave, traversing Germany once more and collecting pleasant impressions that were later to be wonderfully recorded in the *Memoirs*, was greeted in Bischofsheim by a swallow that perched on his window-sill, and finally reached Paris thoroughly stimulated and not in the least tired. Here he was informed that the Duchess of Berry had reached Sicily with her infant, to which she had given the proud but somewhat vague name of 'Child of the Vendée'. He resumed his life at his desk; but two months later Marie-Caroline wrote inviting him to meet her in Venice, as she was now determined to penetrate the Hradschin herself, and needed him to escort her. Up, therefore, and away to Venice.

In the September light he contemplated the strange city, drifting in the brackish waters of time like a deserted galley whose rowers were dead and its gliding tarnished. Of course the Amazon was not there, nor had she sent him any message, so he was obliged to wait, and had time to write long, beautiful letters to Madame

Récamier and to think of her with tenderness. He went out to the Lido and looked at the waves; then he wrote Juliette's name in the sand, and watched the incoming tide destroy it. 'The waves, following one upon another, slowly took possession of the consolatory name; not till the sixteenth surge did they carry it away, letter by letter, as though it pained them.' Thus at all times when sadness grew too great, or his faith in things and men threatened to fail him, he must invoke the protectress without whom his life appeared senseless.

He communed with Venice, appealed to the city and tried to look into it as into a mirror: 'Venice, our destinies were alike! My dreams are paling, as your palaces sink into ruin. The hours of my spring have been dimmed like the arabesques decorating the cornices of your monuments. But you are decaying without knowing it, whereas I am aware of my ruins. Your voluptuous sky, the grace of the waves that bathe you, stir my heart today as they did of old. Growing old has made no difference, I still dream of a thousand fantasies. The energy of my being has concentrated itself deep within my heart. Years have not made me wiser, they have only succeeded in detaching my outward youthfulness and driving it inside me. What dew still falls upon me? What breeze, flower-scented, still penetrates me with its warm breath? Alas, the wind that blows round my now denuded head comes from no happy shore.'

A few days later, driving through Carinthia with the Duchess of Berry, his inward ear caught the answer of the autumnal city. 'You roamed for a week among all my splendours,' whispered Venice to him, 'and could not escape for a moment from my spell. Am I not still just as beautiful as in the days of my power? Do not the memory of it and the radiance of my fame surround me with an aureole that still dazzles every eye? Confess that age gives me only a further charm. I am sinking slowly under the pressure of Time, but I refuse to surrender. Like a city in decay, a life nearing its end can still be beautiful. Adorn your last years with an aureole, erect the statue of your greatest work. It is good to find the promise of immortality in death itself, from the prestige of art. Your living Muse, whose name you wrote lately in my sands, will give you courage. And when she and you are overcome with weariness and fear, look at each other, think of me, and whisper with a smile: "Venice".'

The journey to Prague was as useless as before. Chateaubriand had felt the Amazon's somewhat too categorical summons to escort her importunate, but he was not the man to refuse a service to the woman to whom he had cried 'Your son is my King!' She was accompanied by the young Count Lucchesi, who had been persuaded to marry her 'secretly' on receipt of a hundred thousand francs from the hands of the famous banker Ouvrard. Chateaubriand felt highly uncomfortable in this company, and he was almost relieved when the Austrian police held up the Duchess and her companion and begged them politely to turn back. Chateaubriand let himself be coaxed into going on alone to make a further attempt to mollify Charles X. But again he had no success; Madame de Lucchesi, as the exiled King persisted in calling her, remained excluded from the Royal Family. Chateaubriand himself wrote a decisive *Finis* under his diplomatic activity on behalf of the mother of the 'Child of the Vendée', and went back to work. His *Memoirs from beyond the Grave* were awaiting their completion.

THE FUTURE OF THE WORLD

In his house in the Rue d'Enfer beside the pious Céleste's Home he felt at times as if he were living in a monastery. 'In the morning I wake to the ringing of the *Angelus*. From my bed I hear the clergy singing in the chapel; from my window I can see a Crucifix standing between a nut tree and an elder bush, and near it cows, poultry, pigeons and bees. Sisters of Charity in black penitential garments and white-winged headdresses, old priests and convalescents wend their way among the lilacs, azaleas and rhododendrons of the garden, between currant bushes and vegetable plots. From time to time processions go past, with Madame de Chateaubriand bringing up the rear, rosary in hand. The thrushes flute, grasshoppers chirp, nightingales vie with the hymns.' The aged author was much respected by this pious company, because great ladies often came to have the famous man pointed out to them, in return for a handsome alms, as he worked at his window or strolled in his little garden. The Mother Superior sold quill pens with which he was supposed to have written the famous phrase 'Madame, your son is my King'. The Sisters also manufactured 'Chateaubriand chocolate' which they sold at a high price to visitors, and even the young Victor Hugo, who was as poor as a church mouse, was caught one day as he was going to call on him, and forced, rebelliously, to buy twenty francs worth of 'pious chocolate'.

The masterpiece, the *Memoirs*, the story of his soul, his life and his time, was nearing completion. In the final chapter he considers 'The Future of the World', and cast a sorrowful glance at the lot of Kings: 'Democracy is at their heels, they climb from story to story, from the ground floor to the gable of their palaces, and from there they leap headlong through the skylight into the flood that is to engulf them.' What would the society of tomorrow look like? The inequality of wealth would lead to catastrophes. 'How shall wealth be evenly distributed, how shall wages be weighed against labour, how shall women achieve legal emancipation? I do not know. Humanity will probably become greater, but man, I fear, will become smaller. Some of the principal qualities of genius will be lost: fancy, poetry and the arts will die in the cells of a beehive society, in which each individual will be no more than a bee, a little wheel in a machine, an atom in organized material. . . . In any case I foresee a population getting excited, proclaiming its might, shouting "I will! I shall be! The future belongs to me! I am discovering the universe! Before me there was nothing! The world has been waiting for me! I am unique! My fathers were fools and idiots!" '

The author looked for facts that might contradict such outbursts of baseless self-assertion. But he only found 'a flock of unrestrained generations that have never come to maturity, have no political or religious beliefs, and fling themselves on money and official posts like the poor on free food. It is a flock that recognizes no leader, runs from the plain to the mountain and back again to the plain, despising the advice of the old shepherds seasoned by sun and wind. . . .' He foresaw socialism, but whereas his liberal and revolutionary friends, who were increasingly finding their way to his house, saw in the dawning era and the new order of society a final state, a full stop and the conclusion of a development, Chateaubriand knew that even the New would represent only a stage, a fragment of time, which man, by the force of his desires, drives forward to mingle in the stream of events.

He advocated a Christian solution; but did he do so with complete sincerity? Even his ceaseless attempts to believe, his zealous observance of religious practices, were prompted by an instinct of chivalry. In the silent recesses of his heart he had reached complete nihilism; he flung himself passionately into discussions with his friends of the Left, Lammenais, Carrel, Lamartine, Béranger, but he could never succeed in believing in anything but the irresistible alteration of the world. He had lost faith in monarchy, he was convinced that a free democracy would lead to fresh tyrannies, he refused to join in the incipient idolatry of the People because he believed it to be condemned to purely material interests. In short he had come to the end of all his hopes, but he would not have been Chateaubriand if he had not fought for what he had once believed in. He remained the champion of a cause he had long given up for lost: 'As a prophet about to leave the world I am writing down my prophecy, in my declining days, on light, dry leaves that the breath of eternity will soon have carried away.'

It was a relief to him when in 1838 the Archbishop of Paris announced that he was prepared to acquire Madame de Chateaubriand's Home for the Church. He could thus escape from the atmosphere of a convent for pious old people, his household would have the benefit of a little cash, and he could settle nearer to Juliette. He bought a moderate-sized house in the Rue du Bac, which had a very fine façade dating from the previous century, and was adorned with medallions, sphinxes and chimeras. He lived there to the end of his days, in a little room on the ground floor overlooking the fairly spacious garden. His furnishings were simple, not to say severe: an iron bedstead, a big table covered with papers and books, and by the fireplace a little table with a wicker armchair, that was all. An unpainted wooden chest stood on the floor, in which he kept the manuscript of the *Memoirs*. On the wall hung a crucifix, with a consecrated twig of box behind it, and a Madonna after Mignard that Claire de Duras had bequeathed him. The other rooms in the house, the reception rooms and his wife's apartment, were comfortable, and furnished in good taste.

He rose between four and five in the morning and worked all the forenoon, being then only lightly dressed, in slippers and an old frock coat that served him as a dressing-gown. He wrote and meditated till the arrival of his secretary, to whom he dictated the carefully prepared pages. Pilorge was no longer in office—there had obviously been some disagreement—a certain Danielo had taken his place, who was wont to complain that he was forced to serve the old writer as a 'literary crutch', when he had so much to say himself as an author. However, no original work of his has come down to posterity, only his *Conversations with Chateaubriand*, set down with great charm. At some time in the morning the barber would put in appearance, to shave him, and now and then to trim his white but still rebellious locks. It was said of this loquacious Figaro that he carefully collected the hair he cut off and sold it to feminine enthusaists as relics.

'I'm dying of joy,' wrote Chateaubriand to Madame Récamier when he moved into the new house, 'to think that I only need ten minutes now to reach your door.' He paid her a visit every day. As soon as he had dressed for lunch and eaten it with his wife, he left the house. He still favoured a certain elegance, and wore a smart, very snugly fitting frock coat in royal blue or light brown, was careful always to have a flower in his buttonhole, and carried an ebony stick with a gold top. On the stroke of three he was at the door of the 'Abbey', where Madame Récamier had her apartment. He climbed the stairs with a little effort, and remained alone with her for an hour and a half, no other guests being admitted meanwhile. What did they talk about? Nobody knew, though some asserted that they remained silent the whole time. Certain it is, however, that they enjoyed their time together as the Peace of God, that all sadness and tension fell away from time as soon as they were alone together. If she was absent for a day he wrote to her, saying 'I don't know what to do; Paris is a desert without your beauty. Come back to me soon, I miss you sorely. Your absence disheartens me so that I can't even write; I haven't the strength for anything. I look forward to a little word from you to help me to live'.

Towards five o'clock other guests arrived, but things were not as lively as they used to be. Madame Récamier herself had suffered a change; her eye trouble was increasing so fast that she was nearly blind. With indescribable grace she sought to conceal her growing helplessness; her hesitant movements and the rapt expression of her listening face made her 'the most beautiful old woman of her time'. She was still intent on keeping conversation going. Chateaubriand sat in his usual armchair by the fireplace, out of which he would stir for nobody. In the presence of visitors he did not know he would not open his mouth, or if he did, it was only to prophesy misfortune or refer bitterly to the development of society. It was evident that he took no interest in encouraging younger people, but he was such an impressive figure, even his silence was still so imposing, that nobody dared provoke him.

Was his ignorance of what was being written in France really as complete as he wanted people to believe? These were the great days of Victor Hugo, Lamartine, Alfred de Vigny, Alfred de Musset, Sainte-Beuve, Stendhal and Balzac. The old man declared he had never heard their names, and asked who this Lamartinière and Hector Rhugo were. In actual fact he dipped into their books a good deal, and with a discerning eye, secretly delighted that they should have learnt so much from himself, and not above picking up hints from them for his own style. But there were days when he entertained the company at Juliette's with a surprising abundance of stories and anecdotes. 'Messieurs, how kind and amusing you have been today!' the delighted hostess would exclaim, 'And you, Monsieur de Chateaubriand, have regaled us with things I had never heard of from you before!'

At half-past five, as a rule, he made a move to leave. 'Good Heavens. it's nearly six o'clock, I shall be late!' he would exclaim, adding with a laugh, 'I'm never hungry till seven, but Madame de

Chateaubriand would like to dine at five; so we have agreed to sit down to dinner on the stroke of six, which means that neither of us is satisfied. That is called leading a good married life.' The couple never went out of an evening. Sometimes an old friend would pay them a visit—Marcellus or Hyde de Neuville—but more often bishops or other religious persons, with whom Céleste kept up a running conversation. He then found it very difficult to conceal his boredom and stifle his yawns, but it was even worse when they dined alone and his wife read aloud to him afterwards from the *Lives of the Saints,* or heaped him with reproaches, at which she was an expert. 'People say you are a great man; I am not a great woman, I don't value fine speeches, only sound judgement. And *I* judge rightly!' 'But of course, *chère amie,*' replied the great man, 'of course!', and gave a secret yawn. 'He was an exemplary husband,' says his secretary Danielo, 'a hero of domestic peace and honourable patience. He would have given anything, I believe, even his fame, to avoid a row.'

Although he was always preoccupied with age and death, although he talked to every visitor about his coming departure and the beauty of dying, his behaviour remained perfectly natural and he was mindful of his dignity. With women he adopted a respectful, self-deprecating tone full of kindly homage. When he first met Rachel, the famous actress, he said to her 'How sad to see something so beautiful arising, when one has got to die!' To which Rachel replied 'But Monsieur le Vicomte, there are men that do not die!' Other women, too, said and wrote the most reverential things to him. Marcelline Desbordes-Valmore read a fragment of the *Memoirs* and declared she detected in his genius 'the flight of the eagle beating the air with its wings'. The poetess Amable Tastu told him in verse that she looked on him as 'an angel, a saint and a prophet', before whom she must kneel. Madame de Girardin talked and wrote about him incessantly, she strewed flowers in the path of the old lion, exclaiming 'What can be more seductive than charm coupled with power!' Speeches of this sort gave him pleasure, but he knew all too well that they were addressed to his posthumous fame, of whose glory these women hoped to snatch a little share. He had no more illusions.

When in 1842 the Duchess of Berry's son, whom he called his King Henri V, offered to pay him the pension of a Peer of France, he accepted gladly. In the following year the young man called the French Legitimists together in London, and begged Chateaubriand to join them. He started on the journey without hesitation, enjoyed the rough Channel crossing, revisited with emotion all the scenes of his earlier years and wrote the most beautiful letters to Juliette. Henri V received him with every mark of respect: 'Please sit down Monsieur de Chateaubriand, so that I may lean on you.' And turning to the rest of the company, he said 'If I have ever thought of the throne of my fathers, it has only been in the hope of serving my country with the principles and sentiments than Monsieur de Chateaubriand has so brilliantly proclaimed'.

But however wonderful this occasion may have been for him, he was longing to get back to Paris, not only to Madame Récamier but to his work. He knew now that his *Memoirs* were his supreme creation, and he had staked everything on giving them the fullest perfection. The description of his own life was becoming enlarged to a picture of the history of his time, and this apparently most personal work, which begins with an account of his childhood, actually contains the finest and fairest study of Napoleon that has ever been written. Thus the expression 'I and Napoleon', originally so audacious, is made to assume a deeper meaning, for out of the closely entangled threads of their two destinies emerges the picture of a great man and his downfall. He decided not to have the work published till after his death. If it were to appear during his lifetime it might have to be 'less candid and less true'. 'Besides, I have always imagined myself sitting in my coffin as I wrote, and this has given the work a certain religious stamp, which I could not efface without spoiling it. I should find it difficult to stifle this rapt voice, rising from the grave, which is heard throughout the whole course of the narrative.'

In order to stimulate their friends' growing interest in the great work, Madame Récamier organized some readings from it in her drawing-room. She assembled the listeners with care, choosing people from widely differing circles, who would be able to spread its fame. Writers such as Sainte-Beuve, Edgar Quinet, Jules Janin, seemed to her the most important, but she also invited old friends and a few clerics and politicians. Someone who could not be invited for want of room reported later 'The reading was a triumph, so we were told by those allowed to attend, and they regretted that Madame Récamier's drawing-room, so famous for her kindness and charm, was not as spacious as the Plain of Sunium'. The author never read from the work himself, perhaps because he was afraid of being overcome by emotion at certain passages of the text. 'But if we missed something of the mysterious intonation because we did not hear his voice,' writes Sainte-Beuve, 'we saw him all the better: we could follow the reflections of the reading on his spacious features like drifting cloud shadows over the crests of a forest.'

The readings were chiefly intended to secure subscribers to the complete edition of the *Memoirs*. This was achieved without difficulty: Delloye the publisher founded a society of shareholders which acquired the sole rights in the work and advanced the author a sum of 156,000 francs besides guaranteeing him a life annuity. He was suddenly free from all material cares; he settled all his debts and delivered up the chest containing the manuscript to the notary. But he was obviously not quite happy over this arrangement; he said it was now 'his thoughts that had entered the debtors' prison instead of his person'. Moreover he was so used to financial difficulties that he felt there was something missing now that they were got rid of. As he could no longer talk of his poverty he took to complaining of his boredom again, upon which Béranger retorted 'If you have always been bored, it's because you've never been sufficiently interested in other people!' With which, of course, Céleste eagerly agreed.

MEMENTO MORI

The day on which the chest containing the manuscript was removed from the house was a day of sudden emptiness, of arrested vitality. What now? Old age keeps itself alive by habits in which a little pedantry is mingled, but also a livelier sense of duty. The passage of the hours that have no more surprises to offer are suddenly audible as steps, or the turning of wheels. The sound is disturbing to one's inner peace, and can only be stifled by further work. For the sake of this inward calm, which is the great gift of old age, Chateaubriand seized a fresh sheet of paper and wrote upon it, in a hand that was still firm and clear, *The Life of the Abbé Rancé*. It was to be his last book, and it has almost the appearance of an epilogue to the *Memoirs,* though it lacks the settled order and sequence of that work. It consists of a medley, sometimes graceful, sometimes pathetic, of incidents in the life of his hero, religious and moral considerations, and a thousand variants of his ever-recurrent self-portraiture. The whole is a glorious misuse of the apropos. Every idea, every fact becomes a magic password, under the spell of which the old rock pours forth fresh springs. It is at once the most imperfect and the most ingenious of Chateaubriand's works.

It was said that his confessor had imposed this labour on him, but the old Abbé Séguin was far too wise to dictate a literary work to him by way of penance; he had carefully contented himself with offering him a few suggestions. At the age of ninety-three he knew a great deal about human nature, and could even see into the soul of a genius. He knew only too well that it was too late to make an ideal penitent of him, but it delighted this pious old man to find that he could gently bend his supreme art to the service of a great religious figure. Chateaubriand had tried once before to attack the subject, but had been prevented by 'a natural antipathy'. Now he suddenly began writing—in different styles, now violent, now religious, now passionate, now sober, just as he happened to feel at the moment, proceeding with all the more freedom because there was not the least resemblance between his hero and himself.

Rancé was a French nobleman of the seventeenth century, who at the age of ten came into the benefice of the neglected Cistercian monastery in the valley of La Trappe. Further clerical property fell to his share, and according to the custom of the time he became an ecclesiastic without feeling the least vocation for it. On the contrary, he soon became notorious in Paris for his vicious way of life, till one day he underwent a spiritual revelation that led him to renounce the deceits of the world. His conversion was certainly one of the most sudden and radical in the religious history of France. Rancé went to La Trappe and transformed what was left there of monastic life to the strictest Order that Christendom had ever known, the Order of the Trappists, whose members must bind themselves to perpetual silence, and have only one greeting: *memento mori.*

How far removed was this reminder from Chateaubriand's infatuation with death! The very fact that the background of the story is so monastically sombre makes the man of the world that he still was, and would remain, stand out the more clearly. In actual fact he could still speak only of himself, and with every sentence he wrote he delved deeper into his own consciousness. He devotes a few pages to the transmutation of the feeling between man and woman as it betrays itself in love letters. He is concerned with the extinction of passion: 'What has happened? Is a new tie beginning or is the old one at an end? However that may be, love dies before its object. Human emotions are subject to the effects of a secret travail; the fever of time produces weariness, destroys illusions and changes our hearts, as it alters our hair and adds to our age. But there is an exception to this decay of human things. Now and again it happens that love endures long enough in a strong soul to become transformed to passionate friendship, to become a sort of duty, to achieve the qualities of a virtue. Then it loses its natural impotence and lives on its immortal foundations.' Thus even in the midst of this story of a stern saint, Juliette receives her homage.

Those who are given to bemoaning themselves, to invoking death and talking glibly of the peace of the grave, may last a long while, often longer than they would wish. In June 1846 Chateaubriand drove out to the Champ de Mars to go for a walk there. As he was getting out of the carriage the horses bolted; he was thrown to the ground and broke his collar-bone. This accident, little serious in appearance, completely shattered his carefully tended constitution. He must have sustained injuries not recognized by the doctors, for he found all movement difficult and his left arm became useless. A contemporary writes 'I found the illustrious old man with his arm in a sling, more crumpled up than

seated, in a chair by the window overlooking his little garden.
From what he told me he evidently spends the whole day in this
condition, sunk into himself, without reading, and without other
amusement than contemplating the little garden, which is much
neglected, but pleases him because, as he says, it resembles a
cemetery. The poor man is frightfully bored; nothing amuses him,
he has no inclination for anything and is increasingly estranged
from the course of affairs. He has no children, no family, and
Madame de Chateaubriand gives me the impression of being
frightfully bored herself. Visitors keep away, more and more,
from a man suffering from boredom to such a degree. It is the
saddest old age one can imagine.'

The worst trial of all was that, when he visited Madame
Récamier, he had to be carried up by two servants and lifted into
his accustomed chair by the fire. Visitors came less often, they
disliked the sight of his helplessness, his silence oppressed them.
Sainte-Beuve paid his visits, as he says, 'out of respect'. 'Monsieur
de Chateaubriand never says a word nowadays,' he notes in
December 1847, 'you can't get a sound out of him. Béranger
declares he is able to make him talk for a quarter of an hour; but
as Thiers justly observes, when Béranger has been talking to anybody, he imagines the other person has spoken.' Soon these
outings came to an end, the old man could no longer leave the
house. Madame Récamier came to the Rue du Bac every afternoon, and Madame de Chateaubriand had the melancholy satisfaction of knowing that her husband could no longer betake
himself to the usual rendezvous, and that the 'Arch-lady' must
come to her instead, if she wanted to see her old friend. Poor,
embittered Céleste had not long to enjoy this modest triumph,
for she died suddenly, without having been really ill. She had been
ill all along, of course, forever complaining and trying cures, but
for that very reason everybody had expected her to live for ever.
Now all at once the old-maidish figure had vanished and a lifelong
tie was broken.

The day after her funeral, which he attended with the utmost
physical effort, Chateaubriand drove to Hortense Allart's house
and sent the driver to beg her to come down, as he could no longer

mount the stairs. 'I stepped into his carriage,' she says, 'he was friendly and amiable. He told me he was bored. . . . He cannot walk now; he is melancholy. He still has his old charm, the distinction, the superior mind, that make him so attractive. Age has not altered the beauty of his face, it has only made it more impressive.' This from the frivolous Hortense, who had given him so much pleasure! How finely and respectfully she speaks of the old man, how much kinder is her judgement than that of many of his old friends! She had never been very near him intellectually and she knew that his sympathy with her literary work was a form of gallantry. He had wanted her company and her willingness to please him by her good temper and light-heartedness. But now, when all desires were extinguished, and the old man could only speak with effort, she listened reverently to his lingering talk, steeped in the bitterness of renunciation and disillusionment: 'I have no more concern with the affairs of this miserable world. I've seen politics at too close quarters. I don't believe in anything or value anything any more; I am content to have been fooled, without regret, by two or three great ideas, Freedom, Loyalty, Honour.'

God makes no appearance in this Trinity, but he had declared often enough that the Christian faith seemed to him the only solution of the perplexities of this world. He was too clearly aware of the torrent of crises beginning to flood the century, to foresee any social way out. Unlike most of his contemporaries of a younger generation, he was no Utopian. Was his adherence to the Catholic faith more than a counsel of despair? Was the practice of religion more than a consolation? Was it the fruit of some perception that allowed him to contemplate calmly the future of the world and the salvation of his own soul? Earlier, when he was extolling the *Spirit of Christianity*, he had revealed the beauty and the social usefulness of the Catholic religion, drifting thus into a side road that might easily have led to error. It was only natural that he should have been unable thereafter to separate religion and politics, declaring, as did Sismondi, that religion was 'necessary to the support of the State'. Such a form of belief has little consolation to offer a man on the threshold of death. Now

x

that the State no longer interested him, he must look upon faith as an autonomous force, or else forgo the security it might afford. 'I believe,' he said, 'as firmly in God as in my own existence; I believe in Christianity as a great and permanent truth—as a religion, as far as I can. I believe in it for twenty-four hours, and then the devil comes back again; he plunges me into the profoundest doubt, extricating myself from which keeps me fully occupied as death approaches.'

Where, therefore, was certainly to be had? He found it in his friendship with Madame Récamier, which allowed no uncertainty and no fears to arise. The mystery of human nearness and intimacy, and the magic of mere presence became increasingly palpable to these two people as their physical life receded. Juliette had had to undergo a second operation for cataract, which had had no curative result. She was now quite blind. Nevertheless she appeared every day in the Rue du Bac to keep her friend company. She felt her way carefully, with graceful movements, through the little room as far as his armchair, and seated herself at his side. They had spent much time in silence together of late years, and now words failed them almost entirely. Visitors seldom came; the frailty of the couple inspired them with fear. Victor Hugo came once or twice. 'It was touching and sad,' he said, 'the woman who could no longer see sought the man who could no longer feel. Their two hands found each other. God be praised! One ceases to live but one goes on loving.'

The bond between them had survived all the storms of time, it had withstood crises and injuries only guessed at by others, for discretion had always been the rule of their life together. They were living to its finish a harmony which had become the law of their love. He, who had never quite surrendered himself, whom nobody, neither man nor woman, could ever quite dominate, who always kept the essence of his being to himself even in moments of deepest devotion, and she, whom no man had ever quite conquered—these two people had found each other in their need to be loved without complete surrender, and had become one through mutual trust and the subtlest harmony. Their capacity for taking pleasure in each other while respecting voluntarily drawn limits, and attuning themselves to each other's subtlest moods, had afforded them a union such as the most passionate surrender could not have achieved.

They lived almost entirely in the dark, for daylight was no longer a boon to Juliette, and he, who could only move with difficulty and could no longer hold a book, was content to give himself up to his dreams so long as he knew she was beside him. Now and then he would recite some famous poem or a piece of prose to her, in subdued tones; she listened with delight, and when his memory failed him, would pick up the thread and continue the recitation. At one such moment he suddenly asked her to marry him, so that she might bear his name for the remainder of her life, and have no need to leave his house till her last hour. The proposal moved her profoundly, and preoccupied her for some time, but it may be that she no longer had the courage to alter the tenor of her life, however completely at his service. In the end she gently advised him to relinquish the idea, since nothing in the world could increase the spiritual depth of their unity. He listened in silence, and never referred to his suggestion again; it may even have faded from his clouded memory.

'For a long while now,' says Alexis de Tocqueville, 'he had sunk into a sort of speechless bewilderment, which at times suggested that his mental powers were extinguished. He was in this condition when rumours of the February Revolution reached him, and he insisted on being told what was happening. He was informed that Louis Philippe's monarchy had fallen. "That's a good thing!" he said, and relapsed into silence.' The great events, the fighting in the streets, Guizot's resignation, the departure of the King and the proclamation of the Republic, news of these hardly penetrated into the slowly darkening life of these two; they scarcely noticed the sound of the heavy guns being fired nearby. Marceline Valmore wrote to Sainte-Beuve 'I pray for the people and for you, I pray for the enchanting ghost of Madame Récamier, and the angels hear me.' That ghost had indeed not yet vanished, it still hovered over Chateaubriand's bed, smiling bravely to his sadness. To Béranger, who paid him a short visit, he whispered 'So you've got your Republic at last.' 'That's so,' answered

Béranger, 'but I would rather have been able to go on dreaming of it than see it as it is.'

What Chateaubriand had foreseen and foretold, ten years earlier, of the future of the world, was beginning to take shape. On his sick bed, to which he was now confined by inflammation of the lungs, he was no longer aware of what was happening, but the spirit of history saw to it that this great man, who had witnessed so many revolutions, should still be alive when the bloody insurrection of June broke out. What had happened? What had come to pass in this ever restless, ever whispering, gossiping, laughing, frenzied city of Paris? It was hardly three months since Louis Philippe had been hounded out; remains of the barricades erected in February were everywhere to be seen. On the Place du Panthéon they had not even taken the trouble to remove the bricks prolonging one aisle of the church to a gigantic rampart. Had not the Liberal Bourgeoisie just incited the Paris workmen to destroy the barricades? Yet now, with trepidation, they saw the city bristling again with these warlike defences. What control had they over the social ideas they had set in circulation so light-heartedly? The upheaval of these June days of 1848 began as a famine revolt, but it did not stop there. The underground current of the Great Revolution was breaking afresh through the thin layer of earth on which the bourgeoisie aggrandized by Louis Philippe were living their care-free lives. The shades of Robespierre and Babeuf arose nightly from their unknown common grave, and whispered to the poor the lethal cradle-song of social vengeance. The machine had entered upon its domination and revolutionized the nature of labour. General franchise had become a reality: at one blow the number of voters had risen from a few thousand to many millions. Every worker had learnt overnight to tremble for his job, and to turn his fear to political purpose. The masses had come of age politically at the moment when they were plunged in an economic crisis the like of which had never been known. Like underground waters the old teachings of the Revolution went murmuring secretly, finding their way among men in the guise of social Utopias, States of the Future, secret Leagues, new Gospels, promises and proclamations.

Enfantin, Considérant, Proudhon ('Property is Robbery'), Raspail, Barbès, Blanqui, Cabet, Buchez, Chatel and Louis Blanc were all preaching their systems, their grand final solutions, their dreams and social structures. The soil on which France was living was riddled with theories, of which that of state employment proved the most disastrous.

'This is war between rich and poor!' cried Blanqui, 'The rich have brought it about, they are the aggressors, living on the sweat of the poor!' The right to work was the insistent claim, born of the February revolution and raised to heaven like a clenched fist. To relieve the pressure the government had set up the so-called National Workshops, in which more than 100,000 workers were to be employed—without any proper jobs having been found for them. These workshops soon became centres of agitation and civil-war schools for the workless. The Director of the Workshops confided his apprehensions to the young Freycinet: 'What will happen on the day when I am told to liquidate the whole thing? There are honest fellows among them, who have no other livelihood and can no longer find work in the factories. What will they do? They are the ideal recruits for revolt.'

On June 21st the liquidation took place. The first great employment experiment of modern capitalism had fallen through. Workers up to the age of twenty-five were allowed to enter the army, the remainder were relegated to the provinces, to rid the capital of these elements of unrest. The government had taken the precaution of furnishing the city with fresh troops, munitions and provisions. During the night the streets filled with endless processions of workers, who were to be carted away early next morning. On June 23rd an immense crowd assembled on the Place du Panthéon, separated into sections and took possession of the barricades to the rhythmic cry of 'Work! Bread! Work! Bread!' The sombre determination of the marchers boded no good.

The battle lasted four days. The bitterness on both sides was indescribable: hatred, despair, revenge, and a mutual thirst for blood rose to white heat. Never before had people destroyed one another in Paris with such gusto as on those days of June. Three

Generals lost their lives, among them General Bréa, who was killed near the Orleans Gate while attempting to parley. The Archbishop of Paris too, while trying to mediate with the furious crowd, was struck down by a bullet. Insoluble enigma of civil war! These people—who only a few weeks earlier had been living at peace with one another—were now falling upon one another with a cruelty such as no foreign army would dream of. The women, especially, proved good shots and inhuman avengers. On the other side it was the Gardes Mobiles that raged most fiercely. These had been called into being by Lamartine only a few months earlier, and recruited for the most part from Catholic youth organizations. They were all young, and the sight of blood had driven them quite mad. 'Those little lads with their green shoulder-straps,' writes an eye-witness, 'were like ravening martens dipping their snouts in blood.'

When on the fourth day Cavaignac informed the National Assembly that the rising had been completely quelled, the streets of Paris were strewn with more than 12,000 corpses. Shooting under martial law went on everywhere: at street corners, in cemeteries, in the sandpits of Montmarte and the quarries of the Butte de Chaumont the vanquished collapsed under the salvos of the firing squads. Blanqui cried in vain to the deputies 'These unfortunates were simply misled. Have mercy on them! Mercy even on those that were merciless! If you were to see as much terrible poverty at close quarters as I do every day, your heart would bleed. For the sake of the wives and children of these unfortunates, Mercy! Mercy!' But no mercy could now mend the rift that spread from that hour through France and through the world. Modern society had suddenly been split in two, class hatred had been born, class war was beginning.

The convulsion of the world became audible to the dying man as a thunder of guns, with cries and tumult in the street. Chateaubriand emerged for a moment from his twilight. The artillery fire shook the house, the crucifix on the wall moved, and fell back into position; the uproar gradually died down. The old man was suddenly wide awake. 'What has happened?' he asked uneasily. Out of the mists of his fading memory a gleam fell on the present.

He was told something of the fighting; the bitterness of it was concealed from him, but the resolute bravery on both sides was hinted at. The death of the Archbishop drew tears from him; he had the story repeated to him two or three times. His hands strayed questingly and agitatedly over the coverlet. 'I must go there,' he whispered.

They had fallen, old priests, young lads, rough soldiers—fallen at Jemappes, and Thionville, at Rivoli and Moscow, at Waterloo, and on the Seine bridges in July 1830. Young and old were gone, and were always coming back, their shades drifted on the stream of history, which at this hour was becoming one with the dying man's flood of memories. 'Breaking with real things is nothing, but breaking with memories! The heart itself breaks when it must sever itself from dreams.' So he had written in *Rancé*. The stream of memory came flooding back, bringing with it great events and the shudder of a changing world; but soon the guns fell silent, the June revolt was over, and the dying man fell back into the secrecy of his last hours.

Madame Récamier hardly ever left the room now. When grief overcame her she felt her way softly out of the room to weep. The sick man, who could no longer speak, followed her with anxious eyes, his feverish glance expressed the fear that she might not return, and his features did not relax till she had resumed her place beside him. His face had become transparent from sickness and pain, he felt continually for Juliette's hand. He who had loved freedom above everything would not let this tie be loosened; he wished to die united with her. She did not see him die: she raised her head with its sightless eyes to listen to his breathing. She could hear it no longer. She sank to her knees and laid her face on the edge of the bed. So she remained for a long while, and so she was found by the young men from the Polytechnic who had come in full uniform to mount guard over the dead. They saw the majestic face of the dead man, with the white hair standing up from the forehead. They saw the kneeling figure of the woman who had watched beside him silently weeping, and now with an uncertain hand feeling for a support to enable her to rise.

INDEX

GEORGE ALLEN & UNWIN LTD
London: 40 Museum Street, W.C.1

Auckland: 24 Wyndham Street
Sydney, N.S.W.: Bradbury House, 55 York Street
Cape Town: 109 Long Street
Bombay: 15 Graham Road, Ballard Estate, Bombay 1
Calcutta: 17 Chittaranjan Avenue, Calcutta 13
New Delhi: 13-14 Ajmeri Gate Extension, New Delhi 1
Karachi: Karachi Chambers, McLeod Road
Mexico: Villalongin 32-10, Piso, Mexico 5, D.F.
Toronto: 91 Wellington Street West
São Paulo: Avenida 9 de Julho 1138-Ap. 51
Buenos Aires: Escritorio 454-459, Florida 165
Singapore: 36c Princep Street, Singapore 7
Hong Kong: 1/12 Mirador Mansions, Kowloon